A STUDY OF REVOLUTION

A
STUDY OF
REVOLUTION

BY

PETER CALVERT

CLARENDON PRESS · OXFORD

1970

Oxford University Press, Ely House, London W.1

GLASGOW   NEW YORK   TORONTO   MELBOURNE   WELLINGTON
CAPE TOWN   SALISBURY   IBADAN   NAIROBI   DAR ES SALAAM   LUSAKA   ADDIS ABABA
BOMBAY   CALCUTTA   MADRAS   KARACHI   LAHORE   DACCA
KUALA LUMPUR   SINGAPORE   HONG KONG   TOKYO

MADE AND PRINTED IN GREAT BRITAIN BY
WILLIAM CLOWES AND SONS, LIMITED
LONDON AND BECCLES

IN MEMORIAM
PATRI MIHI
RAYMOND CALVERT
1906–1959

PREFACE

REVOLUTION is a fashionable word. Like most fashionable words, the more it has been used, the vaguer its meaning has become. This vagueness is wholly understandable. Studies of revolution in our time have concentrated in the main on the concept of revolution as social change. In consequence, they have had to deal with so many phenomena at once that the problem of definition, difficult enough for an author, has become exceptionally so for the reader.

This book is a study of revolution as a political phenomenon. Taking the relatively simple definition of revolution as a political phenomenon as its starting-point, it seeks to establish a unified conceptual base for the study of revolution by political scientists. In writing it, I have drawn on the work of authors in many fields, to all of whom I am very grateful. I should like to think that it can be equally useful to them in return.

Revolution is an emotive subject for scientific study. This study, I admit freely, bears the stamp of an author who dislikes intensely the survival of patterns of violence in human relations. But these survivals have got to be understood; they must not be ignored or blindly worshipped. They are intensely corrosive to the fundamental structure of human society—political organization. And, as they endanger the life of the individual, this means any form of political organization, even one that is individually regulated. I can find no evidence that the benefits attributed to revolution in any way measure up to the appalling destruction of human life that has been carried on in its name. If this book falls into the hands of any who aspire to make a revolution, when they have read it I hope they will stop and consider. There are much better things in life to do, so many more.

One of them is to acknowledge one's debts to others. For this book, and for the conclusions it presents, I am wholly responsible. The initial encouragement to follow my inclination to work in this field, however, I owe to Professor Peter Mathias, my Tutor as an undergraduate and my Supervisor in political theory. Professor S. E. Finer's trenchant criticism of a very partial and primitive draft did much to shape the structure of the present text. The content benefited greatly from the reading and criticism of Professor Joseph Frankel, as well as of other readers. I am also grateful to all those who discussed and criticized those points of the present work that appeared in *Political Studies*, in particular to its Editor, Professor Peter Campbell.

I should like to thank particularly all my students at the University of Southampton, and especially those who undertook our joint Special Subject on Revolution. I benefited greatly from our discussions, and I believe they did too.

Liam O'Sullivan and John Simpson both gave me much useful advice on methodology, and Mike Greatorex some very practical help with computation, coupled with lucid advice on statistical method. Mrs. P. Powell devoted much time and energy to the preparation of a final typescript, which in its complexity was a daunting task.

Diana Marshallsay prepared the index. To all of them I give thanks, and absolve them from any responsibility for what follows.

CONTENTS

Contents

PART I

THE ANALYSIS OF REVOLUTION

CHARACTERISTICS OF REVOLUTION

OBJECT

THE purpose of this study is to provide the basis for the scientific study of revolution in its political aspect. This is done through the construction of a model of revolution defined in terms of power. It is shown that this model has specific advantages for the identification of variables capable of being expressed in precise quantities. The model is then tested in a case study before being used as the basis of a study of revolutionary movements in the twentieth century.

Part II, therefore, begins with a survey of these movements, a check list of which will be found at Appendix A. In the course of this survey, statistical evidence is offered on the significance of the relationships between key variables.

Finally, some observations are made as to the implications of this study both for greater understanding of revolution, and for improved knowledge of the workings of the stable political system. The present volume is the first product of what is planned as an ongoing programme of research. As such, it seems proper to indicate leads for future investigation, as well as to initiate discussion of points on which modification of present ideas may well become necessary.

To begin with, it is necessary to consider the special problems that attend all attempts at the scientific study of revolution.

The most obvious is the absence of an agreed definition shared by both trained observers and the lay public. The former have increasingly tended to limit the term to a rare class of historical events, extending over a considerable time, marked by major social and ideological change.[1] Both forms of change are particularly difficult to subject to precise measurement. The latter use the word indiscriminately for all forms of violent political

[1] Lawrence Stone, 'Theories of Revolution', *World Politics*, XVIII, no. 2 (Jan. 1966), 159–76.

change and, by extension, to refer to sudden changes of course in every aspect of life.[2] They agree only on one thing, that attempts to promote change which fail are not revolutions.

Few people would not agree, however, that certain events fall within all definitions of revolution. (We except, for this purpose, the purely metaphorical, as lying outside the range of an avowedly political study.) One such is the French Revolution of 1789. With it in mind as an example, we can discern no less than four aspects of it, each of which have separately and collectively been termed those characteristic of revolution. These are:

(a) A *process* in which the political direction of a state becomes increasingly discredited in the eyes of either the population as a whole or certain key sections of it. *Such a process may culminate in the revolutionary event classified below, or in a change of government by more peaceful means.*

(b) A change of government (transition) at a clearly defined point in time by the use of armed force, or the credible threat of its use; namely, an *event.*

(c) A more-or-less coherent *programme* of change in either the political or the social institutions of a state, or both, induced by the political leadership *after* a revolutionary event, the transition of power, has occurred.

(d) A political *myth* that gives to the political leadership resulting from a revolutionary transition short-term status as the legitimate government of the state.[3]

Thus, in order to investigate fully the concept of revolution it would be necessary to study in detail process, event, programme, and myth as distinct phenomena. Clearly this is an immense task, and there are a number of good reasons for deciding initially to concentrate on the event. It is therefore with the circumstances of the revolutionary transition that this work will be principally concerned. The reasons can be summarized as follows.

The event is the *sine qua non* of a revolutionary situation that

---

[2] And by definition to a wide range of other activities.

[3] I have made use here of the neat terminology proposed by my colleague, John Simpson; cf. Peter Calvert and John Simpson, 'Attributes of Revolution', unpublished paper presented to International Sociological Association, Working Group on Armed Forces and Society, Conference: 'Militarism and the Professional Military Man', London, 14–16 Sept. 1967.

can be clearly labelled as such. If the event does not occur, no certain identification can be made of any preceding period of disaffection as being 'revolutionary'.

Analytically, the event is the aspect of revolution most open to study as a discrete event suitable for comparative study with other discrete events of the same type. As we shall see later, the number of revolutionary events available for study, even in the limited period covered in the present work, is very considerable.

This advantage is compounded by the fact that many aspects of revolutionary transitions are capable of being expressed in very precise numerical terms. There is, however, a problem of the availability of information here which cannot be overlooked, and which will be discussed shortly.

Lastly, despite all these advantages, relatively few case studies exist of revolutionary events, compared with the vast number on social and political processes, programmes, and myths. This is the case, furthermore, despite the fact that the event is that aspect of revolution most readily identifiable to the layman. The *OED* definition of revolution, for example, is 'A complete overthrow of the established government in any country or state by those who were previously subject to it; a forcible substitution of a new ruler or form of government.'[4] This is the definition of a revolutionary event. It is with these events that this study deals.

INFORMATION

Any study of political events depends for its raw material on information about certain events. In the case of a revolution, its nature, and the way in which it must be handled, differs substantially according to whether the movement under consideration is a *contemporary* revolution or a *completed* revolution. As revolutions, as defined here, are seldom lengthy in duration, a comprehensive comparative study will consist almost entirely of the latter.

The study of revolution, as such, cannot be described as a popular field of historiography. Many revolutions are, to be

---

[4] *OED;* cf. Alfred Meisel, 'Revolution and Counter-Revolution', *Encyclopedia of the Social Sciences*, 1934.

sure, popular subjects for the historian, but they are these because of their historical significance, and this is extrinsic rather than intrinsic. Hence attention tends to be focused on the large, the spectacular, and the bloody. The neat, efficient, little *coup* is passed over for the consideration of the events which followed it. But the grandiose bloodbath may reflect an error of judgement, while in point of revolutionary technique the *coup* has performed the same job much more efficiently.[5]

The historian has other problems too.

To future generations successful revolutions always appear to have been inevitable. As with all historical events, if they have significance, it is in terms of causes and results. In the case of revolutionary acts, though each of these may be traced as being related to the act, they are not therefore to be taken as being related to one another.

Let us take a hypothetical instance to illustrate this. There is a revolution. The party placed in power by it carry out widespread social change. Social discontent was present beforehand. The aims of the discontented may have been realized by the successor government; they may, on the other hand, have been superseded by others, which the discontented did not initially want. They may have been taught to want them. Or their leaders may have been killed in the course of violent change, and the successor government may have implemented their aims in anticipation of a new call for them, one which had not hitherto rematerialized. Which consequences followed from what?

Given this tendency, it is not surprising that the urge to systematize has led to a tendency to theorize on the basis of assumed inevitability. The reflection of this in its principal form of Marxist romanticism will be dealt with at greater length in due course. Here it is mentioned only to draw attention to the close relation between revolutionary historiography and the political

[5] Literature on the *coup* is very sparse. See however: D. J. Goodspeed, *The Conspirators, a Study of the Coup d'Etat* (Macmillan, London, 1962); Feliks Gross, *The Seizure of Political Power in a Century of Revolutions* (Philosophical Library, New York, 1958); Curzio Malaparte, *Coup d'Etat, the technique of revolution* (Dutton, New York, 1932); David C. Rapoport, "Coup d'Etat: the view of the men firing pistols', *Nomos VII: Revolution*, ed. Carl J. Friedrich (Atherton Press, New York, 1966). On revolution in general special credit should be given to Thames & Hudson's The Great Revolutions series, especially: J. Halcro Ferguson, *The Revolutions of Latin America* (1963); Francesco Gabrieli, *The Arab Revival* (1961); Tibor Mende, *The Chinese Revolution* (1961); Victor Purcell, *The Revolution in South-east Asia* (1962).

sympathies of historians of revolutions. Such movements strike sensitive nerves, and provoke violent responses. Objective assessment of the course of events seems particularly difficult, as, for example, in the case of Lenin's individual, opportune decision to chose the path of *coup d'état* in Russia. In this there was nothing inevitable, since the choice contradicted his former doctrines and assumptions and was made purely on the basis of expediency. Ironically, this bowing to expediency alone supplied the success that made the construction of the Marxist myth possible, and so obscured its own lessons.[6]

The most serious problem for the historian of revolution, however, is the key one of sources.

Documentation of revolutionary movements is in its essence scanty, and the nature of the movements themselves such as to bias the sources they leave behind. Unless a revolution is planned on foreign soil, the chances that records will survive of the preliminary stages must be rated as negligible. Even if the revolution is successful, these documents may well be suppressed by the victors in an effort to conceal certain policy decisions contrary to the maintenance of the 'revolutionary myth' or 'image'. This is particularly true of proof of receipt of financial aid, especially from interested parties such as foreign-owned companies. Thus, though a legal adviser to a revolutionary movement may well have in his possession such documents, it is improbable that he will be able to reveal their contents. In the nature of legal business they are unlikely to be seen by outsiders until they have long ceased to be of interest to anyone in a position to preserve them.

Attempts which fail may be better documented owing to the fact that they have been subjected to that scrutiny of an ordered government which is preserved in the form of official records, but these may well be destroyed on subsequent occasions.

Revolutions, of course, are not the only form of human activity to leave little or no written record. Other forms are known to be very common, such as corruption, for which the absence of documentation poses the same problems. No one can doubt that these activities are preceded by the forms of negotiation described by S. E. Finer in the revolutionary context as *trabajos* and *compromisos*—the preliminary period of bargaining

---

[6] Goodspeed, *The Conspirators, A Study of the Coup d'Etat* (1962), pp. 70–107.

and testing of opinion.[7] They may, in an acquiescent society, be similarly described as 'formalized', and may be so recorded by goverments unable or unwilling to defend themselves, in the files of their police or security services. But the reliability of these records will be questionable indeed if no action was taken on them, unless it can be shown that an executive officer took a conscious decision to regard them as false when his colleagues knew that they were true.

This is not as unusual as it sounds. In many countries, revolutionary acts are sufficiently common for rumours of impending *coups* to be continually in the air.[8] In such circumstances it is not surprising that occasionally choice falls on the wrong rumour.

Once a revolutionary outbreak has actually begun, there are a few contemporary documents which may have some value. To begin with, there are regular press and magazine sources, whose political affiliations are known and whose bias can therefore be counteracted. There are special broadsheets and emergency radio and television programmes, usually under the auspices of the falling regime. There is the revolutionary manifesto, and commentaries upon it; the speeches of revolutionary leaders; photographs of fighting, regular and irregular military units, plans of battle, written messages in military records, and so forth.

Now from this stage onward, it is clear that all reports that purport to claim knowledge of prior preparation must be treated with the highest suspicion; so too must all claims of revolutionary and government leaders who are always glad to have the opportunity of exaggerating the degree of their active support or the numbers of supporters pledged to them. When all these cautions have been uttered and heeded, it may well be that the only remaining evidence of the preparation of a movement is the deduction of it from the actual course of events followed. This in turn is not only open to personal interpretation of probabilities, as observed above, but also liable to distortion from unforeseen contemporary events.

Even with the best of contingency planning, a revolutionary

---

[7] Samuel E. Finer, *The Man on Horseback* (Pall Mall, London, 1962), p. 156.
[8] William S. Stokes, *Latin American Politics* (Thomas Y. Crowell, New York, 1959), p. 111.

movement may still encounter unforeseen obstacles, and, for that matter, may receive help where it was not expected. A further source of bias arises from the rapidity of events. This results in displacement, loss, or reversal of vital pieces of action in the mind of the observer, which in some cases can render the development of an actual timetable of a day's events permanently impossible. Well-meaning attempts to fit the pieces into a framework that is based on incorrect assumptions are not unknown. In some cases, pieces which do not appear to fit have been simply discarded.[9] The excitement of the moment and the limitations of memory, in any case, place a formidable limitation on the capacity of the average observer. Excitement is particularly prone to lead to exaggeration, most conspicuously, in the event of street fighting, in overall and individual numbers of casualties and the amount of damage done.[10]

At every level, even that of the trained journalist, the tendency of revolution to bias its own sources can go even further, and contribute to its own growth and development. No observer is truly neutral in the conditions of violence; he is a participant as well. The act of weighing the chances of a government's survival may, by its effect on provincial opinion, actually bring about a conclusion which hitherto was in doubt. A photographer who is shot while taking pictures of street fighting becomes a casualty statistic. He impeded the action, and he impedes the assessment of it.[11] Finally, since even the best observer cannot see everything, it is the winner's, rather than the loser's, version he will tend to adopt to fill in the gaps in his experience. Perhaps the majority of witnesses are thus impelled, consciously or no, to come to express evidence tending towards the post-revolutionary viewpoint.

The assessment of the written documents is the key to accuracy, but it is far from easy. Again it must be emphasized that the time by historical standards is short in which a revolution succeeds or fails.

[9] This phenomenon is best known in connection with the collapse of Germany in 1918 and the subsequent myth of the betrayal; cf. Rudolf Coper, *Failure of a Revolution; Germany in 1918–1919* (C. U. P., Cambridge, 1955).
[10] Exaggeration has a positive role to play (Lyford Paterson Edwards, *The Natural History of Revolution* (Russell & Russell, New York, 1965), pp. 177–83).
[11] In one revolution in Paraguay, the only casualty was a spectator on the balcony of the hotel in the Calle Independencia.

Regular radio and newspaper bulletins are generally, by definition, suspended for the duration of hostilities, at least in the zone in which they are taking place.[12] They may locally or generally be taken under the control of the government, and whether operated by the government or by revolutionary forces in a so-called 'liberated' zone, they will be operated in accordance with the need to maximize support and establish norms of obedience to the appropriate authority. In a situation in which doubt exists or persists for some time as to the probable outcome, news services are in any case often suspended altogether. They are replaced on radio and television services by programmes of solemn or patriotic music, and little else often exists during this time to fill the gap, but rumour.

Irregular bulletins, or news-sheets issued by the contending parties, and the proclamations and handbills issued by the revolutionary forces have the same tendencies, in an even higher degree. The last-named, indeed, are the only prime source for the avowed intentions and aims of the movement.[13]

Bulletins prepared for foreign publications, then, inevitably assume importance for the revolutionary historian. Even they can be startlingly inaccurate on the most basic points of fact. Elementary considerations are the experience of the reporter, his political outlook, and those of the readers for whom he is preparing his material. In remote parts of the world reports tend to be sketchy and angled towards sensational detail, such as release of prisoners, personal vendettas, and casualty statistics. There, too, the reporter, if experienced, probably arrived only after the beginning of the event. He is a human being, and the respective degrees of care with which his person is treated by the contending parties, not just from the elementary consideration of safety but also from appreciation of the public relations value of a military salute, a special pass, or effusive praise of foreigners of his particular nationality, may be conducive to favourable reporting. Together with the contemporary government records these, with all their disadvantages, must be considered fundamental sources, and their disadvantages accepted as such.

---

[12] They were suspended altogether in Iraq in 1958.
[13] A useful small collection for the Middle East is Hisham B. Sharabi, *Nationalism and Revolution in the Arab World* (Van Nostrand, Princeton, N.J., 1966).

In addition, the student of revolution will have to make use of memoirs and reminiscences written after the event, either in the post-revolutionary situation or from the relative safety of exile, or both. It is hardly necessary to indicate that these are generally subjective in tone, and often largely devoted to the justification of the author's course in the events he purports to describe. Even the best will often omit much that is significant.[14]

The revolutionary historian, it is clear, will often wish that more had been preserved for his information. For the past this is now impossible. For the future it may well be that something more can be done. This, in turn, leads us to a consideration of the needs of the student of a contemporary revolution.

For the effective study of the contemporary revolution two basic conditions must be met. The method or methods chosen must be capable of immediate application, at least in the gathering of information. And they must, at the same time, be accurate, complete, detailed, and scientific, both in gathering and in processing information. This suggests that a basis for any study must involve the assembling of data in numerical or other code form. But, for this, the data have first to be collected, and it is at this point that we are made sharply aware of the singular difficulties of assimilating this phenomenon to the standard methods of the social sciences.

The course of revolution is rapid; its onset sudden. Its essence lies in the interruption of communication and movement, and it involves at its core, as has been emphasized already, no little personal danger to the observer. Assessment is clearly difficult, though essential. From a strictly scientific point of view, the ability to predict would be even more gratifying.

Certain lines of approach, however, have been identified, and may at least tentatively be advanced here.

To begin with, it is at least significant to note that violent political change is extremely common. Over much of the Earth's surface, a preliminary consideration indicates, it may be considered more common, indeed, to change governments by violent means than by any other. Certainly in these areas revolutionary acts may be taken as being normal and customary;

---

[14] An exception like Trotsky's *History of the Russian Revolution* (Gollancz, London, 1966) carries its own hazards in the form of a message which it seeks to convey through the detail of reminiscence.

their development being regulated, in fact, according to certain formalized customs, however vague and general these may be.[15]

It seems possible, therefore, to plan for an observation service to be set up in all likely locales. To act as a central clearing house for the information gathered in this way, an Institute of Revolutionary Studies could be set up in some convenient centre, with access to data-processing equipment and with library facilities on the largest scale. The implication is that such an Institute should be located in a university area, but, necessarily, in a country of considerable governmental stability, and one without a tradition of student involvement in political violence. Otherwise, obviously, the host government—if, indeed, one could be found—might reasonably be concerned about the possible effects on its own polity of enthusiasts attempting practical experiments.

Then, secondly, there is reason to suppose that within those areas, some are, for reasons of governmental structure and tradition—or lack of it—more liable to political violence than others. There are fashions in revolution, both in the terminology used to justify its aims and express them, and in the symbols affected. The interesting wave of de-Gaulle-type governments in Asia is but the latest in a long series of sets, of which the largest might be called the Class of 1789.[16] This tendency, however, extends beyond ideology to the tactics favoured and to the form of political organization considered most able to carry them out. Even a primitive comparative study should sharpen the principal points of resemblance to the point at which early information should enable the skilled observer to 'type' the event much more rapidly than is at present the case.

This consideration—the tendency to adhere to a ruling pattern—clearly strengthens, in turn, the value of the comparative method. In prediction, however, it presupposes a minimum level of diversionary factors on which the original example was predicated. Since the most common form of di-

---

[15] All formal politics are the product of ritualized violence, but for an extreme case see Norman A. La Charité *et al.*, *Case Study in Insurgency and Revolutionary Warfare: Guatemala 1944–1954* (Special Operations Research Office, The American University, Washington, D.C., 1964), p. 92.

[16] Terminating, perhaps, in 1848, whose fifty [*sic*] revolutions, not all successful, demonstrate the association even more clearly (Priscilla Robertson, *Revolutions of 1848, a social history* (Harper, New York, 1960)).

versionary factor is some form of intervention from the extra-societal environment, allowance will always have to be made for the extreme reluctance, particularly of so-called Great Powers, to refrain from it.

It may be said that there is no guarantee that, if one power does not intervene, its rival or enemy will not do so; nor that, if no power intervenes, the revolution will not follow an undesirable course in terms of the interests of one or other of them. All this is quite true. But is a question well worth considering, whether the unpredictability of an uncontrollable, unpredictable revolution is likely to be desirable to any contending power *in the long run*. At least, in terms of pure self interest, it would be wise to attempt a very much more thorough analysis of the growth and progress of any revolution before intervention than is currently the case, but better by far not to intervene at all.

Thirdly, it is a fact that revolutionary movements presuppose the existence of some kind of social and political order. If there is no government to be overthrown, there cannot, strictly speaking, be a revolutionary movement, since there is no one agreed government that it can operate against. The question of defining this state of affairs, and of the nature of the state-building process which corresponds to revolution in it, will be left to a later chapter. Here it is sufficient, for the present, to note that the existence of a government implies in turn a pattern of action which is disturbed by the onset of revolution. It is therefore clear that the student of revolution must first gain a detailed acquaintance with the normal operation of the state machine in the area of time immediately preceding the onset. He must go further: he must establish a historical pattern of development, in which the degree of departure from precedent, if any, may be placed.

This form of study is fundamental, and fortunately a relatively straightforward matter. The conventions of such study are, after all, already well established. Official actions of a legitimate government are generally recognized as being a legitimate object of study, within certain broad limits. The existence of any counter-governmental operation, however secret, must necessarily be reflected in perturbations of the operation of the political system. That is to say, not only does an overt political movement manifest itself most obviously by its effect

upon its rivals, but even a subterranean conspiracy will do like-
wise. It is, indeed, doubtful whether the most secret of conspiracies can exist in a well-organized state. *Prima facie* evidence
suggests that in most, if not all instances, a government which is
overthrown is well aware in advance of the existence of the
movement which is to overthrow it.[17] At the very least, they
know the direction from which danger is to be apprehended, the
reasonable estimate of the amount of force available to be deployed by the disaffected party, and the nature of the means
which they are likely to employ. Yet in a surprisingly large
number of cases the action actually taken to forestall or counter
the revolutionary attempt is weak, ineffective, and perhaps
positively suicidal.[18] This suggests that in developing a theory
of revolution one must necessarily develop a theory of government. Yet the sort of theory of government which we are likely
to obtain from previous consideration of revolution is likely to be
somewhat different from those of existing models; models developed on the presupposition of ordered government.

METHOD

With these problems of information in mind, the present study
was planned to make use of the comparative method, in treating
of a limited number of variables suitable for quantitative treatment.

Though these variables all relate to the revolutionary event,
they were in the first instance selected because of their quantitative nature, rather than for the part they play in the development of the revolutionary event. They are, therefore, in the
nature of indicators rather than true variables, though some
participate of both aspects, and may alternatively be termed its
dimensions.

The model commences by assigning to each revolutionary
event a specific *periodicity*; that is to say, a measure of the time
elapsed since the last transition in the designated political
system.

The transition itself has a *duration* in time, and a *level* in geo-

[17] Denis W. Brogan, *The Price of Revolution* (Hamish Hamilton, London, 1951),
p. 66.

[18] Crane Brinton, *The Anatomy of Revolution* (Vintage Books, New York, 1952),
pp. 48–51.

graphical space. The violence employed in achieving it has a *strength* in terms of personnel and armament, and a *magnitude* in number of casualties resulting from it.

Leadership in this action, which is, after all, a military action, is located in a *directorate* whose size, though perhaps very large in some cases, is at least theoretically capable of measurement as the key leadership group within the movement as a whole.

These *personnel*, whose strength we have already estimated, may be broadly grouped according to whether they are military or civilian or both. Important differences may be hypothesized as being related to this variable. The event may lead to one of a number of types of *succession*, and these indeed may prove to be one of the best indicators by which we can measure the effects of the event itself. The succession may be accompanied by an increase or decrease in the qualitative or quantitative *participation* of individuals in the political process.

Lastly, the event may or may not be accompanied by external *aid* and result in internal or external social *initiatives* on the part of the successor government. If it does, it will be relevant to the question both of the programme of the revolution and of the myth which it may or may not be successful in creating.

We cannot, however, hope to handle all these variables successfully until we have first made an attempt to locate the revolutionary event itself within the general field of the politics of violence. When this is done, we can proceed to identify the power relationships intrinsic to the revolutionary event. By so doing we shall give depth to the choice of variables outlined here. Then and only then can we make use of them to generate further hypotheses about the nature of revolution in our own time.

FORCE

Constitutional government is a substitute for force in intra state relations. It is a development of the etiquette that binds the political community in its primitive state.[19] The informal use of

[19] Lucy Mair, *Primitive Government* (Penguin Books, London, 1962), pp. 18–19; Meyer Fortes and E. E. Evans Pritchard, eds., *African Political Systems* (O. U. P., London, 1963), p. XV; Aidan Southall, 'A Critique of the Typology of States and Political Systems', in Max Gluckman and Fred Eggan, eds., *Political Systems and the Distribution of Power*, A.S.A. Monographs, 2 (Tavistock Publications, London, 1965), pp. 120–1.

force, which we call violence, may either be regulated or suppressed by society, but it must be either regulated or suppressed. If it is regulated, it may either be institutionalized or left in private hands. It is unlikely that it can ever wholly be suppressed: there is an ineradicable minimum.

Since crime rates reflect the degree of disrespect for the law, that is to say the degree to which the social norms diverge from the norms of the ruling ideology, they must be examined by the political scientist as the basis of his assessment of the use of force in social control within the political community.[20] The nature of violence is determined by the nature of political socialization. The attitude towards violence to other members of the community, for example in the school or in the peer group, is determined very early in youth. In this country the legend of Robin Hood is perhaps not taken too seriously, and it is counterbalanced by the authority patterns of such well-known civic pictures of virtue as Dick Whittington and the Mayor of Toy Town. Contrast the situation of the American child brought up on Daniel Boone or Davy Crockett, or the 'bad men' of the West. These variations are the most basic expression of the differences between countries which determine the variations in the patterns of force and violence in the life of the adult communities in those countries. The myth of the frontier setting preserved in the United States is now no longer applicable to a largely suburban or urban community, but its persistence still determines much of the pattern of social life within certain groups more or less alienated from the main stream.

In most mature societies these are the only dominant patterns still recognized by society. In less mature societies force may indeed be largely left in private hands, and the patterns of duel and feud continue to serve ends without imperilling the structure of the community.[21] If necessary, institutional patterns

[20] Indicators for current societies are given in Bruce M. Russett, *World Handbook of Political and Social Indicators* (Yale University Press, New Haven, 1964). A sophisticated extension is Ted Gurr, *New error-compensated measures for comparing nations: some correlates of civil violence*, Center of International Studies, Woodrow Wilson School of Public and International Affairs, Research Monograph No. 25 (Princeton, 1966).

[21] Richard S. Weinert, 'Violence in pre-modern societies: rural Colombia', *American Political Science Review*, LX, no. 2 (June 1966), 340.

such as the bullfight, the football match, or even the Olympic Games may act to divert a proportion of energy from political violence in a given country. These facts are well recognized. What is not always so clearly recognized is the degree to which force persists in the service of the state.

The state claims the monopoly of the use of force within its territorial jurisdiction, as Weber recognized.[22] But it is all too easy to interpret this monopoly in transcendental terms. The use of force on behalf of the state is not just an academic question. The state is continually engaged in a full-scale war upon those elements who seek to diverge from the institutionalized pattern of non-violent action. In short, the war on crime *is* a war. Even in the most 'law-abiding' of communities a considerable measure of physical force is accepted as being necessary, and in some cases indeed desirable, in the arrest of criminals. It is not, however, possible to separate the persistence of physical force in any pattern in the service of the state from its potential or actual impact upon politics. Any use of force can be institutionalized into a pattern of social control, and this implies therefore that it may in certain circumstances be used also in patterns of political control.

We may begin, therefore, with the consideration of the use of regular police force. The type that is meant here is not only that which is used in the making of arrests, but also that accepted as a minimal quantity in the interrogation of suspects or in unofficial or semi-official action against persons deemed to be undesirable. The 1964 action of the Brighton police against 'mods' and 'rockers' was of this type. Traditional targets in countries other than the United Kingdom of this pattern of harassment, targets which might be considered to serve a political function, have been rioters, strikers, and demonstrators. In modern times this pattern, raised to a high degree of sophistication in, for example, South Africa, has been developed into a deliberate pattern of inhibition of the expression of interests held by a substantial section of the population.[23] It is generally considered that in normal circumstances it is inapplicable, in

[22] Max Weber, *The Theory of Social and Economic Organization* (The Free Press, New York, 1965), pp. 155–6.
[23] Gwendolen M. Carter, *The Politics of Inequality, South Africa since 1948*, 2nd edn. (Thames & Hudson, London, 1958), pp. 48 ff.

that it will lead, in an open society, to irritation and social instability.[24] This risk, however, is one which governments still seem quite willing to take.

When this pattern proceeds to a more developed one, it may be characterized separately as partaking of the character of special police force. All countries maintain some form of police organization for security (counter-intelligence) purposes. In the United Kingdom it is well known that this function is performed by the Special Branch. Since counter-intelligence operations involve the safety of the state and small, but critical, numbers of persons and brief times, the temptation to resort to extra-legal methods must be strong where the threat to the state is correspondingly strong. In common-law countries, it is generally considered that the right of recourse to law operates to a high degree against the effective operation of such systems. Countries enjoying the protection of common law and Habeas Corpus as an integral part of their structure are few, and the greater part of countries in the world are far more strongly influenced by Roman law. Roman-law countries do not have the universal right of recourse against the excesses of administrative action, except through administrative law. Furthermore, the urgency of recourse in most countries increases with the value of the secrets which that country seeks to hide and the proximity of those secrets to land frontiers. Where there is a genuine threat, or where a genuine threat is apprehended, this urgency may become such as to lead to a substantial cession of authority to the protective forces.[25]

Where this urge for security is coupled with the existence of the dominant one-party state, this type of force shades off imperceptibly into that exercised by the secret police. In Europe alone, Spain, Portugal, Yugoslavia, and the Iron Curtain countries each maintain some form of secret police.[26] Strictly speaking these organs, though incorporated within the respective ministries of the interior of these states, are entirely extra-

[24] As, e.g., in Ireland, with the Royal Irish Constabulary; Richard Bennett, *The Black and Tans* (Four Square, London, 1964), p. 13.

[25] David Wise and Thomas B. Ross, *The Invisible Government* (Jonathan Cape, London, 1965), p. 4.

[26] Merle Fainsod, *How Russia is Ruled* (Harvard University Press, Cambridge, Mass.; O. U. P., London, 1963), pp. 421–62; Simon Wolin and R. M. Slusser, eds., *The Soviet Secret Police* (Praeger, New York, 1957).

constitutional. They exist for political reasons pure and simple, and their political importance is paramount over any incidental function they may serve in regulating trivial infractions of the law. Any concern that they may have with considerations of criminal behaviour or military security are overshadowed by the dominant need for political security of the ruling elite. As the chief organ of rule-application, therefore, they are supreme, and by the nature of the political structure virtually divorced from the input functions of the political system. They can therefore be regarded as exercising a form of political function which can be termed 'input control'. That is to say, they regulate the process of political socialization and recruitment and interest articulation so that demands and claims, if presented at all, need not be met.[27] Clearly, such an organization, if unchecked, would form a serious threat to the monopoly of the state over it. It therefore follows that it is not permitted to engross a monopoly of force and is counterbalanced in most cases by the military organization.

Before considering the role of the military it will be necessary, however, to consider the role of paramilitary forces, which are frequently found in the particular form of the militia-structured political party in combination with a secret police.[28] They could, of course, exist without it, but no significant example seems to exist. The paramilitary force, although valuable in its way as a counterpoise to the secret police, is more often found in combination with it, as a counterpoise to the military. Certain paramilitary police forces exist for purely strategic reasons unconnected with the dominance of one political party, and are designated to fight a full-scale war against guerrilla forces, for which they are considered to be in some ways superior to the military. The variants on this theme are wide-ranging, from the forces of Malaysia, which are entirely professional and military, to those of Thailand where revolutionary outbreaks have persistently involved clashes between the paramilitary police and the military. In the latter case the paramilitary forces in themselves have been used as a base for the ascent of a military

[27] This is very distinct from Easton's concept of 'gatekeeping' as 'regulation of want conversion', which as he uses it implies some intention to convert wants (David Easton, *A Systems Analysis of Political Life* (John Wiley, New York, 1965), p. 93).

[28] On the militia as a party structure see Maurice Duverger, *Political Parties, their Organisation and Activity in the Modern State* (Methuen, London, 1964), pp. 36 ff.

leader to political power. The classic example of this phenomenon was the *coup* mounted by Luang Pibul in 1947.[29]

The key organ in the use of force by the state in all systems is
the army. The army gains its supreme importance from its role
in the maintenance of the boundary of the state-system, and in
maintaining, indeed, its very existence in the international
community.[30] The state in its international role presupposes
the existence of a separate organ of force. But its existence in
itself poses a question of control to the ruling elite. In a nascent
nation-state the development of role-differentiation requires a
distinct class devoted to military proficiency. As the representatives of the state in its war-making capacity, members of this
body find themselves continuously tempted to assert themselves as holding a prescriptive claim either to regulate in the
interests of constitutional stability the operation of the system or,
in advanced cases, to supplant it.

The political role of the military has been the subject of a
number of detailed studies, both general and regional.[31] In the
divided community it assumes a dual significance. As re-
storers of the constitution the military incline to support the
'conservative' side of politics, and as an internal caste, their
loyalty, which overrides regional loyalties of its members and
those of the community as a whole, does serve a positive function in compelling geographical unity and in maintaining the
boundaries of the political system intact. But in revolution the
army comes into its own. There it is the crucial weight in the

[29] Anthony Short, 'Communism and the Emergency', in Wang Gung-wu, ed.,
Malaysia (Pall Mall, London, 1964), pp. 149 ff.; John Coast, *Some Aspects of
Siamese Politics* (International Secretariat Institute of Pacific Relations, New York,
1953), mimeographed.

[30] Alfred Vagts, *A History of Militarism, Civilian and Military* (Hollis & Carter,
London, 1959), p. 15.

[31] Stanislaw Andrzejewski, *Military Organisation and Society* (Routledge, London,
1954); William Gutteridge, *Armed Forces in New States* (O. U. P., London, 1962);
Michael Howard, ed., *Soldiers and Governments. Nine Studies in Civil–Military Relations*
(Eyre & Spottiswoode, London, 1957); Samuel P. Huntington, *The Soldier and the
State; The Theory and Politics of Civil–Military Relations* (Harvard University Press,
Cambridge, Mass., 1957); John J. Johnson, *The Military and Society in Latin America*
(Stanford University Press, Stanford, 1964); John J. Johnson, ed., *The Role of the
Military in Underdeveloped Countries* (Princeton University Press, Princeton, 1962);
Edwin Lieuwen, *Arms and Politics in Latin America* (Praeger, London, 1963); Finer,
op. cit.; Vagts, op. cit.; Martin C. Needler, 'Political development and military
intervention in Latin America', *American Political Science Review*, LX, no. 3 (Sept.
1966), 616.

balance of power. As the ultimate argument of the ruling elite the army's loyalties become vital to the stability of the regime against whatever patterns of violence may be levelled against it. It is generally conceded that the right of legitimacy possessed by the government extends as far as the use of the military forces in its defence against an overt attempt to overthrow it, and it is frequently so used.

Questions of this kind, however, arise only after the development of a pattern of political threat. The total pattern of violence is made up of a number of lesser patterns, coming under the general headings of sub-revolutionary violence and violence against the state. To these we must now turn.

VIOLENCE

No general agreement at present seems to exist as to where the pattern of violence against the state first emerges from the pattern of constitutional action. Demonstrations, for example, may be either non-violent or violent. The degree of accepted violence used by demonstrators varies a great deal from country to country, and from age to age. In many cases, without proceeding to violence, demonstrations alone have been sufficient to bring down governments, as in France in 1848.[32] They therefore must be held in all cases to imply an element of violence of expression within the norms of the society and to be subject to governmental recognition of them as such. They are not likely to be interpreted as such unless there is a tradition of violent action which leads the government to suppose that it is possible that they may in fact develop into violence. If they do so, they may be reclassified as riots. But the distinction between violent demonstrations and riots is in one sense very great.

Riots are a much more widespread, general, uncontrolled expression of undiscriminating rejection of constitutional values, carrying political overtones of unchecked escalation towards possible future demands for the overthrow of the government.

An extension in geographical terms of this is the endemic terrorist movement. Terrorist movements may be found in most parts of the world; in fact the United States is among the few

[32] Robertson, pp. 30–9.

countries in the world in which this form of action is not traditional.[33] But terrorism, although capable of being subdivided as between riots and demonstrations, in terms of avowed aims and the nature of the political change sought, is in its nature extremely difficult to classify and identify. All that can be said here is that the persistence of terrorism is undoubtedly closely related to the availability of weapons. Where, as in tropical countries, these may be improvised from unspecialized agricultural implements which are freely available, terrorism tends to be particularly widespread.[34]

Described in these generalized terms, however, the levels of violence against the state remain vague and indeterminate, implying that by their nature they resist classification in 'institutional' terms. To make use of them in political analysis we must link them with the sort of functions that are performed by the political system itself. It is reasonable to suppose that these movements, which may generally be classified in the terms of Émile Durkheim's definition as 'anomic', will perform not only the interest-articulation function ascribed to them by Almond and Coleman, but also (sporadically) those of interest aggregation, political socialization and recruitment, and, indeed, political communication.[35] Further, since these movements in some sense supplant the state by virtue of their very existence, they partake of the nature of the political system, and we may expect to find among anomic movements parallels to the regular institutions of organized government, once examination of function has shown us where to look.

If the threshold of violence is attained with the public demonstration, often closely linked with other forms of direct action, such as strikes, which are possibly of private or non-political origin, there we may begin our search. Demonstrations are quite violent enough, within the rules of the game, to be very uncomfortable for the individual opponent unlucky enough to be caught in them. But their purpose is a single one; they have one aim and articulate one interest. The implication that they are the anomic equivalent of interest groups is inescapable.

[33] Examples in Europe alone include Austria, Great Britain, Italy, and France.

[34] Stokes, pp. 300–12, discusses this phenomenon, which in Latin America is called *machetismo*.

[35] Gabriel A. Almond and James S. Coleman, eds., *The Politics of the Developing Areas* (Princeton University Press, Princeton, 1960), pp. 17, 26–38.

In a different order of violence, equally clearly, is the urban riot. These are generalized, undiscriminating in aggregation, perhaps but clearly aggregative, and with the potential of political and even governmental change, when operating in the capital city and directed towards the possession of the machinery of government. They could, therefore, be regarded as the anomic equivalent of a parliamentary party. Like it, they vary widely in the quality of their leadership and the degree to which this has accepted the need for planning and organization in the search for power. Planning, if present, may similarly be amateur or professional.

The anomic equivalent of the 'mass' party would seem to be the generalized terrorist movement. It is, after all, at this level that violence plays the most important role in political socialization and recruitment of members of rural populations with a view to achieving political control. In this way, it is part of the daily frame of reference over large areas of the world's surface. For with the persistence of terrorism the maintenance of order based upon a written agreement or constitution becomes virtually impossible. It is replaced by the local dominance of the terrorist machine. The tendency, naturally, is to concentrate on such dramatic examples of the phenomenon as Morocco, Colombia, or Indonesia in the 1960s.[36] But this, as we have seen, is to miss an important point, its quality of survival *pari passu* with constitutional government in the most advanced political communities.

With terrorism the threshold of revolution would seem to have been reached. But we must remember that there are certain societies in which government has either never developed or has completely broken down. These are the countries that are in the state which we may call 'anarchial decentralism', and in which we can now postulate the existence of a full state of civil war existing through time at the level of sub-revolutionary violence.[37] This is one of the functions of state building referred to

[36] On Colombia see John D. Martz, *Colombia, a Contemporary Political Survey* (University of North Carolina Press, Chapel Hill, 1964); Weinert, loc. cit. On Indonesia after the fall of Sukarno see Tarzie Vittachi, *The Fall of Sukarno* (Mayflower-Dell, London, 1967).

[37] The only current example is Laos, unless Vietnam be allowed despite its developed state. See Roger M. Smith, 'Laos', in *Governments and Politics of Southeast Asia*, 2nd edn., ed. George McTurnan Kahin (Cornell University Press, Ithaca, N.Y., 1964), pp. 527–89. Arabia, Albania, and China have had similar

in the first chapter. At this point we have clearly reverted to the fact that without the existence of a defined government revolution as such cannot exist. It is this scale which we may use as the basis for our classification of the politics of violence. It is likely that some will object that in this sense 'the politics of violence' appears to be a contradiction in terms.

To accept this, however, would be to draw a hard and fast line between non-violent and violent behaviour, which we have already agreed would not be in accordance with the facts. The problem of maintaining an ordered community in an environment in which violent relationships have been normal can be tackled in three ways. The community may make every effort to suppress violence, making no concession to the desire of individuals to make use of it in the natural patterns of their lives. Such a situation would psychologically be one of extreme instability; while the absolute alternative, the voluntary assumption of the duty of maintaining an agreement on the use of non-violence at all times, seems to be equally unrealistic.

The basis of continuing society, even the internally non-violent one, therefore, is an arrangement whereby violence is channelled within given bounds. Most easily, it can be directed outside the territorial boundary of the community on neighbouring communities with which no restraining ties exist. But these communities may be too ordered, too stable, or too powerful to be challenged in this way. Failing the dispersion of individual energies in risky and dangerous activities to reduce violent inputs to the political system to the point at which they can be easily regulated, some agreement will be needed as to use of violence in the political struggle itself.

This may broadly take one of two forms, that is, a geographical or a social delimitation. The latter implies that certain rituals give permission for the use of violence, or that violence is directed against some limited sect or clique within society whose role is to furnish the scapegoat for the acts of the society as a whole. The former, which is rare, implies that violence is by custom restricted to a given area, usually the environs of the

experiences since 1900. Anthony Nutting, *The Arabs, A Narrative History from Mohammed to the Present* (Hollis & Carter, London, 1964); David Howarth, *The Desert King, a life of Ibn Saud* (Collins, London, 1964); Vandeleur Robinson, *Albania's Road to Freedom* (Allen & Unwin, London, 1941); Constantine A. Chekrezi, *Albania Past and Present* (Macmillan, New York, 1919).

capital, but sometimes a provincial battleground of traditional significance but little practical strategic value. In either case, the acquisition of control over the key area brings about a symbolic dominance which is transferred to an actual transition of power by technically sub-revolutionary means.[38]

The political community derives from societies in which the nature of politics is discernible only by the act of boundary-maintenance. In the mature society violence is to be recognized as corrosive, and handled as such. How then can we relate the existence of anomic structures with the duration of the political community through time in any form that we can recognize? The answer is that in the complex interplay of forces which constitutes the community we must recognize significant phases of positive and negative structures, in which the negative structures act to attract compulsions that would otherwise disrupt the community altogether. If violence pure and simple is corrosive to the ordered community, anomic structures are nevertheless present within it, both inherently and in the form of expressions of social disobedience. It is true that the aspects of violence that appear in the political sphere are sporadic and intermittent, and their relationship to one another is as yet imperfectly understood.[39] The relationships between them, however, are not the whole story: it is the overall pattern of relationships between them and the structures of the ordered community that alone gives the total expression of the dynamic pattern.

In the physical sciences a multitude of particles have been discovered, negatively charged and potentially annihilating to the concept of matter as it exists in our universe in the combination of the 'anti-matter' beloved of science-fiction writers. But it does not exist in that particular combination in our universe, and separately these particles fulfil a necessary role in the structure of matter. The study of political 'anti-matter' is a study of relationships of this sort. They have an inner coherence,

[38] The similarity to state-building conditions is most evident in the state of dissolution and reformation of Central Europe in late 1918, particularly in Yugoslavia. See, e.g., Ivo J. Lederer, *Yugoslavia at the Paris Peace Conference; a Study in frontier making* (Yale University Press, New Haven and London, 1965).

[39] Konrad Lorenz, *On Aggression* (Methuen, London, 1966); Richard N. Adams, 'Power and Power Domains', *América Latina* (Rio de Janeiro), IX, Abril–Junho de 1966, no. 2 (Reprint 33, The University of Texas Institute of Latin American Studies Offprint Series).

even if that coherence is incompatible with the maintenance of ordered government.

At the head of the scale of anomic structures, therefore, stands that temporary large-scale phenomenon we call revolution. But what is the non-anomic equivalent? Is it the equivalent of a general election? It is, after all, a structure of choice. It represents the successful culmination, one would think, of the interests articulated and aggregated by lesser structures which we can separately describe as being sub-revolutionary in character. But the parallel does not do full justice to a complex phenomenon. It is an institutional pattern of transfer which lacks only institutionalization, but it is more than that. The deception arises simply from its negative phase in that it represents the annihilation of the political system if carried to a sufficient degree. Revolution is the anomic equivalent of the system.

Since we shall feel the need for a more sophisticated scheme of anomic inputs at a later period of our investigations, it seems advisable to set it out here as the corollary of this identification. This exposition does not imply any specific internal relationships at this stage between an anomic structure and its parallel in the ordered community; but it does suggest, though not with precision, something of the relationships which exist between the structures performing each of the Almond and Coleman functions and those performing others.

Among the anomic structures that operate in the process of political socialization, we find, as we have already suggested, violent crime, oratorical violence or the habit of rhetorical appeals to violence, and the duel and feud. The imitation of earlier anomic movements comes under this category. So too does military training and, even more tellingly, participation in war without glory or indeed with actual ignominy, especially in defeat. The process of political recruitment in the anomic scheme, then, demands more structured functional processes. The most usual manifestation include picketing, informal tribunals and lynching parties, demonstrations, riot incitement and street coercion. With the introduction of terrorist visitations and conspiracies, whether military or civil, we reach forms of functional specialization which lead specifically to potential classes of revolutionary behaviour. They provide the personnel necessary for the development of the interests expressed through other anomic movements and, indeed, of interests that are denied access to the normal process of political action by non-violent means.[40]

The interest-articulation function in anomic terms is expressed through strikes, street and agrarian incidents, attacks on political leaders, on buildings or fitments representing the symbolic authority of the state, or on major interests regarded as being of functional importance in the maintenance of the prevailing regime. Functional specialization is further developed in the support of organized terrorist movements or participation in them or in the consultation among the military which precede interposition or intervention in the affairs of government. This holds good even for movements aiming at something less than a governmental transition, indicating the close relationship between whirlpools of anomic activity and the regular process of governmental interchange. Conversely, non-violent as well as violent interest expressions can be aggregated through the more sophisticated machinery of anomic interest aggregation.

At this point functional specialization involves us in a problem of identification which is of some complexity. Instances of anomic interest aggregation are of great historic importance in many cases; and their study lays corresponding stress on their individual characteristics rather than on their role in a functional scheme. The corresponding societies of the American colonies in 1774–5, the military juntas of Brazil and Argentina, the Peasants' Revolts of the Middle Ages, and the Sections of Paris in 1792 all do, however, have this unity in functional terms. Similarly, specialization in the techniques of revolutionary warfare produce the terrorist bands, guerrilla sections, and lodges of military officers, which in modern times have operated to translate generalized interests into formidably effective presentations, within the anomic context, of demand for political, and hence governmental, change. Institutional specialization is reflected in the emergence of significant roles in political communication for individuals serving as informal news readers, authors of proclamations, and couriers of all types.

[40] Cf. José Ortega y Gasset, *La Rebelión de las Masas* (Revista del Occidente, Madrid, 1962).

If the political system is seen as a mechanism for making decisions or choices between alternatives, then revolution, it cannot be denied, is the anomic process of choice. It is, then, not only the general election, the selection of leaders, or even the cabinet meeting, but in a curious way it goes beyond that, to operate as a political system as a whole. This point will emerge again under conditions of more favourable clarification in the discussion on the revolutionary sequence.

We are now in a position to proceed with our model for the study of revolution, and so attempt to give to the major process of the anomic anti-world of politics something of the scientific basis that has been given in recent years to its equivalent in the ordered political system.

A MODEL OF REVOLUTION

CLASSIFICATION

THE essential difference between revolution proper and sub-revolutionary violence lies in the successful transfer of power. This transfer of power we shall call the revolutionary transition. It is in this actual act of transition that we find the basis for classification of revolutionary movements. This classification, therefore, is integral to the nature of revolution and is not shared by it with any other form of political action. On the other hand, as we have established, sub-revolutionary violence in a sense may amount to a revolution that has been unsuccessful. It will therefore be found that the nature of sub-revolutionary violence is capable of interpretation in the terms of the scheme that is set out here.[1]

The transfer of power from the forces legitimately exercising it within the state demands the exercise of power. That exercise of power, it may be expected, will be resisted, in the case of extra-constitutional means with all the force the state can command. This process of resistance implies that inevitably there exists a close relationship between the strength of the government as a body capable of deploying force, and the strength of revolutionary movements directed against it.

The scheme of classification which we propose may therefore be based either upon the power employed to overthrow the government, or on the power which that government can exercise against it. Both may be expressed theoretically with reasonable ease in standard terms, as units of military capability, and each is related to the other.[2] The use and employment of this power is regulated by the normal considerations of

[1] A summary of this section with additions appeared as Peter Calvert, 'Revolution: the politics of violence', *Political Studies*, XV, no. 1 (Feb. 1967), 1.

[2] The relationship can be calculated mathematically by an extension of the N-square law first propounded by Frederick W. Lanchester in *Aircraft in Warfare, the dawn of the fourth arm* (Constable, London, 1916). See below.

strategy. That is to say, it depends for its effectiveness not only on the actual total amount of force available but also on the rate with which it can be developed to the extent demanded, together with the resources available for developing additional force on any given front as required. It is from the exigencies of strategy, also, that the degrees of classification are necessarily derived.

There are four levels of action on which military force may be directed against a government, provided that force is to be generated within its own national territory. Force may be directed against the executive, whether vested in an individual or in a small collective body. It may be directed against the government as a whole. In view of the fact that government, in a modern developed country, is normally fully effective only in symbiosis with its capital city, at the heart of a formalized network of communications, force may be directed against the capital city and towards the possession of the capital city. Force may also be exercised indirectly on the capital, and hence on the government, by the acquisition of a base in a province or over an area of the country outside the capital region. There are in fact no other ways in which military force may be directed so as to secure a governmental transition, by its effect alone. The exercise of force may, and very frequently does, bring about a loss of will on the part of the government to resist. The resignation of a government under pressure, in face of such force and demonstrations of strength, however, may be assimilated to the respective level on which that force is being applied, and therefore to this extent there is no clearly marked boundary line between each of these categories and a series of shadow forms of sub-revolutionary violence except their success.[3]

Before proceeding to analyse these groupings, three points must be noticed.

The first is that the transfer of power by force is not rare, but

---

[3] For the sake of convenience, we may give each of these levels an arbitrarily chosen name. I have suggested the following, as being vaguely related to the quantity of violence they are supposed to designate, in that they are all existing restricted usages on the given level. Thus a successful exercise of power on the executive I have termed a defenestration; on the government a *golpe*, on the capital a *cuartelazo*, and on a province a *pronunciamiento*. Purists may object, but politics has a long history of borrowings from Spanish, of which 'liberal' and 'ambassador' are not the least considerable. See Calvert, 'Revolution; the politics of violence'; Stokes, pp. 316 ff.

extremely common. Indeed, in historical terms, for many countries it has been more common than peaceful transfer (in other words, than transfer of power regulated through an institutionalized pattern by the guidance of accepted rules and customs). Nor is this surprising since the location of power in the primitive society was determined by force. The primitive society of today exists in so far as it exists at all in virtue of the fact that it is delimited by a boundary beyond which sanctions on the use of force do not apply. Within those boundaries, on the other hand, the community may either choose to regulate or to forbid the use of force altogether. In the last resort, however, in the primitive community and even in the nation states of today, force is still the ultimate determinant of the authority of the ruler. The revolution is simply a challenge to this established pattern, in the language in which it is itself accustomed to operate.

This implies, therefore, that this means of transfer, where it is normal, has developed in most cases its own ritual and set of customs. Where this has occurred, revolution has been assimilated to the pattern of government. Where it has not, it is clear that the resort to violence in securing the transfer of power is liable to be unpredictable and probably savage. It follows that there is injected into the governmental structure a degree of violence that is then incorporated into it and may indeed become a regular part of it. It is clear that in this latter eventuality the relation of it to the pre-revolutionary condition must take account of the degree of force employed in the first instance.

In considering this, an important principle emerges. If the quantity is insufficient, clearly no revolution will have occurred, and the type of violence will remain at a sub-revolutionary level, however important its consequences may be in political terms. But if, on the other hand, the amount is excessive, reactions additional to those necessitated by the transition are inevitable, and may well become unpredictable. If so, the directorate may lose control of the forces that it has generated, the force surplus to its requirements becoming available for acquisition by potential rivals. From the point of view of the revolutionary the use of excess force, beyond the small quantity necessary to meet contingencies, is foolishly unnecessary. Its preparation may well betray the movement, and its use is likely in the most favourable of circumstances to prove beyond its capacity.

The minimum quantity of force needed to overthrow a given government in given circumstances may be termed the Minimum Necessary Force (MNF). It is possible that in some societies, in some circumstances, this quantity may be so great as to be outside the capacity of any anti-governmental group to develop from internal resources, or so small as to fall below the limit of revolutionary as opposed to sub-revolutionary action, even without the operation of constitutional agreements or a belief-system to which the ruling elite normally conforms. But in most cases we may expect it to fall within one of the four levels we have identified, which represents a progression of quantities from the lowest to the highest within the terms of our definition.

On these as we can, therefore, proceed to construct a series of matrices on the basis of qualities in the operation that we consider to be of sufficient importance. One that is of particular interest is the nature of the successor government installed by the promoters of the revolutionary transition. In general the nature of this is quite clear, because if a transition has been achieved at all, the object almost inevitably assumes by that fact the nature of an accomplished result, even if this stage is transitional as a stage to a development of more complex political forms. Needless to say, the real reasons of the promoters may well not accord with their ostensible ones, and their intentions may always change as success in execution raises the possibility of the achievement of goals previously discarded as over-optimistic in the foreseeable pattern of events.

A special complication arises where the achievement of the revolutionary transition is unsuccessful, either because the MNF is not achieved at all, or because it is not achieved in what we may call the Critical Time (CT). In this case a transition may be achieved that was not contemplated and that is in fact achieved at the hands of a third party. In such cases the two sets of actions must be carefully separated, the existence of the former attempt being taken into account in the assessment of the balance of chances of the latter.

When two or more revolutionary transitions can be related in this way the set of transitions will here be designated a revolutionary sequence.

In all cases, the deployment of force requires certain social and material preconditions. These, which will be treated in greater detail in presenting the comparative study, are the directorate, the personnel, the goals, and the facilities of revolution. Lack of any one of them renders the development of a revolutionary situation impossible—a fact known by rule of thumb to every generation of rulers who have succeeded in maintaining themselves in power.[4]

It follows, therefore, that even if the MNF is exceeded in the course of a revolutionary transition, affording the opportunity for a fresh transition to be made, no such further transition can take place unless the excess force can be brought under the control of a new directorate commanding personnel and with fresh goals posited by them for a fresh revolutionary situation. Of course, the variables need not necessarily be the same ones and, indeed, are more likely *not* to be the same ones, as those involved in the original transition. But it is reasonable to expect that they will be more influenced by it than by any other single determinant, until at least a substantial period of years has gone by.

If, for example, potential personnel have been alienated by a potential directorate's conduct in circumstances of violent action, its chances of assuming leadership in a similar situation will depend on its ability either to eradicate this unfortunate impression or to transfer its appeal to fresh groups sufficient in number to outweigh them. The important thing to note, however, is that the *excess* over the MNF is *in every other way* equivalent to a balance of sub-revolutionary violence. That is to say, the consequences of a deficiency are not necessarily different from those of an excess.

Deficiency below the MNF can imply either no change or an attempt to add further force, with or without an attempt to forestall or pre-empt that addition. The excess over the MNF can mean either that the change of government is resisted only by a form of violence which is within its powers to control, or that it is resisted either by an attempt by the prior government to reverse the decision of force or an attempt by other groups to

---

[4] Aristotle's *Politics*, trs. Benjamin Jowett, intro. H. W. C. Davis (Clarendon Press, Oxford, 1931), Book 5, paras. 8:5, 9:5, 10:13, etc.; Niccolò Machiavelli, *The Prince* and *The Discourses* (Random House, New York, 1950), pp. 89–90.

avert the threat of such a reaction by following the example of the successful revolutionaries.

It is safe to say, however, that the existence of an actual revolutionary transition will have one major consequence not shared by any expression of sub-revolutionary violence—the involvement of external powers. The fall of a government implies the raising of the question of recognition of the successor government, and thus affords the opportunity for external intervention. Such intervention might well seem very desirable in a number of other internal political situations, including that of prevalent or persistent sub-revolutionary violence, but only on the occasion of an actual transition do the customs of the international community normally sanction it, though today only in a negative and non-coercive form.[5]

Clearly a great deal will depend on the nature of the successor government. It is a major factor in assessing the nature of the directorate and in determining the subsequent course of political institutionalization.

There are five possible intended consequences of a revolutionary transition. It may be carried out without any particular successor either being desired or provided for, as in the United States in 1963 v.[6] It may be designed merely to strike down an existing government, permitting its regular constitutional succession machinery to operate and the constitutionally designated officer to succeed to the executive functions, as in Brazil in 1955 δ, with the implication that this particular succession is the one desired. It may be carried out in favour of another predetermined successor or group of successors. Alternately, the transition itself formally installs only a transitional government, whether military or civil, to operate the constitutional machinery, as in Egypt in 1952 γ. The choice of successor government is then left to the regular constitutional machinery with the implication that any constitutionally chosen government will be acceptable to the promoters. And, lastly, the transition may be designed to install a convention or constituent assembly, with a view to redesigning the entire structure of the state and of its government, as in China in 1949 ζ.

[5] George Schwarzenberger, *A manual of international law*, 4th edn. (Stevens, London, 1960), I, 66–7, 173–4.

[6] References in this form here and subsequently are to the Check Lists, pp. 183 ff. For notes on the composition of the Check Lists see p. 83.

But it should be noted that any shift within the revolutionary context from one goal to another need not necessarily be the result of revolutionary pressure. It can be the consequence of sub-revolutionary influences or even of a simple change of mind on the part of the leader of the directorate. The latter case of course is only applicable where a leader has been prepared to secure objectives second-best to those actually desired. Nor must it be forgotten that leadership in the directorate of re-volutionary transitions is frequently plural, and such changes can reflect a shift in balance within the directing body.[7]

With these facts in mind, we can now proceed to develop the ranges of options open to the promoters in a revolutionary situation. The simplest of these is revolutionary action upon the executive, the leader of government or the chief executive. It is therefore the most localized form of change, requiring the lowest level of force.[8] In intensity it may range from kidnap-ping, with or without forced resignation, to assassination; and its consequences tend to be limited to the simpler forms of govern-mental change. Thus possible variations are all concerned with bringing about a fairly simple form of political objective. Ex-ecutive revolutions without regard to the successor, in favour of the automatic successor, or in favour of a predetermined suc-cessor only if he is one who has a reasonable chance of succeed-ing in normal circumstances, seem to be the only practical methods.

Of these, the first type is normally seen only in the form of an attempt at assassination; other forms, in fact, being virtually unknown.[9] This follows from the fact that, without the justi-fication of ideological grounds for the total destruction of organized government, this form of political action is so clearly futile, particularly in the circumstances of the modern, highly

---

[7] The most striking instance perhaps is the aftermath of the Cuban revolution of 1959; see Boris Goldenberg, *The Cuban Revolution and Latin America* (Allen & Unwin, London, 1965).

[8] In minimal form it must, to succeed, entail the assassination of the executive; hence, ironically, below a certain point, the less force available the more assured the change.

[9] Some examples are the fall of Deb Shamsher, Nepal 1901; of Estrada, Nica-ragua, 1911; of Alessandri, Chile, 1925; of Ramírez, Argentina, 1944; and of Naguib, Egypt, 1954. See Frederick M. Nunn, 'Military Rule in Chile. The Revolu-tions of September 5, 1924 and January 23, 1925', *Hispanic American Historical Review*, XLVII, no. 1 (Feb. 1967), 1.

organized state, that its employment is normally restricted to the mentally unbalanced. These last act generally on their own, but this in itself has a degree of significance. It demonstrates extremely clearly the very small number of people who are required to carry out a change of this sort.[10]

Similarly, small numbers are sufficient for a successful attempt at kidnapping, and the restraints upon this exercise are obviously almost entirely those of custom and acceptance, rather than the difficulties of securing the limited degree of co-operation and the maintenance of the essential secrecy. Thus on one occasion an attempt to kidnap President Lleras Camargo of Colombia was only foiled by the fact that the kidnappers foolishly drove past the front of the Presidential Palace.[11] As we shall see, assassinations do seem to be indicative of a degree of disorganized dissent which is frequently followed by efforts at organization and canalization. This process can, in turn, lead to the onset of a revolutionary sequence. Success in this sort of action must necessarily depend on speed and timing. Few people, fortunately, are prepared to claim that they could exercise the amount of skill necessary to carry out such an operation, while, without such skill, the small numbers involved are likely to face the deployment of an overwhelmingly quantity of resistance.

In a highly developed modern state, institutionalization is designed to facilitate the replacement of any one individual without undue disturbance. The individual element in government, though of great importance, is sufficiently restrained by it to ensure that a substantial period elapses after a transition before a change of course is seen to have occurred. Even then it is not necessarily clear in advance how great this element may be, since the machine itself limits the expression of individuality to an even greater extent at all levels short of the top. Accordingly, though there remains a high probability that removal of those exercising leadership roles will bring about substantive changes

[10] Even if the assassin (or assassins) of President Kennedy had had the entire Dallas police force as accomplices—a ridiculous idea—the total amount of force generated would still be less than that engaged in any of the *coups* of Latin America in the years 1962–4 (*Report of the Warren Commission on the Assassination of President Kennedy* (Bantam Books, New York, 1964); Mark Lane, *Rush to Judgement* (Penguin Books, London, 1966, with additional material); Edwin Lieuwen, *Generals versus Presidents, Neomilitarism in Latin America* (Pall Mall, London, 1964)).

[11] Martz, *Colombia*, pp. 270–1.

in government, the logic of the system is against attempting a transition of which execution will necessarily be hazardous and the consequences apparently slight during the crucial first stages of acceptance for the successor government.

But executive revolution in practice is only the limiting case of the otherwise less prevalent government revolution.[12] This is revolutionary action on the chief agencies of governmental decision-making, including advisers, that is to say, on the President or Prime Minister and his executive staff and/or Cabinet. It is, in fact, as a type of governmental revolution that most people regard executive revolution; from this, in any case, assassination is traditionally excluded. Politically this assessment of their similarity, in so far as it relates to historical consequences, is correct, but strategically there are significant differences. The most important of these is the enormously increased geographical area over which a governmental revolution has to operate in order to be sure of immobilizing all parts of the government during the Critical Time.

The essence of success in this case, therefore, is pre-planning, to a point at which accuracy and timing are highly developed and the Critical Time is reduced to the minimum. It is relatively easy, though, to plan for the simultaneous immobilization of all members of the government. It is a different question actually to secure access to the crucial points and to co-ordinate the action over any substantial distance. Furthermore, the distances involved are liable to be no less than those separating individual parts of the government (particularly those relating to the defence functions) from sources of military reinforcement. As a result, the calculations involved represent not only a judgement on the balance of forces but also an estimate of the degree to which those forces will develop in the estimated Critical Time. The ultimate advantage in this kind of action, clearly, lies with the pre-existing government.

It follows that this type of political change is not normally undertaken with the object merely of removing an unpopular ruler. Inevitably some form of successor has to be provided for, if only to maintain the forms of legitimacy in the eyes of those

---

[12] Some examples are the Serbian *coup* of 1903; the Pangalos *coup* in Greece, 1925; the Phya Phahon Sena *coup* in Siam, 1933; the fall of Peñaranda, Bolivia, 1943; and the Phoumi Nosavan *coup* in Laos, 1959.

expected to transfer their allegiance to the new regime. The ultimate successor seldom is the automatic one, though the provision of an interim government in order to maintain the constitutional forms of change is quite usual.

Operation on the third level, that is, revolutionary action designed to secure control of the capital city as a necessary preliminary to the overthrow of the government itself, involves fairly significant differences of scale once more.[13] Though surprise is essential as much to effective deployment in metropolitan revolution as at lower levels, speed is much less so. The essence of the operation is force. This is inherent in the fact that it is characteristically a military form; or rather, the one fact is related to the other. As a military form it enjoys great popularity in countries where military intervention by violence in politics is customary. It is not, however, necessarily limited to military use, though unlikely to be successful in civilian instances, unless there is either no army in the state, or unless the army elects to stand aloof from a violent process of political change generated by the development of anomic civilian structures.

The metropolitan revolution depends for its effectiveness on the engrossment of as large a majority as it can secure in the first instance, or of the total military potential of the capital area. The limitation of time, in so far as it is applicable once total potential has been secured, applies only during the relatively lengthy period required to bring up forces as reinforcements from provincial areas. Such a substantial alteration in the political complexion of the capital is unlikely to be practicable for the automatic successor. In general, metropolitan revolutions are designed to secure either the succession of a predetermined successor or that of an interim government, again with a view to maintaining constitutional forms. This interim government normally takes the form of a military junta in the predominant military type.

But it must be clearly understood that the securing of the possession of the capital is a general term covering a wide range of activity, of which not the least important is the compara-

---

[13] Some examples are the fall of King Manoel of Portugal, 1910; the Kondylis *coup* in Greece, 1926; the fall of Ayala, Paraguay, 1936; and of Villaroel, Bolivia, 1946; and the Massu *coup* in Algeria, 1958.

tively rare, but much studied, spontaneous uprising of substantial sections of the capital population. In modern times these are often organized and led by intellectual groups, and in particular by university students. Given this kind of political pressure, it is more than probable that the military will determine to conform to the prevailing pattern of public opinion, though it can, and very frequently does, attempt to secure control of the situation again at a later date.

Naturally, these simple forms can be, and are, used simultaneously and consecutively, according to desire and support, just as the conventional political party may engage in conflict on the issue chosen by its rival, or seek to find another with which to turn the flank of its rival. A power play on one level may, according to case, be countered either by one on the same level, or by one on a different level. In some countries this has, indeed, attained the standing of a formal ritual, but the search for power is not any the less violent for being ritualized.

A good example of a complex power play (a term which we may adopt to designate a revolutionary sequence of short duration in which violence is continuous), occurring in the course of a larger combination of events generally termed a major revolution, is the set of events which took place in Mexico in February 1913. In this case an abortive metropolitan revolution led by one general caused the threat of a government revolution from another, which in turn induced an executive revolution by a third (1913 γ). The subsequent assassination of the deposed President constituted an excess of the MNF and led in turn to the declaration of a new revolutionary movement in a provincial centre.[14]

Two points must be noted. Firstly, although complex changes of power play—ones extending through more than three or four instances—are rare, examples of individual ones and of pairs are extremely common, and few countries in the present century can boast of complete freedom from any of

[14] Peter Calvert, *The Mexican Revolution, 1910–1914; the diplomacy of Anglo-American conflict* (C. U. P., Cambridge, 1968), pp. 106 ff. Stanley Robert Ross, *Francisco I. Madero, Apostol de la democracia mexicana* (Biografias Gandesas, Mexico, 1959), pp. 263 ff. See also Robert E. Quirk, *The Mexican Revolution, 1914–1915; the Convention of Aguascalientes* (Indiana University Press, Bloomington, 1960); Roberto Blanco Moheno, *Crónica de la Revolución Mexicana*, 3 vols. (Libro-Mex Editores, Mexico, 1965).

them. It has been suggested that there is a relationship between the reasons for success or failure in a specific context, that of military intervention, and the extent of economic or social development in the appropriate society.[15] Yet although some correlation may be detected, there seem to have been sufficient instances in the present century, and even in the last few years, to cast doubt on this.

Secondly, though military influence is undoubtedly significant, and in some instances overwhelmingly so, it can be exaggerated. Predisposition to intervene is not a measurable quantity, but sufficient examples of intervention exist to suggest that it is always a possibility, however remote. It will not occur, however, unless the military body actually has the capacity to intervene.

It is at this point that many governments seem to have been markedly lacking in common sense. The almost total freedom of Great Britain from military intervention, above the level of influence, in the past century *may* have been wholly due to the country's economic development, or it *may* in part have been the not entirely unintentional result of stationing trained troops well away from the capital and preferably on the North-West Frontier of India. A foreign policy conducted in such a manner as to provide a continuous occupation for the military in the form of overseas adventures, if successful, brings about a degree of physical expansion of the national territory to the point at which it becomes extremely difficult to carry out the simpler forms of revolution at all.

The essence of military action, whether on the government or on the capital, is simply to provide the necessary conditions for the transfer of power. This can be provided—at a cost—by civilian forces, or by civilian agreement; and the paradox is, that where a government is unaccustomed to intervention by military forces it is actually more, not less, vulnerable to similar civilian actions. On the other hand, military action is essential where it is normal. It is therefore at least arguable that militarism, in the revolutionary sense, is only an interesting custom, however important it may be as a phenomenon in its own right.

The most extended level of revolutionary action is in the

[15] Finer, pp. 87 ff.

province.[16] A provincial revolution is action designed to build up a base for the exercise of pressure to secure the overthrow of government. Its essence, accordingly, lies neither in speed nor in force, but in its attractiveness and its distance from the centre of possible retaliation. This distance must be understood as meaning distance in terms of the rapid and effective deployment of military forces. It may consist less of physical remoteness in the geographical sense than in separation from the governmental body by difficult or inconvenient terrain.[17] In either sense, distance provides the protection for the movement.

Its attractiveness, whether real or artificial, is designed to draw in sufficient recruits to achieve overall superiority against government forces in all reasonable circumstances. This force may then be deployed against the government in such a way as to bring about a formal military victory, representing the achievement of superiority within the state. In consequence, it will be clear that a provincial revolution without a predetermined goal, though imaginable, cannot be successful. It is clear, also, that a movement so widespread is usually one demanding wide-scale political change. Accordingly it favours the establishment of interim government or even of a constituent assembly, as preliminary step on the way to large-scale and thoroughly thought-out political action.

The question arises as to whether within the national territory there is an overall possible total reserve or 'bank' of force, of which a revolutionary movement must, if it is attempting this method, succeed in pre-empting a majority share. This concept undoubtedly has value in the assessment of the instantaneous position, particularly with regard to the armed forces. It remains useful in forecasting the position expected over a space

---

[16] Some examples are the fall of the monarchy in China, 1912; the Nationalist Revolt in Turkey, 1919; the Brazilian Revolution of 1930; the Indonesian Revolution of 1945–6; and the Cuban Revolution of 1959.

[17] This was raised to a principle by Ernesto (Che) Guevara, but in a restricted sense, which impedes its efficient use. See Mao Tse-tung and Che Guevara, *Guerrilla Warfare* (Cassell, London, 1964), p. 127. The consequences are graphically described between Régis Debray, 'Latin America: The Long March', *New Left Review*, 33 (Sept.–Oct. 1965), 17–58, and the same author's *Revolución en la Revolución?* (Casa de las Américas, Havana, 1967), in the striking contrast of his opinions on Bolivia. See also on guerrilla warfare generally Charles W. Thayer, *Guerrilla* (Michael Joseph, London, 1963); John S. Pustay, *Counterinsurgency Warfare* (Free Press, New York; Collier-Macmillan, London, 1965).

of hours or indeed days. Over the longer periods in which provincial revolutions usually operate, however, the 'bank', as an economic analogy, must give way to the 'economy' in which production and consumption provide the dynamic elements.

It is theoretically possible, but thoroughly unlikely, that a total national ascendency, outside the capital area, could be achieved by an internal political force without bringing about a governmental transition. Examples, however, of outside intervention securing such a predominance, without, however, being able to achieve governmental control, are sufficiently numerous to suggest that the possibility cannot be entirely discounted. Famous examples of the latter state include Spain under Napoleon (1808–12) and Mexico in the time of Benito Juárez (1864–7). In both cases, the governments externally imposed attempted to represent themselves to the nation at large as being internal manifestations of political change, but in neither case were they successful. It should be said, though, that in small states a provincial ascendency may occur by its nature over so large a section of the national territory as to be virtually indistinguishable from such an assembly, and a long line of cases from the Republic of Haiti (e.g. 1902 δ, ε, 1908 θ, 1911 ζ) are very relevant here.

Numerous examples of provincial revolutions can be cited, though certainly a high proportion fail. An even higher number, for reasons of the vast scale of the preparations required, never come to fruition. Furthermore, once under way, the power play must, by definition, take place in the open. In such circumstances, it takes strong nerves to maintain defiance against potentially overwhelming forces. In modern times the development of weaponry has considerably reduced the areas of the world's surface in which the terrain is sufficiently difficult to maintain this sort of movement. Accordingly it can be said at once that the popularity of the provincial revolution is out of all proportion to the risks involved. These considerations may give ground to some doubt as to the ability of most revolutionaries, and some surprising assurances about the stability of most governments.

A number of interesting speculations can be made about the existence of special cases within these categories. For example, if a government were very unstable and unable to maintain the police power within its own capital, one could conceive of a 'provincial revolution' in the capital itself, while the government proper was in flight, perhaps.[18] But the technical problems involved in maintaining such a movement in an ordered state would still be those of applying a particular level of force, namely that needed for control of a city. The effort required to secure control of the capital remains the same even when, for example, the chief executive or, indeed, the whole government is absent from it, either on holiday or for reasons of national policy. The indirect effect of securing control is no less great. It may, indeed, owing to the difficulty in securing an effective degree of retaliation, be more effective. Examples of very different types of such revolutionary phenomena are as disparate as the Siamese Revolution of 1932[19] (1932 ε) and the overthrow of President Nkrumah of Ghana in 1966 (1966 ζ).[20]

QUANTIFICATION

Having thus established the main outlines and broad classification of inquiry, we must next turn to the problem of quantification. This is a task that is of very great complexity, owing to the great disparities in the effectiveness of weapons. In comparing the efficiency of ground forces we may make use of the N-square law discovered by the distinguished engineer, Frederick W. Lanchester. The N-square law provides that 'the fighting strength of a force may be broadly defined as proportional to the square of its numerical strength multiplied by the fighting value of its individual units' or

$$Rn^2 = Bm^2$$

where n and m respectively stand for the numbers of the 'red' (or revolutionary) and 'blue' (or government) forces, and R and B for their respective fighting values. Calculations extending

[18] This appears to be necessary precondition for the 'Urban guerrillas' praised by Debray, loc. cit.

[19] Coast, op. cit.; H.R.H. Prince Chula Chakrabongse of Thailand, *Lords of Life; The Paternal Monarchy of Bangkok, 1782–1932, with the earlier and more recent history of Thailand* (Alvin Redman, London, 1960), pp. 309–17; see also Fred W. Riggs, *Thailand; The Modernization of a Bureaucratic Polity* (East–West Center Press, Honolulu, 1966).

[20] Colonel A. A. Afrifa, *The Ghana Coup, 24th February 1966* (Frank Cass, London, 1966).

over a substantial period must also allow for the time element, and involve the calculation of the rate of build-up of forces on any given front.[21]

The N-square law is applicable, and indeed easier to operate, in the case of conflict between ship and ship or between aircraft and aircraft. But the conflict that is engendered by revolutionary warfare seldom involves this sort of confrontation. The value of an air force in revolutionary circumstances lies for the government in its role of detecting and destroying ground forces. Using the law, it is possible to calculate with a reasonable degree of ease the relative value of opposing air forces in destroying their corresponding opposing land forces. It is a very different matter to relate the efficiency of an aircraft as a weapon against land forces to the value of an individual soldier. We cannot, in fact, expect to find a constant value, valid in all circumstances, to describe this relationship.

Fortunately, as it happens, under revolutionary conditions the differences between forces, in so far as they relate to such advanced technical equipment as aircraft, are normally very great. Revolutionaries themselves very seldom enjoy air support comparable with that of the government with which they are in conflict, and to all intents and purposes most revolutionary conflicts therefore involve ground forces alone.

Since the relative effectiveness of ground-based weapons is fairly well determined, the only question that then arises is whether general considerations of advantage may be rendered inapplicable by tactical inconveniences, such as the impossibility of obtaining access to certain determined strongpoints.[22] In addition, a constant must be built into the equations to allow for the fact that most weapons in modern times give a distinct advantage to the defensive as against the offensive user.

To summarize the process, therefore, we begin by ascertaining the total number of forces available to the government and to the opposition respectively at the outset of the action, which we can call m and n respectively. In the case of the government, this will be a proportion of a larger force, M, which is the total available to it on concentration of forces, part again of M', the

[21] Lanchester, op. cit.

[22] An important factor in the Serbian *coup* of 1903, cf. Goodspeed, p. 8; Wayne S. Vucinich, *Serbia between East and West, the Events of 1903–1908* (Stanford University Press, Stanford, 1954).

total mobilized force of the nation. A military revolt, by definition, is subtracted from this force to the extent that it contributes
to n.

The relative effectiveness of these forces can only be judged
arbitrarily. If that of the government, B, is normalized so that
$B = 1 \cdot 0$, then we may expect the efficiency of revolutionary
forces to be less than that quantity, in all cases except those in
which massive defections have occurred from the regular forces.

Lanchester was concerned to show that the disadvantage to
the numerically weaker force was so great in a given arena that
it was essential for that force to concentrate its forces to the
greatest possible extent. This it can do either by summoning
reinforcements, or by narrowing the arena chosen by it. Only
the latter option is normally open to the revolutionary force,
and if additional forces are available, their efficiency is normally so low that they impede the action.

Of the variables taken into account in assessing R and B, the
military values of the revolutionary and government forces
respectively, the criterion of efficiency is clearly most significant.
It is for this reason that the type of *personnel* as well as their
strength was selected as a key variable in the comparative study.
The quality of leadership, which cannot be so easily assessed, is
estimated to some extent by the size of the *directorate*, subject to
considerations to be discussed further in Part II. The nature of
weapons is, of course, not homogeneous even through land forces,
as large formations are stronger per man than small units in
terms of fire power and destructive capability. On the other
hand, where small groups are concerned, even an 'unarmed'
man has a significant level of force capability. At the least he
may, by stratagem or otherwise, detain significant bodies of
armed men until armed reinforcements are brought up.

Finally, the overall strength of the contending forces should
be plotted through time to the point at which the transition is
actually successful.

Two points should be noted. Transition depends not only on
the actual balance of forces as it was observed by impartial observers or as it can be plotted in retrospect. Governmental
decisions to change the arena of conflict, bring up reinforcements, or resign their offices all depend on the situation as the
government perceive it. As was stressed earlier, revolutionary

actions are brief in the main, and not easy to disentangle while they are in progress. Governments may, and often do, make mistakes in their assessments. Secondly, really efficient use of surprise may well ensure that no efficient countering force is developed at all.

The point at which a build-up of force passes through the MNF point may be termed the 'force threshold'. The question naturally follows whether there is not just one, but a number of force thresholds, each being in some way related to a different set of post-revolutionary consequences. These forms, whose origins we must either link to, or separate from, the basic use of force to promote the transition itself, we may call the 'initiatives'.

SOCIAL INITIATIVES

The initiatives divide in a number of ways. Some are non-violent and others violent. Some may be classified as 'internal' and others as 'external', either in origin or application. These initiatives are what many people mean when they talk about 'revolution' as such, but as we have already seen, the vast majority of revolutionary acts, even if successful, are not in fact followed by a level of initiatives rising above the norm for the society, whether or not those acts occur singly or as part of a revolutionary sequence. This is understandable, since the revolutionary act is primarily concerned with the transfer of power, and those who are successful in carrying out revolutionary transitions tend only to be concerned with that transfer.

From time to time, however, it does happen that a revolutionary act results in the accession to power of a person or persons who has, or have, positive aims beyond the assumption of power, and aims which are considered by them to be a coherent part of the revolutionary act. We have already seen something of the ideological background which makes this sort of thing possible, and, indeed, in present circumstances, probable. Though in violent as in non-violent transitions the leader who succeeds in achieving power is not necessarily the leader best fitted to exercise that power, it does not necessarily follow that he is not. The chance of such a leader achieving power is greatest where the old order's power is least. In other circumstances the effort to reach power and to attain power can in itself demand the full capability and attention of one man or of a group. In the extreme case, where the government has no support at all, even to the extent of a residue in favour of the system under which it operates, the widest opportunities occur for post-revolutionary initiatives; and it is from such cases that the most spectacular instances tend to be drawn—those of the so-called 'Great Revolutions'.[23]

It is unlikely that the revolutionary leader, who has, after all, to undertake at least a minimum amount of personal risk in choosing the path of violence, will not wish to make some change in the established order. This minimal change will probably be directed in the first instance towards securing his position, and in its broadest form may be termed 'reform'. In using this phrase, we employ no value judgement, meaning only a form of non-violent social initiative which is broadly within the norms of the society but has not previously been attempted. Such changes occur, if for no other reasons, as a result of the passing of generations, and hence are due to the biological nature of man. They cannot therefore be considered characteristically 'revolutionary'. In most circumstances, in most states, a fairly wide range of reform is possible without the essential continuity of the political system being disrupted; this is, indeed, the operation of what rudimentary survival mechanism the system, *qua* 'system', may be considered to possess.

But the emergence of a revolutionary leader who had definite social aims and regards these as being part of his mission, is of particular significance, for two reasons. On the one hand, he has to reckon with those who desire no further change, and on the other, with those who desire more. It has been suggested that under the Brinton model are to be subsumed all 'true' revolutions, as has been said.[24] Under this form, the special circumstances of the revolutionary state are considered to render 'reform' (in the 'moderate' sense) an unstable form of reaction, leading to a *coup* of the 'extremists' that ushers in a

[23] Originally the 'great social revolutions', Edwards, p. 2; the current phrase we owe to George Sawyer Pettee, *The Process of Revolution* (Harper, New York, 1938), p. 3, and Brinton, op. cit., p. 2.

[24] For example, Hannah Arendt, *On Revolution* (Faber & Faber, London, 1963), p. 27. See also Lucio Mendieta y Nuñez, *Teoria de la Revolución* (Instituto de Investigaciones sociales, UNAM, Mexico [1958]). But cf. Brinton, p. 7.

full range of initiatives. Under the present model this conclusion has already been excluded. The range of possible consequences of 'reform' does include on the one hand the violent initiatives, but it also includes on the other a state of normal satisfaction. It is opportune to record how subjective an assessment of actions as 'reform' may be, even under the present definition, while the failure of a moderate regime may well be due to its bad example in the use of force to secure transition rather than to its predilection for any particular form of legislation.

Different considerations arise when we turn to the question of violent initiatives, of which we shall first consider the internal ones.

Here the use of force by government to secure its initiatives is clearly related to its own inclination to achieve power by violent means. This in turn implies that the use of force will be directed against any elements in society, whether within the revolutionary elite or not, whose enforced state will benefit the consolidation of the regime. The identification of these groups etc. will depend on the aims intended by the application. Internal initiative may be broadly classified in Aristotelian fashion as being directed towards individuals, towards minority groups, or (rarely) towards majority groups. But equally importantly it may be classified as being directed towards their past, present, or future, behaviour, and each of these actions influences the nature of support obtainable or necessary from others, and thus the employment of alternate initiatives to redress the balance.

The initiatives conceived in terms of past behaviour are inevitably negative, directed towards punishment of past actions, and may be classified as revenge, reprisal, and sanction.

Those concerned with present behaviour aim to check it. They too are negative in action, and may be characterized as arrest, restraint, or repression.

For the future, coercion can only be intended in positive terms, to elicit some desired response; yet, as is well known, it is in this fashion that it is most unreliable and poses the greatest problems in terms of assessment. The degrees of positive violence that are future-directed are torture, coercion, and terror.

If set up in the form of a matrix, it will be observed that the escalation of intensity of these forms occurs in both axes, the natural tendency being towards the lower right, i.e. to terror, given that the initiatives are embarked on at all. The peculiar circumstances of revolutionary terror lie in its association with a form of political change that is capable of bringing to power, without impediment and even with encouragement, the individual leader who has ideals exceptionally far removed from reality. The state of mind and feeling in which they are most strongly present may be characterized as 'utopianism'.[25]

The revolutionary leader who seeks utopian ideals must first reconcile reality with theory. The people and their leaders have to be brought into line with one another somehow. If the government has been brought into line with the real, because unexpressed, desires of the people, and the people do not seem to enjoy the experience, it seems to the leader that there must be something wrong with them. Violence offers itself as the obvious cure. There is, in any case, a wild fascination in the application of violence that is more basic to the human instinct than many people like to think.[26]

Terror is a method of reshaping the social order through the systematic application of force.[27] Though not directly related to revolution, therefore, it is likely to exist in modern societies only in association with it. The only other leadership situation in which it can reasonably be expected to develop in any other circumstances is that of absolute monarchy. If it does occur, it is directly related, in addition to the possible reactions of those victims of lesser forms of initiative, to a peculiar effect. The occasions on which the most spectacular resort to terror has occurred appear to have been those on which logically there would seem to have been the least *physical* need for it.

It seems, therefore, that it is related to a desire in some leaders to show themselves as demonstrably leading by heroically battling against a foe.[28] If there is no foe, so much the better.

---

[25] This is separately identified in the useful social typology of Chalmers Johnson, *Revolution and the Social System*, Hoover Institution Studies, 3 (The Hoover Institution on War, Revolution and Peace, Stanford University, Stanford, 1964).

[26] Lorenz, op. cit.

[27] Brinton, pp. 185 ff.

[28] Sigmund Neumann, *Permanent Revolution; Totalitarianism in the Age of International Civil War* (Pall Mall, London, 1965), pp. 44 ff.

The artificial foe is superior to the real thing in that it affords less actual danger and can be turned on and off at will. The creation of enemies, through their destruction, is the price that has to be paid.[29] Terror is maximized by the uncertainty surrounding the leader himself when he no longer knows whether or not he is master of his creation.

It will be seen that the possibilities of internal initiative are considerable. If these phenomena are not related to the presence of a revolutionary transition, to what are they related? If they are only fostered by the revolutionary act, as we have here tentatively hypothesized, how many violent transitions occur that do not produce them? These questions become even more pertinent when we consider the presence of a second set of initiatives, having an external, instead of an internal, impact. These initiatives, too, are paralleled by a series we may call the 'complications' of revolution, i.e. intrusions from other states corresponding to the revolution's possible range of impact on its environment.

Propaganda is a familiar phenomenon, vitally related to the standing of any government in the international comity.[30] But of course a revolutionary government has a particular need to employ propaganda, and to employ it effectively. The revolutionary government requires recognition, as the foreign countries that can afford it are in a sense regarded as neutral sources of legitimacy. It must give reasons both for its assumption of power and for its claim to be the legitimate successor to power.

But if countries are unable or unwilling to recognize a new government, it is not unreasonable for the new government to go further and to attempt to 'make itself at home' by encouraging others to follow its example and thus to create a body of friends in surrounding communities, whom it hopes will in due course assume the burden of government and place themselves in a position to lend it aid. It may not do this consciously. Long before the time of Burke or Metternich, the governments of the *anciens régimes* in Europe were very conscious of the probable

---

[29] Hannah Arendt, *The Origins of Totalitarianism*, 2nd enlarged edn. (Allen & Unwin, London, 1958), pp. 351 ff.; Jacob L. Talmon, *The Origins of Totalitarian Democracy* (Mercury Books, London, 1961), pp. 98 ff.

[30] Cf. Neumann, *Permanent Revolution*, p. 205.

effects of continued propagation of libertarian ideas in Switzerland and the Netherlands.[31]

The insidious nature of revolutionary propaganda is not that it converts a few activists and drives the masses to desperate deeds. The activists are there already; normally they are impotent for lack of the elements necessary to carry out a successful transition, and more frequently, perhaps, they lack the capacity to bring those elements together. Propaganda secures its full effect on the largest number of people when it induces them to make a compromise between the views it expresses and their own. The suspension of disbelief is all that the activist requires to secure his necessary temporary superiority in force.

Technically the use of propaganda designed to bring about forcible action may be regarded as an actual use of force; and certainly it cannot be regarded as non-violent. The lowest degree of actual force that is transmitted across the boundary of a national revolutionary state into a neighbouring community takes the form of aid to revolutionaries there, and forms a natural progression from the positive use of propaganda. The next level may be termed that of infiltration and subversion, and at the extreme of violent interposition we find war in all its various forms. Again, none of these phenomena seems to be specifically revolutionary in origin. But it could not be denied that they gain their peculiar impact from the fact of pre-existing successful transition. Again, too, they are related to the theory that a revolutionary government must not only be obeyed, it must also be actively liked.[32] In this sense, they are, like terror, attempts to bring reality into line with theory, and like it, too, are unpredictable in their results.

In the light of this, a special role has been attached to the role of the convention, which, as Verney demonstrates, is an expression of total democracy in institutional form.[33] It permits, in unusual conditions of stress, the free growth and transfer of extreme opinion. For external relations this implies the emergence to political power of the non-expert with a simplistic

[31] Voltaire and Rousseau were among the most distinguished men of the century, living in exile and with their works subject to censorship.

[32] Talmon, pp. 104–5.

[33] Douglas V. Verney, *The Analysis of Political Systems* (Routledge, London, 1961), pp. 57 ff.

view of the reform of all human relationships, and not least those over which he has no control. His relation to the urban crowd strengthens the formalization of violence in these best-defined of circumstances,[34] when the total removal of the state structure in time of crisis favours the emergence of new concepts extending even to the geographical formation of the state itself. The removal of the leader, even of the government, need not lead to this degree of disorientation, and neither need the disruption of the capital, provided local government leaders or mechanisms remain intact.

It follows that great resistance to revolutionary extremes is to be expected in states that are accustomed either to a genuinely federal structure or a strong tradition of autonomy in local government. Logically, as an extension of this, we find that the greatest possible resistance is to be expected in those circumstances in which we have decided by definition that revolution, as such, is impossible. These are the systems which exist in the state of anarchical decentralism.

INTRUSION AND REACTION

Phenomena of a very similar character may, in the post-revolutionary situation, result from the external intrusions that we have termed above the 'complications'. This is not to say that traditions of geographical division, social incompatibility, or the survival of pre-revolutionary issues are not in themselves complications of the post-revolutionary situation, but it is to say that these external intrusions produce marked changes in the degree of internal violence, which in turn invade the political system from within. All the so-called 'great revolutions' have been shaped by external interference, though not all cases of interference produce 'great revolutions'—far from it. Some indeed have, in the eyes of some observers, actually cut short 'great revolutions'.[35] The observer of the great revolutions, on the other hand, may well argue that the peculiar development there originated not simply from external intrusion, but from a combination of external intrusions and internal initiatives. The combination of these was such that by no normal means did it

[34] Talmon, p. 98.
[35] Goldenberg, pp. 57 ff., e.g. Bolivia and Guatemala.

seem possible for ordinary men and women to direct government to resolve both.

Such a combination means that the decisive point is that at which an external influence begins to assist a force of internal dissension. Without that combination a 'great revolution' is improbable. This, it may be noted, *could be averted by the external government* where the internal government is by definition inadequate to do so. The interventions, like the external initiatives of the revolution, must be essentially violent in character, but they need not necessarily be 'successful' or 'unsuccessful' in terms of its avowed ends in order to produce a serious diversion of violent energies within the revolutionary system. Propaganda alone is unlikely to complicate revolution, unless it takes the special active form of non-recognition, which we may take as the threshold of 'complication'.

Non-recognition represents, therefore, the least severe form of forcible action directed upon a revolutionary government. The alien government may choose in addition three more levels of interposition: aid to opposition, subversion, and war, corresponding to the external initiatives open to the revolutionaries themselves.[36] They are likely to retaliate in kind, as well as develop internal resistances of a complex sort.

Dangers lie in any action whatsoever against revolutionary governments. Take the minimal example of propaganda: propaganda can deceive the propagator as well as the propagatee, and is well placed to do so when confused conditions prevent adequate check on the response to it. What is taken as a cry for help may be no more than feedback from the alien nation's own deception; there is no certainty. To embark on any intervention, therefore, is to run a special risk of being deceived as to actual conditions and, on inaccurate evidence, embarking on the use of force under the impression that force is not force until people are actually killed by it.[37] The response in terms of social unification against the intrusion is then likely to be severe and sudden.

[36] See Robert E. Quirk, *An Affair of Honor* (McGraw-Hill, New York, 1964), pp. 53 ff.; Theodore C. Sorenson, *Kennedy* (Hodder and Stoughton, London, 1965), pp. 296–7; Robert Scheer and Maurice Zeitlin, *Cuba an American tragedy*, revsd. edn. (Penguin Books, London, 1964), pp. 202–3.
[37] Quirk, *An Affair of Honor*, p. 68.

In any case, even propaganda may give rise to internal consequences by a very simple chain of events. The revolutionary
government notes that alien propaganda implies the existence
of a strong counter-revolutionary movement in its territory. It
will reasonably feel impelled to extirpate it. The consequences
are unification of sentiment, pressure towards uniformity, and
likely use of terror, to ensure positive response to proposed
reforms. When this stage has been reached, the use of terror
creates an opposition to the government; and the opposition on
the one hand feels compelled to support the government in
resistance to the foreigner, but on the other reacts violently
against the pressure to side with the government even for the
most laudable motives.

The outcome in all cases, forces being relatively evenly
balanced, is likely to be war. In turn, this creates in the alien
nation a sentiment of justification for intervention, thus further
confusing its appreciation of the real position in the neighbouring country.

Foreign governments do, however, have positive as well as
negative roles to play in neighbouring revolutions. Not only do
they confer the mantle of legitimacy (and so lead many revolutionary movements to devote considerably greater sums to the
maintenance of suitable representation in sensitive capitals than
to any other item of necessary expenditure), but they can also
supply or purvey financial aid in the original transition, as well
as armaments, recruits, or any combination of these, in the
form of covert or overt military assistance. But it may well be
sufficient for them to permit or prevent, according to case, the
legal importation of arms into the country concerned from their
territory. As legal authorities they can indeed go even further,
in imposing restrictions of movement on conspirators located
on their soil or in turning a blind eye to their activities. Rarely,
they have been known to show active support for such movements and, patriotism being what it is, such overt sympathy
produces its own opposition.

It is now, in conclusion, desirable to examine the concept of
reaction. For many purposes this may be seen as being comparable with its namesake in the world of the physical sciences.
Social reaction is the consequence, roughly proportionate in
extent, of social displacement. But the term 'reaction' is also

applied to the period or periods in which reaction dominates and subdues the revolutionary impulse, and particularly that period which ends any sequence of revolutionary acts collectively known as 'a Revolution'.[38] There seems to be no substitute for time in determining whether or not a post-revolutionary norm has been established, though a fairly short period may be sufficient to illustrate that a bloc of support formerly attached to the *ancien régime* has become firmly attached to the new. It is possible that in many instances even this type of post-revolutionary norm may not exist at all. Accordingly the problem of ascertaining the limits of revolution between which a definite sequence of events may properly be studied as a whole is one of great difficulty. It is true, of course, that revolutionary movements can be crushed by force.[39] This force, normally exercised by the government threatened, has in some cases been extended to neighbouring or hegemonic powers. Hitherto we have called it simply 'countering force', and may well continue to do so.

Effective countering force may be seen as akin to that which it seems to meet. It is, then, best secretly prepared, sudden in onset, and minimal in extent. In other words, counter-revolutionary action, for success, should follow the rules of revolutionary action. The state, however, has a freer hand, as it is not by definition limited by Critical Time when, in its normal condition, potentially superior to any opponent in the long run. It can therefore be prepared for reasons of choice, not easily imaginable, to embark on a long political struggle. If it does, the excess or deficiency of countering force can have as serious consequences for the equilibrium of the state as can be expected from the excess or deficiency of revolutionary force.

It is true that psychologically, if in no other way, the pre-existing government must *always* benefit in some degree from its theoretical (if transitional) right to the monopoly of force. But this right has to be exercised within the accepted norms of the system if power and respect are both to be preserved.

The current fashion for guerrilla warfare has its origin in

---

[38] Brinton, pp. 215 ff.
[39] Lawrence Stone, 'Theories of Revolution', *World Politics*, XVIII, no. 2 (Jan. 1966), 159; cf. Katherine C. Chorley, *Armies and the Art of Revolution* (Faber and Faber, London, 1943).

doctrinaire views as to the necessity for the forcible conversion of the mass of the peasant population, in countries of predominantly agrarian economies and very little global significance in terms of power resources or power mobilization. By implication its proponents deny the significance of a concept of MNF.[40] Faced with the reality of guerrilla war with revolutionary intention, however, the traditional military mind reacted with the development of a theory of counter-guerrilla war which is defective if pushed to its logical conclusions. It is wholly irrational in its disproportionate deployment of fighting forces and material, large-scale civilian resettlement, and control of food supplies.[41] Only the richest powers can finance and support such a vast operation, and even they cannot do so in more than one or two places at a time.

It is the contention of this analysis that although theories of 'guerrilla revolution', such as those of Mao Tse-tung and, more recently, Truong Chinh,[42] are doctrinaire in origin; they obey the usual rules. Their proponents' power is effective in so far as it is sufficient to overcome countering force during the Critical Time. The Critical Time under these theories is indefinite. The dilemma therefore which the guerrillas face is this. They cannot strike effectively below the maximum level, even if they wish to do so, for leaders in countries such as these tend to be very well guarded, in some cases by foreign advisers. The capital is heavily garrisoned because the troops mainly operate from there, and the troops are loyal within limits because they are relatively well paid and are encouraged to follow their favourite vocation with every facility for initiative or reward. None of

[40] Peter Paret and John W. Shy, *Guerrillas in the 1960s*, revsd. edn. (Praeger, New York, 1962); Mao Tse-tung and Che Guevara, op. cit.; Stuart R. Schram, *The Political Thought of Mao Tse-tung* (Praeger, New York, 1963). A critique of 'guerrillism' is contained in the perceptive study by Andrew C. Janos, *The Seizure of Power: a study of force and popular consent*, Research Monograph no. 16 (Center of International Studies, Woodrow Wilson School of Public and International Affairs, Princeton University, Princeton, 1964).

[41] This derived from a misleading interpretation of the successful campaigns of the British in Malaya and the Americans in the Philippines, in each case with the support of a large section of the population guaranteed because of strong internal divisions.

[42] Dang Xuan Khu ('Truong Chinh'), *Primer for Revolt, the Communist takeover in Viet-Nam. A Facsimile Edition of The August Revolution and the Resistance will Win*, intro. and notes Bernard B. Fall (Praeger, New York, 1963). See also Vo Nguyen Giap, *People's War, People's Army*, 2nd edn. (Praeger, New York, 1965).

these factors, be it said, need necessarily be permanent, and where they have failed, as in Vietnam at the time of the Japanese surrender, leaders of revolutionary movements significantly have (following Lenin's earlier example) overcome their inhibitions against *putschism.*[43]

Even in Vietnam they have not persisted in their lapse since the re-establishment of traditional presence; instead they have made a virtue of what they erroneously believed was an obligation to act only on the provincial level. For this, their manpower, financial backing. and logistics were, and are, in the main sufficient to resist countering forces, but insufficient, after all, to achieve dominance, so as to complete the transition. They have therefore failed.

At the same time the governments have not won. How can they do so?

We have already considered, and rejected, the possibility that they could use non-violent means. Such means seem, we recall, more likely to bring about the rapid dissolution of the government than to restore its hopes for the future. It remains to ask whether we can incorporate within the theory of violence and its reaction, a theory of countering violence. If we are to do so, we must postulate, as in the case of revolutionary action itself, a number of levels on which that force can operate. Four suggest themselves as being within the internal capacity of the political system. Force may be directed against the revolutionary leader, against the entire revolutionary force, against an urban society fostering the movement, or against a rural society doing so. This assumption we will have to test in actual practice. One preliminary observation, however, may serve at this stage to reinforce the grounds for hypothesizing that this classification will be found serviceable: the fact that so many occasions are known on which an even higher level has come into play, that is to say, action directed by an alien country against total national support to a revolutionary movement. With this encouraging thought in mind, we may now proceed to develop an actual case study in political change through violence, illustrating the utility of the basic concepts of confrontation between forces inherent in the present model.

[43] Kahin, op. cit.

3

A CASE STUDY

POLITICAL CHANGE IN GUATEMALA

THE subject of our case study in violent political change will be the Republic of Guatemala. Guatemala is a small country. Like other small countries it tends to receive less than its share of the world's attention. In this century it is only in 1954 that it has been the focus of the world's headlines, and then only because it momentarily became the scene of an incident in the Cold War. Otherwise its history has been, if not peaceful, at least reasonably commonplace, and most people know of it, not for its politics, but as the seat of the historic Maya civilization, the 'Land of Eternal Spring', or the homeland of Miguel Angel Asturias.

For the political scientist, however, its interest derives in the first instance from the fact that as a country it is representative of some of the most persistent of Latin America's (and the developing world's) social problems. In its 42,042 square miles (108,889 square kilometres) it contains a population of 4,278,341 (April 1964), representing an estimated increase in the previous two years of over 200,000. Of this population, 54 per cent were of pure Indian blood, but divided into no less than 21 linguistic groups. The rest, whether white or *mestizo*, are customarily referred to in Guatemala as *ladinos*. It is the *ladinos* who hold the political power within the country. A very high proportion of them live in the overgrown capital, Guatemala City, whose population is 572,000; the next largest town, Quezaltenango, contains only 56,000 people.[1]

This disproportion is accentuated by the fact that the country is divided by natural geographical features into three well-defined regions. To the north there is the tropical rain forest. In the centre there are high mountains, reaching in places 13,000 feet above sea level. To the south there is the low-lying hot

[1] *The Statesman's Year-Book, 1965–66* (Macmillan, London, 1965), p. 1080.

country, in which the main crops of the country, coffee and bananas, are grown. The majority of the population lives on the southern uplands and foothills of the mountain range and, though they are dependent on the land in that region for their subsistence, the country relies for its income basically on the crops cultivated on the great plantations to the south. These plantations are either under *ladino* ownership or else in the possession of one great foreign corporation, the United Fruit Company (UFCO) of the United States.

The problems of land distribution, urban concentration, racial division, etc., which one finds in Guatemala, are common to all the Central-American countries, but in Guatemala they occur together in a higher degree. This holds good also for the type of political system. Guatemala, for a long time the seat of the Captaincy-General of the colonial Spanish Empire, has tended to attempt periodically to assert a political dominance over its neighbours, and its meddling in its neighbours' internal political affairs has tended to communicate to those neighbours the problems which it itself has had to face. This inter-relationship is peculiar to Central America among the major areas of Latin America, and is not to be taken as representative of the problems of the countries to the south, but it has, owing to the proximity of the area to the United States, its own peculiar interest.

Furthermore, the political system of Guatemala is a simple one, not only because the country is small, but because, despite internal barriers it has a degree of unity which is obtained only on provincial level in many other parts of the world. This simplicity of political structure makes it peculiarly suitable as a site for a case study in political change. It is evident to the most casual observer that the possibility of a change in ideas in Guatemala is dependent on a previous change in political personnel, whether or not this may be so in a more complex society.

This chapter, therefore, is a study in the 'style' of Guatemalan politics, and this style is what elsewhere has been called the 'real' constitution of the country. Certainly this 'real' constitution is very much distinct from the written constitutions, of which Guatemala to date has had six: those of 1824, 1851, 1879, 1945, 1956, and 1966. These constitutions provided in each case for a form of government modelled on the Spanish Constitution of 1812 and the United States Constitution of 1787, with later influence from that of Mexico (1917). They each provided for a President who exercised the executive power with few checks, a Congress which in the last two Constitutions had been a unicameral body of sixty-six members, and a judiciary which was appointed by the executive and only nominally was independent.[2] Each document was representative of the trend in Latin-American constitution-making of the time, except in the feature of the unicameral Congress, peculiar to Central America. They were not unimportant in that they reflected the ideals and aspirations of the people who wrote them, but they do not indicate how government, and in particular political change, actually worked.

To define the working of the 'real' constitution we must first briefly sketch the history of Guatemala from the date of its separation from the Central American Republic.[3] The Government of that Federation, which lasted from 1824 to 1838, was extremely loose in structure. The individual territories had each separately proclaimed their independence from Mexico and each set up a presidential form of government as if they really were the sovereign states which they were in the process of becoming. When the young Rafael Carrera, therefore, led the revolt against the Government of the Federation in 1838, the presidential form of government was already well established in the country. The 1851 Constitution reflected this, and was distinctive only in its conservatism, implying as it did an unusual degree of clerical ascendancy.

In the century or so which followed independence Guatemala was dominated for the greater part of the time by four men, of whom Carrera himself was the first. The dictatorship of this conservative, illiterate, and unsympathetic personality was ended in 1865 by his natural death. He was succeeded by a nominee of the General Assembly (Congress) who was displaced by a two-year Liberal revolt in 1871. In turn, this successful revolt ushered in a period of Liberal dominance, in which Justo Rufino Barrios, as President from 1879 to 1885, was the princi-

[2] See the excellent summary by John D. Martz, 'Guatemala, the search for political identity', in Martin C. Needler, ed., *Political Systems of Latin America* (Van Nostrand, Princeton, 1964).

[3] This sketch follows Chester Lloyd Jones, *Guatemala, Past and Present* (University of Minnesota Press, Minneapolis, 1940), pp. 39 ff.

pal figure and the man who introduced the first elements of real constitutionalism into the country. But he had one overriding ambition—the reunification of Central America under his leadership—and in pursuit of it met his death in battle against the forces of Honduras on 2 April 1885.

His constitutional successor, Manuel Lisandro Barrillas, prolonged his term by *continuismo*, but after an election in 1891 transferred power peacefully to José María Reyna Barrios, nephew of the President of the same name. The younger Barrios was assassinated in 1898 with the bizarre consequence that his legitimate successor as First Designate, Manuel Estrada Cabrera, was able to become president peacefully and, once in possession of his new powers, to secure the foundations of a dictatorship lasting for twenty-two years.

The circumstances of his deposition in 1920 were not without their interest. Quite simply, he seemed no longer to be up to his job and besides, he had roused the opposition of the United States by his persistent attempts to turn the disunity of Central America to his own account. These two factors culminated in a formal deposition by Congress and the simultaneous defection of a substantial fraction of the army, after which he had to go into exile.

Of his successors in the next ten years the legitimate one, Carlos Herrera, resigned in face of revolt; José M. Orellana died of a heart attack in 1926; Lázaro Chacón resigned for reasons of ill health in 1930; his First Designate, Baudillo Palma resigned after two days, and was replaced under military pressure by the Second Designate, Manuel Orellana; and he in turn, under the influence of the United States, by José María Reyna Andrade. The last-named held constitutional elections which returned a new figure, who was to make himself dictator with the constitutional powers of the Presidency.

Jorge Ubico, President from 1930 to 1944, may not have been able to equal Estrada Cabrera in length of office, but in every other way he was enabled to exceed him by virtue of the benefits of modern technological progress.[4] He ruled, as it has been said, over a 'model gaol'. The symbol of his despotism was the increase and growth of plantation agriculture, assisted by a law

---

[4] For the rule of Ubico see Ronald M. Schneider, *Communism in Guatemala, 1944–1954* (Praeger, New York, 1959), pp. 1–10.

compelling peasants to give 180 free days labour in the year, to be controlled through a system of work cards. The success of his system seemed assured when the Second World War brought a boom in coffee which gave great prosperity to the dictator and his supporters. But it also brought a conflict of interest.

Up to that time the greater part of the coffee plantations, as distinct from the banana plantations, had been owned and operated by German companies. Under United States pressure Ubico was made to expropriate these plantations, and this act challenging the sanctity of private property naturally made some Guatemalans question why they should not do the same with the properties of the United Fruit Company. This questioning spirit was enhanced by the fact that Guatemala, nominally one of the allies, saw an influx of United States military personnel and the propagation by them of the liberal ideas of the Atlantic Charter and of the new United Nations. The alienation of the majority of the population, as at the end of the First World War, reached a climax with the defection of a substantial proportion of the army, and Ubico was forced to resign on 1 July 1944. This time, however, events subsequently followed a very different course.

A small group in the army at once attempted to restore the Ubico-type dictatorship under a different leader. The defection of a further group of younger officers from this effort turned what might merely have been a change of dictators into a new departure in Guatemalan politics. These men were supporters of Juan José Arévalo, a university professor who in exile had been teaching at the University of Tucumán in Argentina; he professed a doctrine which he called 'spiritual socialism' and displayed influences from José Enrique Rodo and José Ortega y Gasset.[5] Arévalo, who became constitutional president and served from 1945 to 1951, was enabled to survive as much by his own political awareness as the fact that his opponents were divided.[6] Under his presidency the first Guatemalan social

[5] A description of Guatemala at the beginning of Arévalo's presidency may be found in Vera Kelsey and Lily de Jongh Osborne, *Four Keys to Guatemala*, 5th printing, revsd. (Funk & Wagnalls, New York, 1946).

[6] Accounts of Arévalo's presidency are Schneider, op. cit., pp. 11–34; John D. Martz, *Central America, the crisis and the challenge* (University of North Carolina Press, 1959); Samuel Guy Inman, *A New Day in Guatemala, a study of the present social*

security legislation was enacted in 1946, and a Labour Code in 1947; the development of the rapidly growing labour force into the counterpoise in the capital to the army, together with the expansion of the Government bureaucracy, were important to the stability of a regime which withstood, as is said, some thirty attempts to overthrow it.

In these years control of the army was vested in Colonel Francisco Arana, who had recast the officer corps in favour of the pro-revolutionary and clearly expected the reversion of the presidency in 1951. His assassination in 1949 left this to his chief rival, Colonel Jacobo Arbenz, whose wife's car was used in the attempt. Care was taken to ensure that no alternative choice could be registered by the 1950 election, and that election duly reflected the real transfer of effective control.

Under Arbenz the tone of political action in Guatemala took on a pronouncedly more nationalist and revolutionary note. Marxist terms became the customary vocabulary of political discussion, and the small, legal Communist Party merged into a larger organization called the *Partido Guatemalteca de Trabajo* (PGT), which became a visibly institutional base of the structure of expanding government. The long-promised land-reform project, unveiled in 1951, was found to embody the expropriation of a substantial section of the property of the United Fruit Company. The Company contested the decision, claiming that for the purposes of banana cultivation large areas of land had to lie fallow at any given time; but they did not satisfactorily explain why their holding had to be vastly in excess of the necessary surplus. Opinion in United States Government circles became minatory and hostile, citing Guatemala as an example of Communist penetration of the Caribbean area; and the Guatemalan Government contested these allegations on nationalist grounds, receiving as a result much sympathy among other small nations and especially Latin-American ones. After a crescendo of charges and countercharges of subversion and threats of invasion, a military revolt was led by exiles against Arbenz in 1954, and within days the President resigned.[7]

Revolution (Worldover Press, Wilton, Conn., 1951). See also Juan José Arévalo, *Discursos en la Presidencia* (Guatemala, 1948).

[7] A brief summary of the Arbenz period is given by Schneider, pp. 35–43, as a prelude to his major theme, the growth of Communist influence in Guatemala. For

The leader of the revolt, General Castillo Armas, had been an unsuccessful candidate at the 1950 elections and unsuccessfully had led a revolt in the same year. Imprisoned in the capital, he had made a spectacular escape which had won him much admiration. Now he emerged as a basically conservative leader, though one who did not nullify the real advances that had been made since 1944. United States aid was forthcoming, and with it some modest improvements were made in the transport system, but little else had been accomplished by July 1957 when President Castillo Armas was assassinated by a member of the palace guard.

Castillo Armas had not been prepared to submit to a formal election, holding only an unopposed 'plebiscite' to prove his rule, together with the revised constitution. In the confused situation which followed his death it appeared that army leaders were, after all, not hostile to the idea of an election. They did, however, dispute the results of the one held by the First Designate acting as president, whereupon he resigned under pressure and his successor held another, with inconclusive results. The choice constitutionally devolved upon the Congress, which awarded the office to the army leader, Miguel Ydígoras Fuentes.

Ydígoras ruled again as a conservative, in an atmosphere of hysteria generated by the Cuban revolution and a smoke-screen of 'Communist plots', until 1963, when he permitted former President Arévalo to return to the country to contest the elections and was promptly deposed by the army and succeeded by his Minister of Defence, Colonel Enrique Peralta. In this *coup* it was even suggested that Ydígoras was a Communist.

Enough has been said so far to make it clear that the pattern of political change in Guatemala since 1838 has basically been one of violence. Constitutions have existed during this period and perhaps have exercised a normative influence; elections

an *arbencista* version see Guillermo Toriello, *La Batalla de Guatemala* (Editorial Universitaria, Santiago de Chile, 1955), or Manuel Galich, *Por Qué lucha Guatemala; Arévalo y Arbenz: Dos hombres contra un imperio* (Elmer Editor, Buenos Aires, 1956); Luis Cardoza y Aragón, *La Revolución Guatemalteca* (Ediciones Cuadernos Americanos, Mexico, 1955, No. 43) is more temperate. Daniel James, *Red Design for the Americas: Guatemalan Prelude* (John Day, New York, 1954) is controversial. For a factual statement of Guatemalan government at 1954 see Kalman H. Silvert, *A study in government: Guatemala* (Middle American Research Institute, Tulane University, Publication 21, New Orleans, 1954).

have been held, but basically as acts legitimating previous transfers of actual power. And yet when we come to apply our model, a curious fact emerges; that in this period constitutional election has actually been the most common *single* method of achieving political power in Guatemala (Table 1, p. 197). As a method, it has existed only together with the much widespread methods of forcible change, but these methods of forcible change have been varied among each of the four possible levels according to the varying fortunes of instrumental groups.

If we concentrate on the recent period (since 1944), the following changes, and major attempts at political change which have failed to achieve a revolutionary transition, have taken place (Table 2, p. 197).

In only one instance has action limited to the person of the President been successful, in 1957.

In four instances violence has been directed against the Government: twice unsuccessfully, in 1950 and 1962, and twice successfully, in 1957 and 1963.

But in no less than seven instances attempts have been made to secure control of the capital by violent means. Of these, the attempts of July and October 1944 have been successful, while those of July 1949, July 1950, July 1952, February 1953, and January 1955 have not.

In eight major instances attempts have been made to secure political change by establishing control of a province. In two cases, June 1954, this was apparently successful. In another case it is still going on. In five it has been unsuccessful, twice in 1948, and once each in 1949, 1953, and 1960.

In examining the actual circumstances of each of these events one fact emerges and that is the substantial role played by the army. In fact, on all occasions on which revolutionary attempts have been successful a substantial proportion of the army has taken part or become involved in them. What sort of organisation is the Guatemalan army, and how does it fulfil the political functions which it has so clearly assumed?

To begin with, the actual force is not a large one, though in proportion to the size of the country it is as large as might reasonably be expected. Its members are estimated in the 1960s as being between 7,000 and 8,000, and this figure has been constant throughout the period under review. At its upper limit the force constitutes only 0·0019 per cent of the population; and the significant fraction, the 900 members of the officer corps, are numerically even less significant. But they form a tightly integrated body which in the political elite represents that fraction from which potential presidents are most often recruited. There has been no study of this elite as a whole, if indeed it has an existence separate from that of the officer corps, and the precise relationship must accordingly be considered a matter for conjecture.[8]

What is known is that most of the officer corps are graduates of the military academy, the *Politécnico* in Guatemala City, of which, for example, Colonel Enrique Peralta himself was a prominent alumnus and a distinguished figure in Guatemalan life as long ago as 1945.

The army is armed with good, but not especially modern, weapons of United States origin, including in addition to semi-automatic rifles and machine-guns a small force of Sherman tanks.[9] Not too much significance should be attached to the fact that the arms are of United States origin. This in itself would be natural in the Caribbean area, where Second World War surplus arms are so cheap. In fact, United States military aid to Guatemala in the twelve years from 1950 to 1962 amounted to only $4,311,000. In 1960 this aid formed only 2·8 per cent of the Guatemalan defence budget.[10]

What is significant is that the army is the dominant political force in the country, and the socialization process of the Guatemalan is orientated towards maintaining that dominance. Latent socialization is provided for the *ladino* in the family and peer group through the assertion of the traditional Hispanic pattern of male dominance. Overt socialization is provided in the school through instruction in the past military glory of the state, and subsequently through the system of selective military training which males between the ages of eighteen and fifty may be required to undergo. While in training their labour is applied to the community in the form of communication, reafforesta-

[8] See, however, Peter Calvert, 'La formación de las actitudes políticas; testimonies de Guatemala', *Aportes*, no. 7 (Jan. 1968), 65.

[9] *The Statesman's Year-Book, 1965–66*, loc. cit.

[10] John Duncan Powell, 'Military Assistance and Militarism in Latin America', *Western Political Quarterly*, XVIII, no. 2, pt. 1 (June 1965), 382 ff.

tion, and agricultural improvements, thus completing the circle of obligation.[11]

The Indian is assimilated to the *ladino* pattern through a complex inter-relationship of his traditional religious/social hierarchy and the political one of the formally Hispanic state.[12] This is not to say that the Indian thereby develops any great respect, still less liking, for the *ladino*, whom he regards as a foreign usurper. But at the same time he may rise, or be torn, out of the local political structure altogether, through the acquisition of Hispanic cultural values.[13] When he does this, he becomes himself a *ladino* and is separated from his peers who remain unassimilated.

This necessarily entails the acceptance of the military role, and the tendency for this element of the cultural pattern to receive especial emphasis is greatly enhanced by the fact that the military itself offers the best opportunity available to the Indian for the acquisition of those very values. Once within the pattern of the *ladino* culture, the newcomer then becomes aware that the army has a further social function in being self-consciously the principal reservoir of technological skills in the Guatemalan system.[14] In this role its only rival as a political force is the student body, some 6,300 strong, of the Universidad de San Carlos de Guatemala, situated strategically in its own 'University City' in the national capital.[15] Recent events have repeatedly shown that the students lack only arms (or the support of a portion of the army) to become a formidable rival to the traditional elite, of which, otherwise, in due course they will become a part.

The inter-relationship of the student body with the political elite is well defined in that though their education is free, their

[11] For military values in Guatemalan soldiery see Mario Monteforte Toledo, *Guatemala, monografía sociológica*, 2nd edn. (Instituto de Investigaciones Sociales, UNAM, Mexico, 1965).

[12] Roland H. Ebel, 'Political Change in Guatemalan Indian Communities', *Journal of Inter-American Studies*, VI, no. 1 (Jan. 1964), 91–104.

[13] Richard N. Adams summarizes many years of research in 'Social Change in Guatemala and US policy', in Council on Foreign Relations, *Social Change in Latin America Today, its implications for United States policy* (New York, 1960).

[14] On this subject, see Lieuwen, *Arms and Politics in Latin America*, pp. 137–54, and 91–4, 163–8.

[15] Figure from *International Handbook of Universities and other institutions of higher education, 1965* (Paris, 1965).

faculty members are part-time members of the various professions whose skills they transmit.

Otherwise, the army is the only effective land force. Although the *Policia Nacional* is organized along paramilitary lines and numbers between 2,000 and 3,000 men, it appears to confine its activities to the regular and special police roles. In this respect it must not be confused with the secret police, the *Policia Judicial*, which functioned with great effectiveness in maintaining the unpopular regimes of Ubico and Arbenz.

The major rival to the army, therefore, is the air force. For most of the period under review this has consisted of a squadron of F-51D Mustang piston-engined fighter-bombers, a squadron of B-26 Invader light bombers, and a squadron of C-47 Dakota transports. To these, after 1959, were added a small flight of T-33 jet training units, the standard jet training aircraft for the United States Air Force. This armament is to be considered fairly representative of Central-American conditions, though larger than the air forces of the countries immediately to the south of Guatemala. The total personnel of the air force amounts to approximately 500 men, of unknown fighting quality when operating on the ground.[16]

The Guatemalan navy was founded as recently as 1959, nominally 'to rout poaching fishing boats and smugglers'. It consisted, and consists, of one gunboat, the *General José Francisco Barrundia*, named after the military hero of Guatemalan independence who was President for a brief spell in the year 1830. Only once in recent years has it had the opportunity to play a significant political role, during the rebel capture of Puerto Barrios in 1960, when it remained loyal to the Government and stood off shore during that *coup* to guard against the landing of potential reinforcements from Cuba.[17]

It is clear from these figures just how in any armed conflict within the country the army holds a commanding position. The

[16] Present day figures from *The Stateman's Year-Book, 1965–66,* loc. cit., with other information from *Jane's All the World's Aircraft, 1947,* comp. and ed. Leonard Bridgman (London, 1947) and subsequent issues.

[17] *Jane's Fighting Ships, 1964–65,* comp. and ed. Raymond V. B. Blackman (London, 1964), gives her displacement as 310 tons and armament as two 3-inch cannon and two 25-mm. A.A. guns, with a complement of 40, and notes that in addition Guatemala possesses 'four small patrol craft'.

navy can for most purposes be discounted.[18] The air force must achieve a decision using air power alone and secure it before its airfields come under effective military attack. The police is restrained from attempting tactical superiority in the capital by the proximity of substantial military forces, the nearest being some 350 feet from the Presidential palace.[19] In the face of army opposition, command of the capital could only be achieved by arming a number of civilians sufficient to overcome both the inherent disadvantage of lack of training and the tactical disadvantages imposed by the rule of concentration by the N-square law with their natural weakness of communication and manoeuvre. The following examples should make the major relationships clear, while at the same time giving illustrations of the sort of factors that operate to complicate the mathematical calculation of advantage.

Most controversial among all recent transitions of power in Guatemala is, of course, the deposition of President Arbenz in June 1954.[20] The operation, which, it will be recalled, operated under the leadership of a military man, General Castillo Armas, took the form of a *pronunciamiento*. The forces employed were assembled in Honduras, the ground forces embarking on a three-pronged attack across the frontier on 18 June. Their military objective, it appears, was the capture of the main rail communication net joining the capital to Puerto Barrios and both to the Salvadorean frontier. The total number of forces on 'each side' was estimated by Schneider as being between 5,000 and 6,000 men, but *The Times* (London) reports suggested at the time that the balance of advantage lay with the Government and imply that the author of the account of the incident for the *Enciclopedia Universal* may be correct in suggesting that on the 19th, the day following the invasion, the Government disposed of 7,000 ground forces and the rebels of only 5,000.[21]

By 25 June the invading forces had advanced only some 25 to

---

[18] For its role in the 1960 *coup* see Miguel Ydígoras Fuentes, *My War with Communism*, as told to Mario Rosenthal (Prentice Hall, Englewood Cliffs, N.J., 1963), p. 167.

[19] La Charité, op. cit.

[20] The following account is based on Schneider, pp. 301–17. See also Wise and Ross, pp. 165 ff.

[21] *Enciclopedia Universal Ilustrada, Suplemento 1953–54* (Espasa-Calpe, Barcelona, 1957), pp. 980 ff.

30 miles. But this means that they had succeeded in capturing the strategic positions on the railway and established a 'provisional government' at Chiquimula on the 21st, after that town had been captured in a desultory skirmish which was the only important event of the war.

Meanwhile small, individual insurgent aircraft were operating over Guatemala City. They bombed the airport at La Aurora, seven kilometres to the south, the fortress of Matamoros, just outside the city, and the barracks by the Presidential Palace. The number of these aircraft has been estimated variously as between two and 'a Squadron', but the actions described could all have been carried out by the lesser number. Nor were the capabilities of the aircraft, described by the representative of the Arbenz Government before the Security Council of the United Nations as 'P-47 aircraft of North American make',[22] as impressive as the innuendo would suggest. *The Times* correspondent described them tactfully as 'fairly recent'. That is to say, they were Second World War machines roughly comparable with those that at that time made up the Guatemalan air force, and much inferior to them in strength of numbers. In any event, it is clear that any local margin of superiority was not enough to give the rebels actual or potential command of the air, and they were at a substantial disadvantage on the ground.

Despite this favourable position, which must have been known to the President, he evidently was not satisfied with it and on 26 June gave orders to the military to arm 5,000 workers from the capital and send them to the front. The arms that were to be used had been imported from Czechoslovakia for this particular purpose in anticipation of just this sort of emergency. Their arrival at this timely moment brought to the fore the question of whether the army was to be outflanked by an organized, paramilitary, possibly Communist, civilian force. When the military leaders refused to distribute the arms, there was no alternative left to Arbenz but to resign, which he did on the evening of 27 June.

Two points emerge clearly. The first is that by 25 June, in

[22] British Parliamentary Papers 1953–54, Cmd. 9277, XXXIII, Guatemala No. 1 (1954), *Report on Events leading up to and arising out of the Change of Régime in Guatemala, 1954* (HMSO, London, 1954), Document No. 6 (Minutes of Security Council, Sunday, 20 June 1954).

strategic terms, the invading forces had in fact already effectively been contained by the army. The air attacks had more moral than physical value, and the only serious threat they seem to have posed to the Government was that a lucky bomb might touch off the vast store of mines which the Czechs had provided as part of their revolutionary arms outfit.[23] The second is that the leaders of the workers were well aware of this tactical and strategic advantage, and bitterly disputed the President's decision to resign with the aid of sporadic disturbances in their stronghold town of Escuintla, which lay between the rebels and the capital. In this dispute they were right and the President wrong, but the President had little alternative in view of his previous serious error in advocating the arms distribution in the first place.

An attempt by civilian and military rebels to gain control of the capital by occupying La Aurora military airfield on 20 January 1955 was even more unsuccessful, and that it was attempted at all can only be attributed to the fact that among those implicated was the Minister of War of the Castillo Armas' administration, Colonel Elfego Monzón, and the forces were led by a former chief of air staff, under Arbenz, Colonel Francisco Cosenza.

It is clear that the object of this attempt was to win over members of the air force, and it is equally obvious that it was unsuccessful. This failure left only a small number of men facing the overwhelming power of the army, the number arrested immediately following the attempt only amounting to about 100. Only two were actually tried and imprisoned, the rest being released, except for Colonel Monzón himself, who was forcibly dispatched to 'a South American diplomatic post'.[24]

But, as we have been reminded, superiority of force depends not only on numbers, but also on the Critical Time, the time in which force can be brought to bear. This lesson is the principal one to be learnt from the next significant attempt at political change, the successful assassination of President Castillo Armas on 26 July 1957.

---

[23] Philip B. Taylor, Jr., 'The Guatemalan Affair: a critique of United States foreign policy', *The American Political Science Review*, L, no. 3 (Sept. 1956), pp. 787 ff.; *The Times*, Sat., 19 June to Mon., 5 July 1954; Wise and Ross, p. 173.

[24] *The Times*, Fri., 21 Jan.; Sat., 22 Jan. 1955.

This attempt was simplicity itself. At 7.30 in the evening as the President and his wife, unarmed, were going in to dinner, one of the palace guards, Romeo Vásquez Sánchez, stood to attention, presented arms, and shot the President through the head. He immediately killed himself with the rifle with which he had killed the President. It was said afterwards that documents had been found on his body implicating others, and subsequently eight members of the guard, of whom two were officers, were arrested on suspicion. But it is quite evident that, even if they were not implicated, there was little or nothing they could have done to forestall such an action.[25]

The subsequent political change, when the army intervened in the elections of 1957, resulting in the eventual transfer of power to Ydígoras, has no special features of interest. The first major attempt to overthrow the new regime came on 13 November 1960, when dissidents seized the port of Puerto Barrios, together with a nearby radio station, and extended their control as far as the town of Zacapa, on the railway to the capital. The leaders of this attempt were army officers, Captain Arturo Chuc del Cid and Captain Rafael Sessan, and among their number was Lieutenant Marco Antonio Yon Sosa, subsequently leader of a dissident guerrilla movement in the north of the country.

At first they seemed to have been successful in their objectives. But in seizing Puerto Barrios, which is as far away from the capital as one can be in Guatemala and still hope to exercise pressure on it, the dissidents clearly hoped to form an alternative base of power, for they relinquished control of a barracks in the capital to do so. They failed to allow for the chance that both the air force and the army would remain loyal to the President. The former bombed and strafed strongpoints, and the latter took part as paratroops dropping behind the rebel lines; after three days of hard fighting the last positions were reduced in the port itself. The leaders of the attempt fled to Honduras. Yon Sosa returned a year later (6 February 1962) with 60 supporters and established himself in the Sierra de Minas, but

[25] *The Times*, Mon., 29 July; Tue., 30 July 1957. For this and subsequent events, see as well Mario Rosenthal, *Guatemala, the Story of an Emergent Latin-American Democracy* (Twayne, New York, 1962).

failed to become a major political force until the fall of Ydígo-ras.[26]

The following period, marked by a number of violent inci-dents in the capital and the assassination of the chief of the *Policía Judicial*, among others, saw also the alienation of the air force from the regime. On 25 November 1962 it attempted its first direct confrontation with the traditional pattern of army dominance.

From their base at La Aurora the air force continued from the point at which the 1955 rising had failed. They used their machines to attack both the army barracks and the Presidential Palace, making full use of both fighter-bombers and bombers. Four civilians were killed and 51 wounded. Within three hours the army had surrounded the airfield, bombarded it from the hills with artillery, and ended the revolt. Two of the leaders took refuge in the Salvadorean Embassy and three others flew straight to El Salvador in one of the C-47s. The rest of the air force, some 500 men, were arrested by the army, but subse-quently all but 17 were released.[27]

This decisive result well illustrates the weakness of air forces on the ground, arising from their need for refuelling facilities and paralleled by their incapacity to achieve a decisive result without land support except in unusually favourable circum-stances. In this case, in operating from La Aurora, the air force paid the penalty of that proximity to the military noted above. They had little alternative, it is true, as it was the only opera-tional military airfield in Guatemala.

Their defeat left the army the sole arbiters of political change, and this they put to the test only four months later when, on 31 March 1963, then surrounded the Presidential Palace with Sherman tanks, broke down the gates, seized President Ydígoras and deported him to Nicaragua, whereupon the Defence Minister, Colonel Enrique Peralta, proclaimed himself 'head of government'.

An interesting sequence of events preceded this *coup*. The pre-election tension was already great when it was announced

[26] *The Times*, Mon., 14 Nov.; Tue., 15 Nov. 1960; *Hispanic American Report*, XV, no. 2 (Apr. 1962); Ydígoras, pp. 160 ff. *Keesing's Contemporary Archives*, 17798A.

[27] *Hispanic American Report*, XV, no. 11 (Jan. 1963); no. 12 (Feb. 1963); Ydígoras, pp. 224 ff.

that ex-President Arévalo was to return, and some five days before that return, the President proclaimed a state of siege. To enforce it, he borrowed the Nicaraguan air force from President Somoza; and it was, indeed, on one of their machines that he was dispatched into exile. It has, therefore, been suggested that there was no real *coup*, and that the resort to violence merely registered an agreement between Ydígoras and Peralta to avoid the holding of elections by transferring power in a more traditional way. Against this must be set the fact that Peralta had enjoyed a leading position in the country much longer than Ydígoras, and a number of other details which suggest that the ostensible account is correct.[28]

However, it was certainly in the belief that the *coup* marked a distinct reaction that the northern guerrillas resumed activity and linked it with a determined series of terrorist attempts in the capital.[29] Their numbers were at that time quite small, some twelve sections or so, and subsequently grew, though not spectacularly. Undoubtedly, their activity has a high degree of nuisance value and has increased military expenditure and numbers in the recent period. But the containment of the movement has isolated it from the opportunity to secure effective change, and the reaction to the 1966 and the preliminary stages of the 1970 elections suggests that the next violent change in the Republic would be of a more traditional type.

The statistics of these recent attempts, expressed in terms of the N-square law, are summarized in Table 3 (p. 198). As the enabling pressure implied in 1954 η and 1957 θ (see Appendix A) was not made operational, these events are excluded from consideration.

To take the simplest instance first, we find that throughout the active phase of the successful 1957 attempt (1957 ζ) the revolutionary force remained constant ($Rn^2 = 1 \cdot 0$). Until success had been achieved it was well in excess of the only available governmental force, which if we assign a value of 0·2 as the effective value of an unarmed man in such circumstances, gives us a value for Bm^2 of 0·8. Since Government reinforce-

---

[28] *Hispanic American Report*, XVI, no. 3 (May 1963); no. 4 (June 1963); Ydígoras, Introduction.

[29] *Hispanic American Report*, XVI, no. 6 (Aug. 1963); XVII, no. 1 (Mar. 1964); Lieuwen, *Generals versus Presidents*, pp. 37–45, cf. Ydígoras, pp. 183–7.

ments were throughout within close range (less than 250 feet or, say, twelve seconds) the success of the attempt was only attained through the use of surprise; governmental strength thereafter peaking at something in excess of eight men ($Bm^2 = 64\cdot0 + 0\cdot2 = 64\cdot2$).

Represented diagrammatically in Table 4 (p. 199), distance w represents the period in which the revolutionary force became aware of the arrival of the President; x that in which action was initiated before the President became aware of it; y the duration of conscious conflict ($y = 0$); and z the time elapsed before Governmental reinforcements arrived. During the interval z the revolutionary withdrew from further conflict by the only means open to him.

Time was not important in determining the outcome of the unsuccessful attempt of 1960, where the revolutionaries could only have counted on success in the event of substantial defections from Government forces. What was significant, however, was their decision to choose the largest possible arena for the confrontation, since with their small numbers they would have stood a much better chance of success had they narrowed it.

This is well illustrated by the successful attempt of 1963 (1963 ε).[30] The professional military men who planned it began by establishing the arena as the narrow area of the Presidential Palace, the access to which was commanded by tanks. These tanks served the dual function of giving their troops a very high quotient of force potential, so high, indeed, that it outweighed the fact that the defenders of the Palace were armed with automatic weapons. The combined disparity of numbers and potential was such that control of the arena was established in a very short time.

This was important, for troops engaged in a limited battle on a narrow arena necessarily risk being trapped in a double ring by reinforcements (though there is no evidence that such reinforcements would have been available in the 1963 case, for the political reasons outlined above). This was, in effect, what happened a year previously in the unsuccessful attempt of 1962 by the air force.

In 1962 the air superiority of the revolutionaries was overwhelming, since there was virtually no resistance to it. It was,

[30] See Appendix B.

however, limited to a fixed time, that determined by the need of aircraft to land and refuel. On the other hand, control of the airfield at which this operation had to be performed was entirely governed by the balance of advantage on land. Though here the Government, owing to surprise, was initially weaker, it had unlimited time in which to generate its full force potential, and for political reasons could generate it in full. Ultimately its superiority reached a point at which the theoretical balance of advantage $(Bm^2 - Rn^2)$ reached the large figure of 63,800,000 units. By that time, however, the resistance had already been broken by heavy shelling and the consequent deterioration of the airfield.

In the 1954 instance (1954 ζ) the strength of air forces was roughly equal, while that of the ground forces was slightly in favour of the Government. Normally one would, however, have expected the force potential of the revolutionaries to be significantly lower. This was probably not the case, since the Guatemalan army had no operational training for the previous six years and suffered the disadvantage of weak leadership, following the assassination of Arana. On the other hand, the revolutionaries are said to have benefited from United States military aid. The balance of the intangible factor of morale would have been in their favour too, since the officer corps was, as events showed subsequently, very dubious about the policies of the Arbenz Government.

As a result the numerical superiority of forces on the Government side was, if not ample, sufficient to check the revolutionary advance. It was the defection of these forces, in the person of their higher officers, that so decisively reversed the advantage and won the day for the Castillo Armas forces (Table 5, p. 199).

To sum up, therefore, the normal style of political change in Guatemala is one of violent action. This violent action takes the form of brief, set pieces of activity in which each side is organized before the action begins, and no significant accretions of strength take place afterwards. Violence is formal, rather than actual, the number of casualties being fairly small in each case.

We can go further and advance the hypothesis that, in view of the theoretical model advanced here, this pattern of political change will prove to be general in the world at large for the period of the twentieth century which we cover here in the comparative study. Furthermore, statistical examination of these incidents should show that other aspects of the Guatemalan scene are relevant to the study of political change in general.

The Guatemalan army, who regard this pattern of violence as being very much their perquisite and are jealous of any attempt to democratize the base of violence within the state, are not necessarily averse to casualties on principle, but avoid them in general among their own numbers, the military code of etiquette incorporating such characteristically Latin-American features as the acceptance of the right of asylum. As has occurred elsewhere, the air force has to some extent been incorporated into the traditional pattern established by the army, with which it shares certain general objectives and values. It has, however, tended to be inherently unaware of its natural limitations and has, therefore, attempted, unsuccessfully, a direct confrontation with the army.

The guerrilla movements which have been active recently in Guatemala have been led and organized by military men, and rely upon an external base. In this respect they follow a traditional Central-American pattern. There is as yet no reason to suppose that ideological differences have made any substantial difference in the degree of their success, since their advances compare unfavourably with those made on the same time scale by the Liberal revolt of 1869–70. The only revolt of this type which has been successful was significantly conventional rather than guerrilla in character and successful through the mistakes of its opponents rather than through its own inherent virtues.

But there are other lessons, too. The events of 1944–54 are traditionally regarded as forming part of a 'Revolution'—in the sense of 'social revolution'. It is therefore interesting to note that in pattern they exhibit substantial differences from that to be expected under the Marxist model, or for that matter under the currently favoured Western model.[31] They were initiated in 1944 by the transfer of allegiance of the army, which alone gave meaning to the social revolt of the capital. The succeeding years, though, were not in historical terms marked by an increase in political violence or in the extension of

---

[31] Brinton, op. cit.

social controls in any defined sense. Instead there was a diminution to the point at which violence was no longer successful in attaining political change, and the transition from moderates to extremists did not occur as such: Arévalo moderating in office, transferring power peacefully to Arbenz, and Arbenz becoming more extreme. Furthermore, even the extremism of the land reform was conservative enough to be accepted by successor governments, and this represented a real transfer of power within the system.

1954 reinstated violence in its traditional form, cutting short the apparent tendency of social institutionalization towards a basic reshaping, before that reshaping could be achieved, if, indeed, it had been intended. It is in the interests, therefore, of the Arbencistas, especially the Marxist-orientated ones, to see Arbenz as having been overcome only by external force, in this case of United States neo-imperialism expressed through that mysterious monster, the CIA. It is, unfortunately, also in the interests of the CIA to allow this to be thought.[32]

The power model does not profess to give a complete explanation, but it does enable us to give its true value to the crucial miscalculation of the balance of forces by Arbenz himself.

In these terms, the resignation of Arbenz did not end a 'Revolution', it ushered in a revolutionary sequence. This sequence, down to the present, represents a causal chain of violence of some length, and it does have an internal coherence beyond that. The successful governments of this period have characteristically been moderate to conservative. They have maintained the Arévalo reforms, while representing a narrow band of differences on the merits of specific measures of the Arbenz period. This band, in fact, is so notably narrow that it could easily be comprehended within a process of non-violent change, while the challenge represented either by the person of Arévalo himself or by the guerrillas has not represented, and does not now represent, a challenge to the maintenance of a system of ordered government. In the Arévalo case, at least, the choice of a violent rather than a non-violent transition in 1963 resulted simply from the establishment of violence in the traditional political vocabulary of action.

[32] Wise & Ross, p. 166, quoting from a speech by ex-President Eisenhower on 10 June 1963.

In the long term, we may expect the style to be maintained, in view of the consideration, speculative as it is, that the reduction of political violence would lead to a transfer of its energies into the social sphere. This transfer, with the consequence of alteration or even dissolution of the existing social, and hence by extension political, order, would no doubt be welcome to some Guatemalans, but if it were achieved, they would still have to cope with the problems of violence in politics in circumstances markedly less favourable for their solution.

Finally we may attempt some observations on the role of the external relationships. In the microcosm, Guatemala forms part of a Central America whose history has been one of disunification and reunification. In view of the fact that this style of Guatemalan politics has been one of violence, it is necessary to consider these periods in terms of violence. In particular, some consideration must be given to the thesis of Professor Quincy Wright that in periods when attack is supreme over defence there is a tendency towards political unification, and when the opposite is the case, disunity results.[33]

The calculations involved are at best abstruse and usually vague for lack of objective data. But it can be said that the dissolution of the Central American Republic came at the beginning of that long period of improvement in firearms which by 1900 had made defensive fire some five times as effective as attacking. This position, for Latin America as a whole, would seem to have remained essentially static until the mid-1930s, when the introduction of the aircraft reached the point at which, for governments, this advantage could be reversed at least on favourable terrain. The defeat of the revolt of Saturnino Cedillo, the last of the Mexican caudillos, in the deserts of the north in 1938 is generally ascribed to this cause.

In the case of Guatemala, however, the build-up became a reality only in the 1940s, and in the 1950s was complicated by the issue of the growing democratization of all forms of warfare. In 1954 this issue was at the heart of the political conflict, and it was decided, in effect, in favour of centralization. The political parallel in non-violence to the borrowing to the Nicaraguan air

[33] J. F. C. Fuller, *Armament and History* (Eyre & Spottiswode, London, 1946), pp. 33–4; Quincy Wright, *A Study of War*, 2nd edn. (University of Chicago Press, Chicago, 1965), pp. 380–97.

force by President Ydígoras has been the development of the Central American Common Market; and it is not a coincidence that both developments have proceeded together, within the traditional sphere of influence of the United States threatened by the ideological conversion of Cuba.

It is not proved possible to devise a test for the assumption of George Modelski that in states of what he terms 'internal war', external intervention is inevitable.[34] Inevitability takes a long time. But within the scope of this inquiry, it is possible from the data to question the absoluteness of James N. Rosenau's schematic presentation that requires that intervention result from 'authority' and not from 'personnel' wars.[35] In a small state no accurate boundary can be drawn between these two concepts. In Latin America, in theory as well as in practice, they are, in any case, inextricably intertwined.

In the case of a small state as near to a great power as Guatemala is to the United States, it might rather be postulated that intervention is a continuous quantity rather than an intermittent act. If a reservoir of additional power is available for the asking outside the political system, it is in the interests of the weaker party in any internal dispute to engage it on its behalf, provided always that in doing so it does not alienate its existing actual or potential support.

This is so obvious a qualification that it is easy to forget that nationalism or self-importance may easily blind individuals in particular cases to its significance.

[34] George Modelski, 'The International Relations of Internal War', in *International Aspects of Civil Strife*, ed. James N. Rosenau (Princeton University Press, Princeton, 1964), pp. 14 ff.

[35] James N. Rosenau, 'Internal War as an international Event', in James N. Rosenau, op. cit., pp. 45 ff.

PART II

REVOLUTION IN THE TWENTIETH
CENTURY

4

REVOLUTION IN THE TWENTIETH CENTURY

I. THE CHECK LIST

IN this section it is proposed to introduce a comparative study of sixteen variables in revolutionary patterns since 1901. The purpose of this study is to test hypotheses advanced in earlier chapters and to give guidance on the value of certain areas for further research. For reasons of convenience it was decided to cut short the period covered in 1960, and the study will therefore serve the additional purpose of offering data against which the nature of events since 1961 can be assessed. Needless to say, no claims are made for its value as a basis for prediction as it stands.

The hypotheses to be tested were formulated on the basis of impressionistic evidence drawn from preliminary reading over a wide area. A preliminary list of events was drawn up to serve as the basis for further reading and the reduction of superfluous questions; in the course of this, the general guidance of the broad definition of revolution given in Chapter 1 was made operational in the form of a number of working rules. On this basis the check list given in Appendix A was elaborated.

The operational rules took the form in the main of limitations to the inclusion of events. While all events involving the presence (not use) of force were included for initial consideration, four categories of rare events were excluded from the final list. A separatist government had to fulfil the artificial condition of survival as a distinct entity for a period of one year or more to justify inclusion. The deposition of a president or other ruler as the result of a formal constitutional process of impeachment was treated as a use of force not exceeding the level of the sub-revolutionary norm. The deposition of a ruler on the grounds of insanity was treated as revolutionary where the ruler was not known to be insane before taking up his rule, since the charge of insanity could not otherwise be regarded as proved. Where there were good grounds to suppose that he did have a previous history of insanity, his disposition was treated as being a non-revolutionary act. Cases where the action was carried out mainly by foreign troops were excluded unless there were good grounds for regarding the action as being initiated internally. Otherwise any case of military action could be regarded as being either revolutionary or an act of external war was included for treatment under its revolutionary aspect.

The completed check list was used as the basis of research on sixteen aspects of revolutionary action which were subsequently recorded in plain and code form.[1] Finally these code statements were used for tabulation and the generation of matrices, the results of which are given here. It should be noted that though every effort was made to see that the code would be compatible with subsequent programmes of analysis of numerical statements and indices, the categories used here are nominal and hence not suitable for advanced statistical treatment.

The exception lies in the initial calculations of periodicity. For this purpose each revolutionary event was assessed as being the successor to a previous revolutionary event occurring x years before, where x was a whole number. Apart from the limitations on the check list mentioned above, this raised a number of other problems which were decided empirically.

The previous revolutionary event sought was normally, and in the vast majority of cases, that occurring in the same country or territorial area. In most cases this was quite obvious; for the first seven on the list (1901 α to 1902 ε inclusive) the years being 1885, 1881, 1898, 1871, 1899, 1899, and 1902 respectively. In the case of the normal separatist movement, such as Panama (1903 γ), this was the last such movement in the parent country, in this case the fall of Sanclemente in 1900. In the case of a colonial territory achieving independence by the use of violence, however, the choice often lay between the most recent events in the territory and in the colonial state respectively. In

---

[1] The principal sources used were: *The Annual Register; Bank of London & South America Fortnightly Review; Enciclopedia Universal Ilustrado; Encyclopaedia Britannica* (13th edn. and 1966 revision); *Keesing's Contemporary Archives*, and the files of *The Times* (London). For Central America considerable help was given by Dana Gardner Munro, *Intervention and Dollar Diplomacy in the Caribbean, 1900–1921* (Princeton University Press, Princeton, 1964).

this case, the more recent of the two was selected, so that for the
1945 *coups* in Cambodia (1945 β), Vietnam (1945 γ), and Laos
(1945 ζ), the earlier date chosen was in each case 1940 and not
1862, 1885, and 1781 respectively.[2]

When this had been done there were still some anomalies. A
country was not normally treated as having a separate existence
as an entity when it was subsequently re-absorbed by its parent
territory within a ten-year period. This permitted territories
changing hands, for example Fiume, to be distinguished in the
period under review, but would not be relevant to non-contiguous colonial territories. The cases of the Dominican Republic in
the last century or of Rhodesia since 1961 would have to be regarded as successful for the purposes of this analysis. The *coups
de main* in Vilna (1920 ε) and Memel (1923 α) were credited to
Poland and Lithuania respectively, but the reversal of the
attribution would not noticeably affect the overall results. It was
chosen because it seemed reasonable to choose the point of
accession rather than that of secession in these particular cases.
But it should be noted that the peaceful accession of a small
territory such as Fiume to a large one such as Italy was not
taken as transferring the datum point of the smaller territory to
the larger, so that the fall of Zanella (1922 α) did not become the
datum for Mussolini's march on Rome (1922 ε), despite its great
historical relevance to it.[3]

The best that can be said about these rules is that they are
a moderate compromise. Revolutions may have affinities very
far afield; for example the 1948 *coup* in Costa Rica (1948 δ) was
headed by a soldier trained in the Spanish Civil War. They
very seldom have no discernible ancestry at all. Yet two artificial formations seemed to require special treatment: the Congo
(Leopoldville, now Kinshasa) and Pakistan, whose antecedents
were taken as the dates of formation, 1885 and 1947. Both,
certainly, were events involving a great deal of violence, but
neither falls within even the broad definition of revolution
used here.

For the purposes of obtaining an overview of probable and
possible correlations, however, the data of periodicity were

[2] D. G. E. Hall, *A History of South East Asia*, 2nd edn. (Macmillan, London, 1954).
[3] Denis Mack Smith, *Italy, a modern history* (University of Michigan Press, Ann Arbor, 1959).

reduced to nominal categories. It will be convenient to give them together with the other categories for variables used and some explanation of reasons for their choice.

II. CODING

It will be noted that on the check list, for reasons of speed, the astronomical convention has been adopted of identifying each event by a year followed by a Greek letter; a convention which has one great advantage, that the product is not easily confused with any other type of code. The day and month given in the check list is that of *the fall of the government overthrown*. Some reasonable difference in opinion may exist about this, but rarely beyond a day or two in each direction. In this comparative study the country, the area of the world in which it is situated, and the time of year were not used for the purposes of analysis, as these data are to be expanded for examination in the extended study that follows. Leaving aside time, which has been mentioned above, the sixteen variables' categories were as follows:

(i) *Periodicity* This was coded into five categories:

1. Under 1 year;
2. 1 to 3 years;
3. 3 to 10 years;
4. 10 to 30 years;
5. Over 30 years.

These categories were basically self-selecting in that they conform to certain basic obervations about the events being studied: that revolutions often follow each other at very short intervals; that people in any system seem to get tired of their government at some point between three and ten years; and that the dominance of a generation is over after thirty years or so. They can, however, be assimilated to the logarithmic values proposed by Richardson,[4] i.e. o equivalent to 3 or below, 1 to 4 to 31, 2 to 32 to 317, and so on, as these values have been used elsewhere in the study, for the real virtues they possess of impartial delimitation and exactness in calculation.

[4] Lewis Fry Richardson, *Statistics of Deadly Quarrels* (Stevens & Sons, London, 1960), pp. 6–7.

(ii) *Duration* This, which refers to the duration of the assault phase only, was coded into five categories:

1. Under 1 day;
2. 1 to 30 days;
3. 1 to 12 months;
4. Over 1 year;
5. Uncertain.

Again, these categories were basically self-selecting, and much less compatible, though it should be said now that 24 hours does not represent a real time division for this purpose, as it is too long for one daylight period of military action and too short for the limit of sustained human effort without sleep. The 'uncertain' category was included to allow for uncertain information in the early years of the century, from which the 2 per cent of cases that fell into this category were all drawn.

In dealing with the special case of political assassination, the assault, though limited in action to a brief period of minutes, is not regarded as being completed as long as the victim survives, which may, as in the case of Premier Hamaguchi of Japan (1930 η), be more than a year and may include a continuation of office.[5]

(iii) *Personnel* This, which refers to the dominant element in the composition of the forces taking part, was coded into three categories:

1. Military;
2. Civilian;
3. Military/Civilian.

Of these, the first is self explanatory, but it should be noted that members of governments *acting in that capacity*, e.g. as heads of state, ministers of home affairs or of police, *or on their own or with colleagues*, are classified as civilian even if they have military backgrounds or were appointed as serving officers. Military chiefs of staff or heads of police clearly bear a quite different relationship to the forces under their command. The third category includes all cases of joint operations, from mass movements to parliamentary forces trained and led by military leaders.

Three cases of genuine mystery, where the principals were and are unknown, were coded 'civilian'. They were the assassinations of President Leconte of Haiti (1912 δ), of Michael

[5] *Annual Register* (1930), 280; (1931), 280.

Collins in Ireland (1922 γ), and of King Ananda Mahidol of Thailand (1946 β).[6]

(iv) *Direction*   Directorates of revolutionary actions were coded into five categories:

1. Individual;
2. Junta;
3. Party;
4. Assembly;
5. Uncertain.

Unavoidably, these categories are interpreted from statements of qualitative rather than quantitative composition, and may be identified by organizational criteria.[7] Thus 'Junta' includes secret societies where authority tends to be implicitly hierarchical and obedience to the ruling group is a prerequisite of membership. 'Party' implies a larger, but still coherent, organization whose sub-systems play a role in the formation of revolutionary activity. 'Assembly' implies a lack of central authority and includes the concept of crowd, as in the fall of Villaroel of Bolivia (1946 γ), as well as the formally constituted assembly which declared the independence of Bulgaria in 1908 (1908 ζ). A handful of cases of simultaneous action and other doubtful cases fall into the residual category.

(v) *Level*   Levels of revolutionary action were categorized under four headings according to the model advanced in Chapter 3:

1. Executive;
2. Government;
3. Capital;
4. Province.

(vi) *Succession*   The types of succession were similarly coded under four headings:

1. Automatic;
2. Designate;
3. Interim;
4. Convention.

(vii) *Authority*   As a further test of the nature of revolutionary

---

[6] Munro, *Intervention and Dollar Diplomacy in the Caribbean, 1900–1921* (Princeton University Press, Princeton, N.J., 1964), p. 259; Rex Taylor, *Michael Collins* (Four Square, London, 1965), pp. 197–205; Coast, p. 35.

[7] See below, pp. 106–110.

leadership, leaders and leadership groups were classified according to Weberian criteria, as:
1. Charismatic;
2. Legal-rational;
3. Traditional;
4. Unclassifiable.

This classification requires some further explanation. As ideal types, the Weberian criteria are not mutually self-exclusive, and the individual events were therefore judged by the predominant element evoked in the judgement of contemporary onlookers. This assessment is subjective at two levels, and caution must be taken therefore in using this test as an absolute scale. In practice, the classification 'charismatic' tended to become in itself a residual category to the second and third. Where only one person was involved, in the case of assassination, no judgement of leadership could be made; these and a few unascertained cases occupy the residual category.

(viii) *Forces* This variable was added to amplify (iii) (Personnel), and consists of four categories of possible response of the armed forces to revolutionary events:
1. Support government;
2. Divided;
3. for Military, Military/Civilian, Support opposition (part or remainder standing aloof); for Civilian, non-intervention.
4. Uncertain.

This residual category is sufficiently larger than any previous one to be regarded as statistically important as a deficiency of information.

(ix) *Participation* The extent of participation being an objective criterion of a successor regime, and one used in relating the nature of the change brought by revolution to the concept of the political system favoured by Dahl and others of the 'Yale school' of political scientists,[8] three categories of quantitative change were introduced:
1. Increase;
2. Decrease;
3. No change discernible.

[8] Robert A. Dahl, *Modern Political Analysis* (Prentice-Hall, Englewood Cliffs, N.J., 1964), pp. 12 ff.

(x) *Strength* Assessments of the strength of revolutionary forces are hard to come by. Often they have to be interpreted from statements of the units or formations taking part. They do not form part of the journalists' technique of simulating reality, as do casualty figures. Only the first of the five categories employed had a precise connotation:

1. Individual;
2. Detachment;
3. Regiment;
4. Formation;
5. Uncertain.

Of these, 'detachment' in practice incorporated the ranges 1 and 2, 'regiment' 3, and 'formation' anything from 4 to 6.

(xi) *Magnitude* The categories for the number killed in action on both sides were also five:

1. Under 3 (Richardson 0);
2. 4 to 31 (Richardson 1);
3. 32 to 316 (Richardson 2);
4. Over 317 (Richardson 3 and over).

As Richardson points out, magnitude is technically a much more precise tool than strength of forces, but is still subject to severe limitations of information with small magnitudes.[9] It was found in practice that there was a great area for which information was lacking altogether, and that the figures given here must be treated with some reserve in view of the fact that the large number of very small magnitudes ascertained are based on qualitative assessments of actions as 'bloodless' or 'one-shot' revolutions.

(xii) *Weapons* Weapons used in the assault phase of revolutions as an integral part of the action by the revolutionary side were listed in eight groups:

1. Primitive;
2. Infantry and small arms;
3. Cavalry;
4. Tanks;
5. Artillery;
6. Air;
7. Naval;
8. Implied force only.

[9] Richardson, pp. 9 ff.

These groups were not mutually exclusive, except for the last, which excludes all the others. 'Implied force' means that the action took the form of making it clear that force could and would be used, without the subsequent development of a trial of strength. Sometimes this force could have proved to be very great indeed, as in the deposition of President Urrutia of Cuba following his public denunciation by Fidel Castro on television (1959 β).[10] More often it involves only a handful of actors, as in the case of those who brought about the fall of Vargas in Brazil in 1954 (1954 θ),[11] and the force implied is that of the unrestrained action of (unnamed) political opponents if those charged with maintaining the government refuse to do so.

Since the overwhelming majority of revolutions in the twentieth century have involved the use of firearms, it is not considered that the 'infantry and small arms' category serves any useful purpose, all more advanced weapons (3 to 7 above) being only supplementary to them. Though over ten per cent of cases were not listed on account of insufficient information, this ratio is, given the known distribution of arms at all relevant periods, virtually certain to hold good for them also.

(xiii) *Reaction* Governmental reaction to the threat of revolution was distinguished in two ways: by three categories of flexibility and by one of rigidity beyond the norm.

1. Reform;
2. Concession;
3. Co-option;
4. Suppression only.

'Concession' was held here to mean also abdication or resignation where resistance was a practical proposition; 'suppression' was held to mean only that not even non-essential demands were met in any respect and that the initiative was taken in the use of force against demonstrators.[12]

A large residue was expected and obtained.

(xiv) *Goals* Similarly, two specialized types of goals were

---

[10] Rufo López-Fresquet, *My Fourteen Months with Castro* (World Publishing Co., Cleveland and New York, 1966), pp. 122 ff.; Goldenberg, p. 188.

[11] 26: Stokes, p. 118.

[12] For the concept of a co-opted revolution see William Kornhauser, 'Revolution and National Development', unpublished paper delivered at 6th World Congress of Sociology, Evian, 1966.

isolated: one tending towards decentralization and one towards centralization:

1. Separatist;
2. Official.

The nature of these distinctions is further discussed below. These two sub-types of revolution were expected to account, and did account, for only a very small proportion of the whole.

(xv) *Aid*   Foreign aid to participants was classified in three categories:

1. To government;
2. To opposition;
3. Neutral.

Aid given to both government and opposition was classified accordingly, as in the Spanish Civil War instance of 1939 α.

(xvi) *Social initiatives*   Social action by a successor government was recorded in three categories:

1. Internal;
2. External;
3. None.

The existence of both internal and external initiatives was recorded as in (xv) above. In this case, the terms were interpreted very widely, within the terms imposed by the discussion in Chapter 2.

Throughout the consideration of these categories and the study that follows it should be borne in mind that each variable is considered as ideally consisting of only one aspect capable of being measured or assessed at least in nominal intervals on a linear scale. Where possible, therefore, variables not subject to purely numerical treatment are treated for the purposes of this preliminary study only on an either/or basis, as being operative or not operative, present or absent. While only in the case of the Weberian types of authority, as stated above, was a process of conscious choice between alternatives made, it should be said that there is yet another possibility of error against which the reader should be warned.

This possibility is that the choice of variables may make inevitable the conclusions for which the investigator was looking; that, in short, the investigator invents the categories that fit his theory. Obviously every conscious effort has been made here to avoid this form of word play, but it must be seriously suggested that the nature of the field demands that we test even the most elementary assumptions to the best of our ability. It is definition that the study of revolution needs. The tables are reproduced here, and the reader can apply his own tests to the author's more far-fetched statements.[13]

With this caution we can now proceed to consider the results of the study itself.

III. RAW CHARACTERISTICS

(i) *Incidence*

Assessment of the variables had in the first place to be related to the incidence of revolutionary phenomena between 1901 and 1960. As the time graph in Table 6 (p. 200) shows, the annual incidence of revolution fluctuates greatly, and during the period under consideration varied from a low of one incident in 1927 to a high of 18 in 1918. Closer examination does, however, suggest something of a pattern. 'Normal' fluctuations have taken place between a low of 2 and a high of 10. Furthermore, there is a distinct regularity about their tendency to move from one end of the scale to the other.

A smoothed graph of these variations was therefore developed by obtaining the mean incidence for each five-year period of the series. In this graph, presented in Table 7 (p. 200), each point represents the mid year of five, beginning in 1903 and continuing by annual movements to 1958.

Study of these graphs in the light of historical and allied factors suggests some interesting considerations. To begin with, it is clear that incidence peaks in the years 1916–20 and reaches a low for the period in 1937–42. A secondary trough occurs in the late twenties and a secondary peak in the early thirties, while the 1946–50 period was again high. Thus, while there is a close resemblance, as might have been expected, between the aftermath of the two world wars, the actual course of those wars was accompanied by a very pronounced difference in governmental stability.

[13] Pitrim Aleksandrovitch Sorokin, *Social and Cultural Dynamics*, III; *Fluctuation of Social Relationships, War, and Revolution* (American Book Company, New York, 1937), pp. 398–400, is relevant here as justification. As reconsidered in *Sociological Theories of Today* (Harper, New York, 1967), pp. 597–609, it has proved its value, and is based on the author's own experiences in Russia, for which see *The Sociology of Revolution* (Lippincott, Philadelphia, 1925).

Surprisingly enough, this cannot be accounted for by regarding it as the product of the number of states extant or achieving independence, as the scatter diagram in Table 8 (p. 201) makes clear. The relationship is so conspicuously non-linear as to suggest that we shall find the difference in the causes rather than in the effects of the wars themselves. The First World War was fought in a separatist climate of opinion and with the intention of increasing the number of states in the world. The Second World War resulted from attempts to reverse this process and to develop a world of large centralized empires. The type of revolutionary activity in the post-war periods of each was therefore markedly different, even if the incidence was similar.

It is clear, therefore, that incidence of itself is an inadequate basis for future statistical prediction of revolutionary activity, even with a universe of states now upwards of 130. It does, however, offer some interesting evidence.

Firstly, in the thirty years between 1870 and 1900 the incidence of revolution was remarkably low. Despite a remarkable peak in 1876, it was distinctly uncommon, and in some years fell away to zero. This period of minimum activity is closely associated with the age of imperialism and the consolidation of empires. As Sorokin showed, this minimum extended to all forms of violence, and was followed by a value for the first quarter of the twentieth century which represents a near maximum for all the ages and countries studied in his work.[14] So there can be no suggestion that low incidence of revolution is actually *caused* by the existence of a low number of states; only that it is associated with it.

Secondly, associated with the granting of independence to a large number of former colonial dependencies, there has been a further spectacular rise in mean incidence since 1958. The value for 1962–6 equalled that for 1914–18, and in 1968 there seemed every reason to suppose that the value was likely to remain high for the time being.[15]

---

[14] Sorokin, *Social and Cultural Dynamics*, III, 481. For Europe it was exceeded in calm only by 1726–50 and AD 626–50.

[15] Annual figures for the decade so far:

1961	5	1964	9	1967	10
1962	7	1965	10	1968	7
1963	13	1966	13	1969	8

See also Appendix B.

(ii) *Periodicity*

An account has already been given of the selection of data for the periodicity of revolution, and of the criteria governing it. The mean annual number of years between revolutions plotted in Table 9 (p. 202) suggested two immediate observations. The fluctuations were seen to be considerable, but not as great as they might be considering the widely differing types of countries and events involved. And again they appeared to exhibit a distinct alternation in their relationship to the mean for the whole period. As in the case of incidence, therefore, a smoothed graph was obtained for five-year periods, and this is presented in Table 10 (p. 202).

It will at once be observed that this graph gives four distinct peaks; about the years 1906, 1921, 1930, and 1945; and four distinct troughs; in 1914, 1927, 1939, and 1955. There is every reason to suppose that it presents an exact picture of variations in governmental stability: that is to say, that the peaks represent periods in which even the most stable governments were at risk, and the troughs those in which only the least stable governments were.

Here the beginnings of both world wars correspond with troughs, as might be expected from the initial value of war in promoting centralization and acceptance of authority. So too do the boom years of the twenties and the period of maximum rigidity of the Cold War, both periods in which a sharp political reaction is discernible against decentralizing tendencies in the preceding period. The further treatment of these observations will be postponed to the chapter on revolutionary behaviour, where they can be considered more fully and some tentative hypotheses about them advanced.

As far as the peaks are concerned, there is clearly room for provocative considerations of the relationship between this index and times of political change in countries operating non-revolutionary facilities. The coincidence of the peaks with the 1906, 1922, 1931, and 1945 elections in the United Kingdom is interesting, as these elections reported strong changes in public attitudes; these approximate also to years of large majorities in the United States.

The mean interval for the period as a whole is 10·6 years. This means that the average periodicity for any five-year period did not fall below 3·1 years or rise above 18·8, so it has little value on its own. It does, however, invite comparison with Sorokin's figure of average frequency for social disturbances, including both successful and unsuccessful revolutions. He states that 'on the average one notable social disturbance occurs in about six years".[16] Since his data were drawn from a very long sweep of history (from the earliest times of ancient Greece) this suggests once more that the present century has so far been an exceptionally turbulent one.[17]

The remaining raw characteristics were treated for the purposes of analysis by time by blocks falling into twelve regular quinquennia: 1901–5, 1906–10, 1911–15, and so on. For purposes of comparison a frequency polygon for these quinquennia is given in Table 11 (p. 203). It will be seen from comparison with Table 7 that it does represent a satisfactory series of samples from all levels of the time graph, and varies broadly in accordance with the variations already noted. On this basis, the following overall observations were made of the frequency and trends of the chosen variables.

(iii) *Duration*

It will be seen from Table 12 (p. 203) that the overwhelming majority, some 70 per cent, of all revolutionary incidents have a duration of less than one month. It is possible to amplify this statement from the original data and to state that, of this majority, by far the greater part last less than three days, which as noted above is the normal outside limit of uninterrupted human activity. The number that last less than one day still makes a very respectable proportion, averaging 37 per cent of the total over the sixty years.

There has been a definite decrease in average duration throughout this period, measured by these nominal categories.

(iv) *Level*

Table 14 (p. 204) shows the level at which revolutionary action was conducted. Before 1925 the mode was to be found at the level of the province. In recent years it has been at the level of the executive, reflecting the centralization of govern-

---

[16] Sorokin, *Social and Cultural Dynamics*, III, 473.

[17] Divergencies from Sorokin's findings are to be expected, as only *successful* revolutions are dealt with here. Note that it is the political attribute and not the social that correlates with wars.

mental functions and the technical considerations imposed by modern communications. These conclusions are strikingly reinforced by the consideration that the overall pattern remains consistent: that some 70 per cent of governmental change by violence occurs in the vicinity of the capital. It is within this area that emphasis has shifted from the overall control of the capital to the direction of effort towards securing possession of the governors.

It is also clear that though the distinction is a useful one, the category of action on government (as opposed to executive) is limited by practical considerations. Were assassination eliminated from the total under 'Executive', the executive totals would still be higher than might reasonably have been predicted.[18]

As far as these raw characteristics are concerned, therefore, it is clear that their nature indicates that the model we have proposed is one with real analytical value. We can, therefore, proceed to make use of it to investigate in greater detail the actual way in which revolutionary events occur. For this purpose we shall find it convenient to group our comments under the main headings corresponding to the four elements of a revolutionary situation: namely the existence of a *directorate*, the assembly of *personnel*, the enunciation of *goals*, and the provision of *facilities*.

IV. DIRECTORATE

It is the existence of direction, from whatever source, whether pre-planned or not, that makes revolution a political act and distinguishes it from a mere riot or brawl. Co-ordination and leadership form the two related aspects of any directed action having political significance. Thus, though in terms of their actual physical quality there is little to choose between the burning of Newgate Prison in 1780 and the fall of the Bastille in 1789, in terms of historical significance it is abundantly clear that the latter was a revolutionary act and the former was not.[19] In neither case, it must be noted, was the action pre-planned,

[18] There were 43 assassinations counted in the period 1901–60; one, in Burma (1947 γ), of a group.
[19] Christopher Hibbert, *King Mob: The Story of Lord George Gordon and the London Riots of 1780* (Longmans Green, London, 1958).

in the sense of being a product of a 'conspiracy'. The revolutionary quality is not necessarily related to that of spontaneity.

Cases of collective and spontaneous leadership having effective political consequences are rare. This applies to revolution as to anything else. Political parties rarely sprout overnight, and elections are not won by well-meaning but inexperienced amateurs. It is the nature of leadership to be most effective when it is unitary, and in the case of conflict between unitary and collective leadership the former appears to have a marginal advantage if the conflict is otherwise reasonably even. The advantage is most marked in the most intense conflict, in other words, in military conflict. Leadership, however, can only be effective when the leader has at his disposal a staff able to put his wishes into effect. Though its leadership may be unitary, therefore, the directorate of revolution is most often a multiple in which the leader proper is only one element.

In so far as revolution is a paramilitary phenomenon, its leadership will benefit from its centralization and fulfilment of the traditional military requisites. Where conflict is diffuse, in the case of wide-ranging movements for social reform, it may, however, be a positive advantage to have collective leadership as an expression of widespread support. Such social movements, in origin non-revolutionary, find it easier to pass through the region of equality to a position of superiority, though the lack of a clear and present threat which might be effective in stimulating concentrated and effective countering action by the established authorities. This is why the Oath of the Tennis Court of 1789 is so much more important than the excesses of 1789 which Burke so much deplored.[20] It established a collective leadership to which the disgruntled could attach themselves.

Leadership need not necessarily be successful to exist, nor need it be continuous in one man or one group of men to be successful. Provided the overall level of power superiority is maintained, there is room even for dissension of views or countermanding orders, as in the Russian revolution of October 1917 (1917 ε).[21] Its success may be contrasted with the disastrous consequences of the same phenomena in a situation of marginal

[20] Edmund Burke, *Reflections on the Revolution in France* (etc.) (W. Watson and others, Dublin, 1790).
[21] Goodspeed, pp. 94–6.

advantage in Ireland in the previous year.[22] But this is an ideal and improbable situation. For all these reasons, and because of the natural human inclination towards simplification, attention tends to be focused in most instances on one man. He is the leader of the revolutionary forces.[23]

There are no special qualities for being a revolutionary leader, save the position of leading in a revolutionary situation. The *authority* of the revolutionary leader may be expressed in the same terms as that of other leaders,[24] and it is for this reason that we have included authority among our variables. It may be based on acceptance, with or without the recognition of exceptional personal qualities—the so-called 'charisma'. It may even be based on tradition. Indeed, in the conditions of revolutionary conservatism already discussed it seems probable that the stronger the traditional element in the leadership (in contrast to the radical demand of the cause) the more effective the leadership is likely to be. The habit of authority works in favour of a leader with this advantage as against his fellows, and so a Robespierre gains ground over a Danton, and a Lenin over a Trotsky.

This in turn raises the very pertinent question of why a man holding traditional authority should become a revolutionary leader. Psychologists have advanced the theory that it is the classical example of over-compensation for real or fancied slights in childhood or youth. Thus Robespierre was denied his chance to read a loyal address to the Royal Family because the Queen was tired.[25] The young Lenin was denied a career in the Russia of the Tsars because of his birth.[26] George Washington could not receive a commission as a regular officer but only as a colonial one.[27] Ho Chi Minh made his living washing dishes in a London restaurant where the wealthy dined.[28] Emiliano

[22] Max Caulfield, *The Easter Rebellion* (Four Square, London, 1965), pp. 48–55.

[23] Neumann, *Permanent Revolution*, pp. 48 ff.

[24] Weber, pp. 328–9.

[25] Gérard Walter, *Robespierre* (Gallimard, Paris, 1961), I, 26–8.

[26] David Shub, *Lenin: A Biography*, revsd. edn. (Penguin Books, London, 1966), pp. 36–8.

[27] Marcus Cunliffe, *George Washington, Man and Monument* (Collins, London, 1959), p. 50.

[28] Robert Shaplen, *The Lost Revolution: Vietnam 1945–1965* (André Deutsch, London, 1966), p. 36; Bernard B. Fall, ed., *Ho-Chi Minh On Revolution: Selected Writings 1920–66* (Pall Mall, London, 1967), p. vii.

Zapata was punished for being a bandit by being forcibly con-
scripted into the Mexican army when its officer corps was the
preserve of the wealthy families.[29] Slights and restraints of this
kind are not unknown to lesser mortals, but they do not become revolutionary leaders.

In any evaluation of Pettee's theory of social 'cramp', therefore, some account must be taken of the fact that those individuals who emerge as leaders are not only not especially
distinguishable as victims of cramp, but seem on the whole to
have enjoyed a measure of social advantage over their fellows.[30]
It may be that the contrast between the actual condition of the
individual and his ambition predisposes him to a leadership role.
But in social terms, it is his possession of a greater measure of
traditional authority than others still eligible as possible leaders
that distinguishes him. Washington rose to fame because he
was the best general in the colonies. As a lawyer, Robespierre
stood out in an Assembly from which the aristocrats had been
removed, because of his aristocratic habit and manner. When
the generals and the landowners were on the run, Zapata
emerged as the best horseman and the most successful strategist
in the State of Morelos. Primacy depends on the stature of
those around about.

At this point it is undeniably difficult to distinguish between
traditional authority and acceptance, as it is hard to separate
either from the nature of the individual personality and the
quality of selfconfidence. The tendency to accentuate acceptance arises from the habit of mind that continues to attribute
superior traditional authority to figures no longer holding real
political power.[31] Devices for this purpose form a large part of
the preoccupation of a successful revolutionary leader, as they
ease acceptance in the minds of the uncommitted that such a
change has actually occurred.[32] Acceptance in revolutionary

[29] H. H. Dunn, *The Crimson Jester, Zapata of Mexico* (Harrap, London, 1934);
cf. Baltasar Dromundo, *Emiliano Zapata* (Imprenta Mundial, Mexico, 1934).

[30] Pettee, pp. 33–63.

[31] Exemplified by Jacobitism in Scotland or Legitimism in France. The objects
of devotion for such cults are generally conspicuously ill-equipped to undertake the
tasks for which they claim authority. A happy exception is Dr. Otto von Habsburg
—see *Otto of Austria: Monarchy in the Atomic Age* (Monarchist Press Association,
London, 1960).

[32] Thus the Revolutionary Government in Egypt chose to place on its coinage
motifs recalling Pharonic times, including hieroglyphs and the figure of a Pharaoh

terms is circular in form and self-justifying in action. The new government is there and has to be accepted. The simplest of many devices used to secure obedience, therefore, is the deliberate creation of an illusion of acceptance, by which the individual is led to accept in default of reliable information about the intentions of society as a whole.[33]

It follows that the 'true' personal qualities of the leader are equally insubstantial. It is not, therefore, a rewarding task to attempt to assess revolutionary leaders with the intention of securing a consensus as to the type of personality involved.[34] Indeed, taking the ostensible characteristics alone, no consistency in this respect can be observed, except in the common possession of some form of belief in the rightness of their cause, and of that form of unquestioning acceptance of the individual protection of destiny which commonly passes for bravery.[35]

Still, if the qualities are insubstantial, their importance is not. It is even possible that the personal capacity of the leader to govern stands in *inverse* proportion to the scale of the movement he heads. A large provincial revolution may be united only in dedication to a common cause and be led by a figurehead. This follows from the emphasis on military qualities in more direct confrontations. But there are pronounced and important exceptions, and the course of history may be made much smoother by the presence of efficient organization, when a spontaneous uprising is actually in contemplation.[36]

The leader's role can be both positive and negative.

In positive role, the leader takes the situation as he finds it, and moulds it to shape. Naturally, his resources can only be those that are available, as Trotsky realized, calling them the

in a war chariot. Ironically, Ancient Egypt did not use coinage before the First Persian Conquest; hieroglyphs appeared on late period coins only once, and the image of the Pharaoh not at all.

[33] Robert Vincent Daniels, *The Conscience of the Revolution, Communist Opposition in Soviet Russia* (Harvard University Press, Cambridge, Mass., 1960).

[34] The bold attempt of E. Victor Wolfenstein, in *The Revolutionary Personality: Lenin, Trotsky, Gandhi* (Princeton University Press, Princeton, 1967) is worth noting; T. W. Adorno, Else Frenkel-Brunswik, Daniel J. Levinson, and R. Nevitt Sanford, *The Authoritarian Personality*, 2 vols. (John Wiley, New York, 1964).

[35] This protection is not proof against abuse, however, as the fate of General Sanjurjo showed (Hugh Thomas, *The Spanish Civil War*, revsd. edn. (Penguin Books, London, 1967), p. 215).

[36] Karl Marx, 'The Civil War in France', in Karl Marx and Friedrich Engels, *Selected Works* (Foreign Languages Publishing House, Moscow, 1962), I, 473.

'objective' conditions.[37] Finding out what these conditions are, however, and exploiting them in the revolutionary cause are tasks to be set and determined by what leadership there is. If that leadership is incapable of using them properly no revolutionary action will ensue, even if the situation has been correctly assessed or even developed to a point at which a revolutionary initiative could have taken place. This moulding is a continuous process. The revolution must conform to its environment until the revolutionary transition is successfully accomplished, and even at the point of success a good leader can rally a remote cause, and by a correct assessment of the real strength of the opposing forces can succeed, where the odds appear on the surface (and to his followers) to be otherwise too great.[38]

Theories of leadership have been developed from illustrations of such successes that take little or no account of the pre-existing conditions, ascribing all to leadership.[39] While it has been made clear above that in all but a very few cases any situation can be regarded as a starting-point for a revolutionary movement, belief in the total power of the leader does not appear justifiable. It has led to repetition of revolutionary acts for their own sake and the consequent deterioration of the total political system. Such repetition serves no social purpose, being directed towards the exchange of leadership only for another of similar outlook. Nevertheless it must be said that the revolutionary leader must be prepared to take a step that no one else has taken, to make a fresh assessment of the opposition forces, and to take the first step away from the path of traditional legality. At the least, such action demands a certain toughness of mind.

Unfortunately such toughness of mind seems to be fairly common and not sufficiently distinctive as a mark of a future revolutionary leader.[40] The leader who can convert others can

[37] Léon Trotsky, 'Lessons of October', in *The Essential Trotsky* (Unwin Books, London, 1963), pp. 144–52; see also Louis Gottschalk, 'Leon Trotsky and the Natural History of Revolutions', *The American Journal of Sociology*, XLIV, no. 3 (Nov. 1938), 339.

[38] Frank O'Connor, *The Big Fellow, Michael Collins and the Irish Revolution*, revsd. edn. (Clonmore & Reynolds, Dublin, 1965), pp. 42 ff.; cf. Rex Taylor, *Michael Collins*.

[39] Even *fidelismo* is strongly tinged by this.

[40] Hans Jürgen Eysenck, *The Psychology of Politics* (Routledge, London, 1954), pp. 107–42.

first convert himself. He may most easily do so by accepting his break with the present as a reversion to the past, or to an extension of that past along a hypothetical parallel line of development. He may represent to himself that it is more important to maintain a custom or tradition than to obey the law. Seldom does the revolutionary justify his actions, even to himself, purely in the light of self-interest.

In the negative role, the leader affects the situation by his removal from it. This must not be confused with the negative role of the head of government, which, as Pettee points out, is often more important than the positive role of the revolutionary in determining the outcome.[41] It is surprising but true that men apparently weak or ineffective in the positive sphere have, by the circumstances that surrounded their withdrawal from it, created more political impetus than many great and positive leaders. The negative leader may either be martyred, like Francisco I. Madero,[42] or sacrificed, like General Naguib.[43] In the first case, his death gives inspiration to his followers, fixing their loyalty to the cause without the inconvenient day-to-day details of political 'horse-trading' to detract from the simplicity of aim. From the ranks of those followers, further leaders may be multiplied. In the second case, the leader as scapegoat for failure or disillusion functions to shift responsibility from the followers and to enable them to make a fresh start under another leader.

Here again it is clear that the prior recognition of the revolutionary leader from his own innate qualities is a task that is very nearly impossible. The leader becomes a known quantity only at the moment defined as that of emergence. This refers to him in his capacity as leader not as revolutionary, so that the moment of emergence for Oliver Cromwell, for example, is not his seizure of the plate from the Cambridge colleges for the Parliamentary cause, but the Battle of Marston Moor.[44] Analysis of the leader at the moment of emergence is of great importance, though it necessarily falls outside the scope of the

[41] Pettee, pp. 90–4.
[42] Ross, pp. 320–1.
[43] Peter Mansfield, *Nasser's Egypt* (Penguin Books, London, 1965), pp. 50–2; see also Muhammad Naguib, *Egypt's Destiny* (Doubleday, Garden City, N.Y., 1955).
[44] John Buchan, *Oliver Cromwell* (Hodder & Stoughton, London, 1950), pp. 192–3.

8—S.O.R.

present study. It is all the more important because of the phenomenon which may be called 'leader-exchange'.

'Leader-exchange' refers to the tendency which has been remarked upon for the ultimate leader of a post-revolutionary government to be someone other than the primary leader of the initial *coup* or his heir apparent. In the assault phase of revolutions the ultimate leader may be found (in retrospect) to have been in a position well placed to succeed the primary, but not so near as to be an immediately obvious successor.[45] The same rule applies however to many other forms of political succession, from Papal conclaves to the customary process of the British Conservative Party. As in those cases, the candidate best placed to succeed among competing equals is the one nearest to the command of the administrative staff of the organization.[46] In the case of a revolution, this means the military command in the field, the administration of revolution being of a military character. In both cases a prominent political figure is at a disadvantage against the coalition of his rivals in opposition.

Where a political revolution is accompanied by leader-exchange, by definition the ultimate leader succeeds the primary leader by sub-revolutionary means, otherwise he becomes the primary leader of a new revolution.

It is possible, however, to have an able revolutionary leader whose displacement has been planned from the beginning. Such planning, however, is almost inseparable from full control of the revolutionary staff. Succession of this type forms the classic instance of the exceptional case of the inheritance of the heir apparent, as, for example, in the inheritance by Stalin of the position and place of Lenin.[47] In this case, however, in the *coup* the function of leadership was divorced from the role of planning. The existence of such a separation should not be too difficult for a trained observer to detect. He will then, if he wishes to develop this branch of revolutionary studies, examine the record of the planner with greater care.

Such a study seems generally to be remarkably easy. A sur-

[45] An interesting study of the political lieutenant, or 'No. 2 man', is contained in Neumann, *Permanent Revolution*, pp. 73–95.

[46] Weber, pp. 367–8.

[47] Isaac Deutscher, *Stalin, a Political Biography*, revsd. edn. (Penguin Books, London, 1966), pp. 232, 249–75.

prising proportion of those who have planned or led *coups* have left voluminous literary evidence of their views and habits of thought from times well before the onset of revolutionary activity. Naturally these records may not always have received the attention which they deserved, and this is particularly true of the making of speeches. The 'History will absolve me!' speech of Fidel Castro is a rare exception.[48]

With current developments in psychology and the computing sciences, it could be that the future will hold governments who have at their disposal new techniques for detecting the sort of character formation which could predispose an individual to revolutionary activity, and match it in anticipation to a range of possible political, economic, and social conditions related to the positions those individuals actually occupy. For the moment, however, it is clear that they find it difficult enough to keep an adequate check on those likely to sell the secrets of state to foreign powers.

The importance of the directorate to the study of revolutionary events, then, lies in its relation to the succession and thus to the future development of political institutions within the state.

Revolution is characterized by a rapid growth-cycle of institutions. These institutions are formed to provide *ad hoc* solutions to two major classes of problems: general problems, i.e. those relating to governments in general; and specific problems, i.e. those relating to revolution in its institutional aspect.

The centralized character of revolution means that both sets of problems are dealt with through the same organs, and thus confused. This confusion is often deliberate. We may, however, identify certain problems as relating specifically to revolution; these are, apart from those relating to the organization and delivery of the central *coup*, those essential to the defence and consolidation of the *coup*. Since practically all modern governments claim descent from revolutionary formations, it is clearly of some importance to have an understanding of the basic theory lying behind the circumstances of their creation. The extent to which institutions for specific problems retain a function in a regular governmental order deserves particular attention.

[48] Goldenberg, pp. 150–3.

The actual preparation and delivery of the *coup* is made operational through the anomic structures covered in detail in Chapters 2 and 3. The directorate forms the link between these structures and the institutions with which we are concerned here. It, and it alone, holds a continuous existence throughout the *coup* and into the new order. At the instant of success it is the directorate that has assumed the responsibility for exercising the functions of government, and the institutional structure that depends upon it initially falls under one of four main headings, depending as to whether the directing body is of one or another of the four types mentioned above (p. 88), the *Assembly*, the *Junta*, the *Military*, or the *Party* type.

The *assembly* is usually a *convention*. The convention is a large assembly with a considerable claim to be considered as being representative of the wishes of the nation as a whole. This is not necessarily because it has been chosen either by 'the people' or by some large proportion of them, nor because it has been chosen by some third party on the basis of representation of the people by interests or other groupings. Its claims to be representative may well rest only on the self-acclaimed function of filling a gap that no other body is available to fill.[49]

A convention has, naturally, to be convened by someone, but it may well have been convened for some purpose other than that of assuming power, as was the Annapolis Convention of 1786. It is the act of assuming authority that transforms it into a revolutionary body, presupposing the further stage of attempting to secure power, but in practice the distinction is often of merely legalistic significance. The act must necessarily occur under the influence of leaders, but again these may well not be those who originally summoned it or who were intended to guide its proceedings. Convention-directed revolutions must be characterized by minimal forward planning and tendencies to rapid and complete changes of course.[50] These changes need not necessarily involve the replacement of the leader or leaders, but in themselves they have major significance in the light of the claim of the convention to a high degree of legitimacy.

[49] It therefore includes the body of the population of the capital in anomic grouping; cf. Goldenberg, pp. 175-7.

[50] For example the French Revolution of 1789 and the October Revolution in Russia, 1917; cf. the fall of Eulalio Gutiérrez in Mexico, 1915 (Quirk, *The Mexican Revolution, 1914-1915*, pp. 132-70).

For this reason the convention commands a high degree of consent from the regular (i.e. pre-revolutionary) organs of state. In turn, this tends not only to accentuate the effects of sudden changes of course, but even to make them more likely; for in taking over the pre-revolutionary governmental machine the convention is spending a 'bank balance' which it cannot readily restore, drawing on the reservoir of traditional skills of the bureaucrat while denouncing him for his former association with those who have now become the enemies of the people.[51] Furthermore, even if the convention is restrained in its treatment of pre-revolutionary officers, it is not in a position to use the loyalty they bring to its service in the sophisticated way in which modern government operates. It is too large, too loud, and too argumentative. The effect of attempting to use its power is to cause the entire machine to disintegrate rather than to rally it to the new cause.

In the first instance the convention tends to subsume all power in itself. Sub-committees may be appointed to plan given tasks, but neither they nor their chairmen are given direct control over the appropriate departments in the executive, which are, therefore, left headless. Lacking direction, the departments continue with routine until some vigilant watchdog denounces it either as time-wasting or as counter-revolutionary plotting.

At the same time the convention has somehow to exert its authority outside the capital. As Pettee has pointed out, the problem is not that it cannot give orders, but that no one who receives the orders has been given the new code.[52] It therefore sends out members of its own body to form similar, lesser organs for local and provincial government; yet at the same time these lack, or are intended to lack, real executive authority, and form merely a transitional stage towards the development of an organism planned in executive rather than legislative terms. Sometimes a similar structure is applied to the capital itself. In this case the fragmentation of authority is carried to the theoretical limit, and the maintenance of public order is likely to be virtually impossible.

[51] Pettee, p. 103, talks of the 'dull minds of functionaries' who keep going in revolutionary times. But Civil Servants do have to eat like everybody else.
[52] Pettee, pp. 107–14.

Finally, the relationship of the convention to the armed forces is of particular concern for study of the emergence of leadership-patterns of a counter-revolutionary spirit.[53] One commander at a time, however brief his term of office, is the maximum an armed force is inclined to obey. The institutionalization of command in one person becomes inevitable if the forces are to meet any serious internal or external challenge. This step is the end of convention government, however much the fiction of subordination to the assembly may be stressed.

Junta, military, and *party* organs can all be classified in apposition to the convention as being characterized by prior planning, selection of personnel through testing of opinion in key positions, and the use of inducements of various kinds.

The *junta* is a self-chosen group, small in size, whether of civilian, civil–military, or purely military, composition. It seeks to run the governmental machine through wholly or partly civilian mechanisms.

The *military* pattern, very rare indeed, is one in which civilian government is entirely supplanted by military personnel, seeking to rule through the military command structure.[54]

The revolutionary *party,* similarly, has a pre-existing command structure, which it can use wholly to replace the national government, and enjoys the advantage over the military that in its formation it has had to recognize and promote the monitoring of popular responses.[55] As already observed, it is not necessarily a revolutionary party in the sense that it was formed to plan or carry out the *coup,* but neither is it sufficient for it to be the residual legatee of a *coup* made by others.

The *coup* by which any of these three organs actually achieves power is carried out with the proposed succession, an alternative government however temporary, already in mind. To be a fully effective one, it should, moreover, be ready to take office without further delay. We can except that delay necessitated by the operation of devices registering or simulating approval which are customarily recognized in the society as conferring

---

[53] Edwards, pp. 146–55.

[54] Not to be confused with the displacement of civilians by military personnel, termed 'supplanting' by Finer, pp. 110–39. The classic example is Cromwell's rule by the Major Generals (Sir Charles Firth, *Oliver Cromwell and the Rule of the Puritans in England* (O. U. P., London, 1961)).

[55] For example the Paris Sections or the Soviets in Russia.

legitimacy, or which may be represented as doing so after the event.

This post-revolutionary government then is *not* necessarily the directing organ of the revolution. If the latter continues to have an existence, it is probable that it will retain the specific functions in its own control while delegating the general ones. A junta, for example, frequently maintains the pre-revolutionary machine to carry out the conventional functions of maintaining food supplies and public order while it appoints sector leaders with police jurisdiction and devises mechanisms of punishment and reward designed to modify the operation of the political system in the interest of the revolutionary cause.

It does not always happen that, when a successful transition has occurred, the planned, pre-formed government takes office. One or more of its members may have been killed or incapacitated in the course of action, as in Mexico in 1913 γ, or for security reasons may not have been warned in advance and hence refuse to serve, or, alternatively, may bargain for a position other than that originally allocated. Such confusion is frequently a contributory cause to the development of a further revolutionary transition designed to secure power for a more integrated group.

There are two residual categories of revolutionary transition in which this activity is of particular importance in determining the political consequences. One is the least conceivable form of the junta type, that in which the transition is planned and carried out by an individual. In the *individual* type no pre-planned succession is possible, and the succession is left to the automatic operation of the system.[56] The other is a subdivision of the assembly, the *crowd* type, where the transition is entirely achieved by an anomic group lacking sufficient stability to be subjected to the process of identification, as in the case of the Bolivian revolution of 1946 (1946 γ).[57] The effect is, however, so closely related to that of an assembly that the only difference in treatment is the disentangling of the relationship of the transition to the post-revolutionary government. A

[56] In the case of a high military official this may ensure succession, as in the succession of Rojas Pinilla in Colombia, 1953 (Martz, *Colombia*, pp. 162–9).

[57] Robert J. Alexander, *The Bolivian National Revolution* (Rutgers University Press, New Brunswick, 1958), p. 37.

pointer to the difficulty is the deceptive similarity between the Bolivian instance and the Iraqi revolution of 1958 (1958 δ); the latter was carefully pre-planned and designed to result in the succession that did take place.[58] The crowd type is therefore treated as being synonymous with the assembly, a vacant succession being technically filled by sub-revolutionary means, unless specifically stated.

In all cases the actual acquisition of power is followed by three stages of institutional development.

In the first stage interest articulation takes place purely through the anomic structures developed for revolutionary purposes. This period may last a long time, as in Mexico between 1914 and 1917 or in China between 1916 and 1928.[59] The aggregation of these interests is achieved by structures whose rapid growth from the moment of successful transition demonstrates the emergence of a specifically revolutionary executive. If the first stage is lengthy, this means that this executive function has failed to achieve unity throughout the political system, and interest aggregation is taking place in disparate areas by disparate organs. It is the aim of the members of these organs to bring this state of affairs back to normality as soon as possible, and the revolutionary executive is charged with the task.

It has the function, in home affairs, of obtaining effective control of the police and of restoring public order to a basic standard, the imposition of price control and the rationing of scarce or essential foodstuffs, and the licensing of transport and provision for the safe conduct of essential supplies and services, especially medical, power and lighting. In finance, it must ensure the capture of the treasury reserves, if any, in order to ensure the payment of the troops and irregular forces, and subsequently must arrange for the collection of loans and other tribute vital to the interim maintenance of the individuals who make up the continuing material of the governmental machine.

[58] Majid Khadduri, *Independent Iraq, 1932–1958*, 2nd edn. (O. U. P., London, 1960), *passim*.

[59] For Mexico, see Peter Calvert, 'The Mexican Political System', *Journal of Development Studies*, IV, no. 4 (July 1968), 464; for China, Li Chien-nung, *The Political History of China, 1840–1928*, trs. and ed. Ssu-yu Teng and Jeremy Ingalls (Van Nostrand, Princeton, 1965).

In defence, the revolutionary command must guarantee the protection of their own headquarters and governmental centre, and maintain the closest links between the two. If applicable, they will detail detachments to oversee the provisional government, and will in most cases have an addition to organize the full neutralization of surviving units of the army and other service branches of the pre-revolutionary regime. Their task may of course go beyond this to the location of rival revolutionary forces in the field and the pacification of local and provincial centres of counter-revolutionary activity.

In foreign affairs, the revolutionary cause must hasten a settlement with its backers and secure diplomatic recognition from appropriate sources. This serves the dual function of reinforcing its claim to legitimacy and at the same time enabling it to free the assets held abroad by the defunct government for its own use. It also enables it to undertake useful ancillary propaganda functions, tending to strengthen its position in the international community.

All these are activities of primarily revolutionary significance and are directed towards the consolidation of the revolution. As such, they do not take into account the welfare of the political community as a whole, and may, indeed, be positively detrimental to it. At this stage the revolutionary government devotes its maximum energies to the degree of reconstruction that it wishes to undertake in the circumstances afforded it. Over and above this, it undertakes only the essential functions of normal government, if indeed, it has not handed them over entirely to a provisional regime.

It is a striking comment on the utility of government as an institution that so few of its functions *qua* government seem to be essential. Banks need not stay open, garbage need not be collected, burglars need not be arrested, and parking meters need not function. Life continues somehow, just as it used to do in the preceding two million years or so of man's history. Still, civilization brings with it a certain dependence on complex machinery, and the maintenance of water supplies and sewerage is vital. In addition, overt looting has to be suppressed, and a minimal degree of defence envisaged in the most probable eventualities of hostile invasion from outside the national boundaries. At that, it is less necessary for government to encourage the continuance of these functions than merely to ensure that they do not come to a halt.

It would, however, for quite other reasons than those of physical survival, be erroneous to suppose that the revolutionary government would be wise to restrict its intervention in conventional processes quite to this extent. The removal of the burden of modern life, of jobs and taxes, or queues and chequebooks, encourages a youthful feeling of irresponsibility. Whatever the opinions of philosophers on the natural state of man, there can be general agreement that, in revolutionary conditions, in the excitement of freedom and under the stimulus of violence, he is inclined to behave badly.[60]

Such behaviour, tending against the assumptions of improvement on which revolutions are based, is in the strict sense as well as the general, counter-revolutionary. This fact has much to do with the evolution of the second stage: the fission of the revolutionary legislature and judiciary from the parent body of the revolutionary executive, once this is functional to its own satisfaction.

In point of fact, the need for a judicial organ is felt first. It takes the form of one or more units of 'revolutionary justice', to investigate departures from the new norm which may be brought to their attention either by fiat or by delation. They are usually empowered to deal also with non-revolutionary derelictions discovered in the course of inquiries.

Generally regarded as being tribunals rather than courts, these units are characterized first by their dual function of investigating as well as of ordering punishment, and secondly by their simplicity of operation. There is a single qualification for membership—membership of the revolutionary movement and loyalty to its cause. Lay status is generally regarded as being a positive advantage, since it retains the minimum of preconception relating to the very different rules governing the operation of courts or justice in a conventional society. There is a single offence for which the accused stands liable to conviction—that of being charged before the tribunal. There is a single punishment for all persons convicted—death.

The separation of the revolutionary legislature usually

---

[60] Erich Fromm, *The Fear of Freedom* (Routledge, London, 1960).

comes somewhat later, when dissatisfaction with the wholesale nature of the tribunal develops. In small movements, however, no separation of the judicial function may take place at all on the revolutionary side; the functions of revolutionary justice being considered sufficiently manageable through the revolutionary directorate itself. Consolidation of this position through formal law will need a new legislature also. In each case the legislature is revolutionary because it is designed or intended to legislate in a particular fashion, and is therefore designed or intended not to be representative of real feeling in so far as those sentiments may be counter-revolutionary. This is no problem, since legislatures do not have to be representative, only authoritative. The authority of the legislature will in each case be derived from the fact of power of the revolution itself.[61]

The nature of the institution itself varies with the central organ of direction. The convention has no problems; it conflates in itself the legislative and executive authority and exercises each as it chooses. The junta may issue ordinances on its own authority, either subject to later confirmation by a new legislature or by leave of an interim authority in lieu of the head of state. In either case it cannot with any ease continue to combine both functions for strictly revolutionary purposes for very long, or it does so at the risk of neglecting its urgent preoccupation with its own immediate survival.

The military body in the age of *levée en masse*, as Vagts points out, is in a more favourable position. It can, and often does, in its own right claim to embody the ultimate emergency power of the state.[62] It is particularly well fitted to use those powers, once assumed, since it has no internal check on the enforcement of decrees handed down from above. Civilian bureaucracy requires a looser rein, though for short periods it can be made to operate under the immediate threat of loss of occupation or of ration privileges. Demonstrable legitimacy is important to the bureaucracy in assuring it of a continuity in responsibility, which might otherwise devolve uncomfortably upon itself.

An existing legislative body may, of course, be tailored to a

[61] The key to this authority is the dropping out of politics by the ordinary citizen noted by Brinton, p. 160.
[62] Vagts, pp. 360 ff.

new purpose by a suitable blend of purging or duress, or be replaced, as opportunity affords, by a fresh term of reliable supporters through the vast range of methods of electoral manipulation that has been devised in modern times to reconcile the will of the people with that of their representatives.

The final stage of development is the expansion of the provisional revolutionary control, thus developed, into a permanent successor government. This process may indeed not be discernible at all at the time, owing to the supersession of the government by a further *coup* or counter-*coup*. It must therefore be remembered that the actual assumption of the title of 'provisional government' is no guide to either that government's intentions or the length of its eventual term of office.[63]

The successor government may be imposed by force or fraud on the one hand, or freely permitted to supersede the interim government on the other. But it is safe to say that both extremes are in themselves rare, owing to the conflicting interests of the members of the interim regime and of the revolutionary council. Some *modus vivendi* has to be arrived at between them. But as far as outsiders are concerned, the most common position is that the successor government is 'forced', in the sense that a conjuror uses the word. In other words, it is not imposed, but the people have no effective alternative to choosing it.

Broadly speaking, the possible paths for the regularization of anomic political systems in an institutional pattern are four. These are: the violent ascendancy of an institutionalized group, a stalemate between anomic interests yielding to articulated institutions, an informal arrangement between anomic interests to accept hegemony from one of their number, and the establishment of a formal contract as the basis of settlement.[64] In practice, the nature and velocity of political conflict are such that no one of them is likely to have permanent application as against the others.

We may now examine the observed variations in aspects of direction of revolutions in our test sample. These aspects are *direction* itself (the dimensions of the directorate), the *authority* of the leadership, and the type of *succession* imposed.

[63] Stokes, p. 393.
[64] Cf. Pettee, p. 117.

(i) *Direction*

Table 15 (p. 205) sets out the fluctuations in directorates observed. It is clear from it that there is a premium on small group organization, which is associated with an increase during the period in the concentration of authority.

It shows up definitively the inadequacies of 'convention' leadership, whether of the crowd or assembly variety. Of the fifteen successful during the quinquennium 1916–20 all succeeded in a 'power vacuum'. These instances account for just under half of all sampled. Of the rest, those of Crete (1908 η),[65] Bulgaria (1908 ζ),[66] and France (1940 β)[67] were made possible only by the complete support of foreign powers, outweighing the influence of other powers and domestic opponents.[68] Spontaneous mass action as in Bolivia (1946 γ), Iraq (1948 α), Haiti (1956 ε), and South Korea (1960 α) has been effective only against governments which have felt obliged to take it as representing a force of public opinion to which they must yield.[69]

(ii) *Authority*

It has already been explained what the limitations on this test were (p. 89). In practice, the interpretation of the raw figures (Table 16, p. 205) must be regarded as inconclusive for these reasons, and the statements made here are therefore cast in the form of comments about coding.

Almost half the incidents could be classified as having leaders judged as holding legal/rational authority, and a quarter as having leaders holding traditional authority. The charismatic category, often taken as a characteristic of revolutionary politics in the broadest sense of the word, accounted for less than a fifth of all instances and showed a marked tendency to fall off with the passage of time.

The unclassifiable cases were mainly assassinations, where

[65] *Encyclopaedia Britannica* (1966), 6, 739–40.
[66] *Encyclopaedia Britannica* (1966), 4, 391; 6, 739–40.
[67] Paul Farmer, *Vichy, Political Dilemma* (O. U. P., London, 1955), pp. 127 ff.
[68] Kornhauser, op. cit., suggested a category of 'imposed' revolution which could have useful analytical value here.
[69] The government did not yield in Colombia after the *Bogotazo* of 1948: Martz, *Colombia*, pp. 59–61.

charismatic could have been used as a catch-all, had it not been considered that for authority to exist it has to have some evidence of being accepted. It is this lack of acceptance which distinguishes the political assassin from other political actors. Besides, as in the realm of individual action the pre-conditioning effect of personal factors must not be overlooked, and must indeed be held responsible for the decision of the assassin to diverge to such an extent from the norms of obedience held by his fellows.[70] Personal rivalry and similar motivations cannot be graded as carrying the authority to act on them as an automatic result of their existence.

(iii) *Succession*

The type of succession resulting from transitions is tabulated in Table 17 (p. 206). The table confirms the heavy predominance of the category 'designate', as might be expected from the drastic nature of revolutionary action. Succession types did not show a definite overall trend, beyond disclosing that convention succession has latterly been extremely unfashionable. This fact reflects the ideological rigidity of recent political doctrines, but it is not necessarily the result of them.

Some fluctuation within the categories was, however, considered to be of interest. Designate succession was highest for the quinquennium 1926–30, a period in which the incidence of revolutionary activity, it will be recalled, was low. Interim succession was correspondingly lowest for this period, and highest for the period 1946–50. Yet in all periods it was very significant, reflecting the fact that it is much easier to eliminate an unpopular government than to establish another in its place. Whether interim governments derive from basic disagreement on post-revolutionary goals and organization, or whether they are used as a legalistic device to cover the imposition of a predetermined or agreed regime, they still serve the fundamental purpose of providing a breathing-space for revolutionaries to redirect their attention towards securing the consent of the people at large.

---

[70] The revolutionary can be very law-abiding in everyday things and interpersonal relationships; cf. the case of the leader who bought 57 tram tickets for his men on the morning of the Easter Rising in Dublin, 1916 (Caulfield, p. 19).

V. PERSONNEL

In the study of personnel the most important thing is to distinguish them from members of the directorate. This seems a truism, but in practice it is not generally done, and is seldom even attempted. Personnel may be studied as a group, but this does not mean that the leader or directorate can be regarded as necessarily being part of that or any other group. Their functions are entirely different, and so, we may assume, are their psychological attitudes. Revolutionary personnel however, may, of course, include potential leaders or by agreement conceal actual ones. This is the logical consequence of the interrelationship between leader and follower recognized by Merriam, by which the leader has effectiveness as such only so long as he shares basic attitudes and approaches with those over whom he wishes to exercise influence.[71]

The isolation of a leader or directorate exercising leadership functions has to be followed by an estimate of the groups within the society supporting that leadership, of actual numbers in each support group, and their equivalence in what may be termed an 'effective support value'. Though it is normal only to distinguish in the first instance between government and opposition forces, each of these will normally be a complex of lesser groups with differing degrees of loyalties to their primary leaders. It is necessary to assess where their loyalties lie, not only in the first instance but also given the various chances of overt conflict in all probable future circumstances.

While it is commonplace to identify certain of these lesser groups, and newspaper writers speak freely of such units as 'the army', 'students', 'the urban workers', and so forth as having a value in a given situation, it is rare that this estimate is either adequate in depth or serviceable enough for more than a short period, to be considered as in itself having sufficient analytical value. Investigations in retrospect therefore tend to concentrate on such estimates from a specific standpoint: that of identifying the first recognition of strategic or tactical moves, or of success or defeat.

For the social scientist such estimates must, however, be

[71] Charles E. Merriam, *Political Power* (Collier Books, New York, 1964), pp. 48–9.

made the raw material for a continuous probability analysis in terms of the basic rule of maximization of support. This rule is well known by rule of thumb to every potential or actual leader. It is, in fact, the ability to apply it which creates or identifies the leader, and many leaders appreciate the corollary, that the best way to gain support is to demonstrate that one has it already. Estimates of actual numbers of revolutionary supporters, as every reporter knows, are consequently notoriously inaccurate. It is even more difficult to take into consideration, as our model would require us in all cases, the factors of armament, location, protection, disposition, and morale necessary to arrive at an approximation of fighting value applicable to each specific instance. This is true even though, as the military strategists indicate, over a long sequence of battles fought with similar armament and accoutrements it is possible to ascertain with a very fair degree of accuracy the relative effectiveness, say, of cavalry and infantry.[72]

In other words, effective support has to be defined, not just by counting noses, but in terms of force deployed, its rapidity of movement, location, objectives, discipline, coherence and enthusiasm, and armament. Only one group normally taking part in revolution is easy (relatively speaking) to classify on all these grounds, and hence to assess. This is the regular army.

Now, in normal cases, the amount of force disposed of by the army is so disproportionately large compared with any force that may be levied and deployed against it that revolution is possible only if it has been alienated from the pre-revolutionary regime, and impossible if it is uncompromisingly opposed to change.[73] This is well known, and is indeed the basis for the intensive study of the role of the military in politics that has become fashionable in recent years. Concentration on the role of the military leads to assessment of the probabilities of revolution in terms of the disposition of the military to intervene, and for this we have an indicator only where it has already happened.

[72] Colonel Frederic Natusch Maude, 'Strategy', in *Encyclopaedia Britannica*, 13th edn., states that these relationships were clear by the time of Frederic II of Prussia.

[73] This statement must be heavily qualified, e.g. Chorley, p. 20. Pettee, p. 104, states that 'there is general agreement that a revolution cannot commence until the army is no longer loyal to the old regime', which reverses definition and explanation.

Leaving aside the cases in which no previous intervention has occurred and those in which military intervention escaped prediction because of natural optimism about the degree of its adherence to traditional legality, there is, however, some cause for concern in the fact that it is precisely those occurrences that have had the most profound political consequences that have somehow escaped interpretation in those terms. They may have done so either because the degree of civilian participation was too great for assessment, or because the imminence of revolution was too great for assessment, or because the imminence of revolution was so obvious to all but the members of the pre-revolutionary government. We are concerned here, therefore, not with criticizing these principles, but with extending them to give an overall assessment of the military-civil situation. The first problem will be to reach a satisfactory approximation between the two. This is best done in current examples by provisionally assuming neutrality on the part of the army and reaching an assessment of the opposing civilian forces, modifying this later in the light of possible inclination by military leaders towards one side or the other.

The army itself, and indeed all forces which are neutral or uninvolved, may technically be disregarded in summing up the basic balance of power. Group separation, however, is one of role, and if groups are neutral *per se* it does not follow that their members will be, especially if in their individual social roles they become involved in fighting against their will. Care must be taken, too, to avoid over-estimating degrees of support by counting roles twice. This warning is particularly important when the social origins of the military are under consideration, and especially if they are deployed in or near their own home towns or provincial areas.

All groups offering potential support to revolutionary movements, furthermore, have pronounced antitheses. Every politician knows or, rather, ought to know, that his election platform cannot appeal simultaneously to two diametrically opposed groups. But not all revolutionary leaders are politicians in this sense. Some at least are driven to revolutionary action by their contempt for 'politician's politics' or their own lack of success in achieving their goals. Many are carried away by their own urgency to maximize support, producing specious manifestos which fail to carry conviction, and relying often on *esprit de corps* or patriotism to carry them through.[74] The same phenomenon is common among amateur politicians of the kind that form Ratepayers' Associations.

The various alternative and often antagonistic support groups can, however, be broadly classified in general categories.

(i) *Categories of support groups*

1. *Professional armed forces* Under the general heading of 'professional armed forces' we find the army and, apart from them and very different in kind, the navy, the air force, the police force or forces, and other paramilitary organizations of various kinds. The nature of these will vary according to the political culture of the country concerned. If armament is restricted or non-existent, the value inculcated by membership of a disciplined body trained to common tasks is correspondingly more important.[75] The idea of the Boy Scouts overthrowing the British Government is comical, but youths of the same age organized in religious or patriotic movements have shaken the Government of Singapore, fatally damaged the regime of Sukarno in Indonesia, and actually overthrown the Government of Syngman Rhee in South Korea (1960 α).[76] No disciplined body, therefore, should be underestimated. On the other hand, the more widespread the holding and the use of arms, the more important becomes the role of the regular army or an armed police force, as in the United States.

Navies and air forces have often shown themselves as being in opposition to army initiatives, and vice versa. The overthrow of Perón in Argentina (1955 α), in which the air forces took part in bombing the Casa Rosada, is a recent example.[77] Some writers have hailed the growth of these competing forces with enthusiasm, seeing in their technical training a form of political indoctrination preferable to that inculcated by the traditional

[74] The literature is vast but accessible collections are rare, Sharabi, op. cit., is one of the best.

[75] Where it is weak it can be challenged by any organized group; see Amir Habibullah, *From Brigand to King* (Sampson Low, London, n.d.); George M. Haddad, *Revolutions and Military Rule in the Middle East: The Northern Tier* (Robert Speller, New York, 1965).

[76] *Annual Register* (1960), 374–5.

[77] George Pendle, *Argentina,* 2nd edn. (O. U. P., London, for Royal Institute of International Affairs, 1961).

military polytechnics. The rise of Colonel Barrientos in Bolivia has been seen as a progressive step (1964 θ),[78] and that of General Ky in South Vietnam (1965 γ), as being a belated retreat from total disaster.[79] Whether fortunately or unfortunately, however, as H. G. Wells recognized more than half a century ago, air forces may threaten an area but ground forces are required to occupy it,[80] and traditional rivalries seldom allow the army to yield primacy in this sort of fashion.

Consequently in Brazil the pattern has been set by which the principal contending forces, the Army and the Navy, traditionally agree to remain neutral in order to avert action by the other.[81] They had the example of the Civil War of 1891 in Chile to demonstrate the consequences of doing otherwise, though this is one of the very few instances in which a regular army fought for the losing side in a revolutionary conflict.[82]

Mobility is less often a problem for the navy than might be thought, since many of the world's capitals are approached by waterways of considerable size, and their advantages in this respect compare favourably with the disadvantages of air forces demonstrated in the Guatemalan incident of 1962 (see above, Chapter 3).

2. *Paramilitary forces* Paramilitary bases for revolution may be official or unofficial organizations. Representative of the former is the police force of Thailand, armed with light tanks and machine-guns, which brought Pibul Songgram to power in 1947 (1947 ζ).[83] The *fasci de combattimiento* of Mussolini and the S.A. of Hitler are notorious examples of the latter.[84]

The 'shirt' movements in general, of course, may be regarded as something more—as revolutionary parties. The revolutionary party must be considered separately, as not all revolutionary parties are paramilitary, and some, such as the

[78] In the limited context of military rule.
[79] Cf. *Annual Register* (1965), 351.
[80] Herbert George Wells, *The War in the Air* (Odhams Press, London, 1921), Preface.
[81] José Maria Bello; *A History of Modern Brazil, 1889–1964* (Stanford University Press, Stanford, 1966), p. 277.
[82] Harold Blakemore, 'The Chilean Revolution of 1891 and its historiography', *The Hispanic American Historical Review*, XLV, no. 2 (Aug. 1965), 393.
[83] Coast, p. 54.
[84] Goodspeed, pp. 147 ff.

anarchist groups of Russia (1911 η) and Portugal (1908 α), achieved revolutionary transitions with only vestiges of formal political organization by uncomfortably accurate perception of the real dynamics of revolutionary change.

Paramilitary forces differ in important respects from military ones. Their training is likely to be less effective. Their armament is never as great, though as noted it may be perfectly adequate for its purpose if used on sound revolutionary principles. Most important of all, the paramilitary organization seldom can claim the mystical status enjoyed by the army as being the special representative of the people in its capacity as defender of the national territory. At their most militant, paramilitary forces are clearly marked as a second line of defence; as police forces they lack glamour, and probably also lack respect.

3. *Civilian institutional groups* If military and paramilitary groups, for whatever reason, are disengaged, fragmented, or neutral, the possibility of support formation devolves on civilian groups alone. As civilian groups, these fall easily into the normal categories used by political scientists and, with Almond, may be classified as institutional, associational, non-associational.[85] As has already been demonstrated, by crossing the boundaries of revolutionary action they do not leave these categories by becoming anomic formations from the standpoint of their political potential.

Armed forces and military and official paramilitary are, of course, institutional groups. But, by definition, the principal institutional groups within the 'state', other than those to whom violence is a profession, are by the nature of functional separation correspondingly reluctant to enter upon revolutionary acts. We do not expect to find embattled bureaucrats on the barricades in a desperate fling to put themselves out of business. There are easier ways. But if there were not, we would not in any case expect them to be the sort of people who would have recourse to violent action.

Religious organizations, on the other hand, however peaceful the official creed, seem much less reluctant. If they are effective religious organizations they need to incorporate the spirit of militancy, not to exclude it. They enjoy, moreover, advantages

[85] Almond and Coleman, p. 33.

of organization. Their command structure integrates a variety of occupations of functional necessity to a successful revolutionary movement, and incorporates a unique apparatus for financing such movements. The role of the Catholic Church in movements as diverse as the nationalist movement in Spain and the anti-Buddhist demonstrations in Vietnam is familiar, so familiar as to lead to an erroneous emphasis among writers.[86] It is not the catholicity of the Church which renders it so effective in revolutionary terms, but the church organization of Catholics which enables them to express their political attitudes in anomic or non-anomic patterns, at will.

Religious organizations can also function as non-associational groups integrating support among supporters for a wholly non-religious revolutionary movement as in Vietnam in the 1960s.

4. *Civilian associational groups*　The three principal forms of associational groups having a revolutionary role are those of the press, organized urban workers, and students.

The role of the press association is self-explanatory. In order for a leader to lead effectively, he cannot spare time to lead his own press. He must, however, control, and by that means encourage and exhort, a significant section of the press in the country at large. Support at this point obviates the need for control measures, which are inclined to produce negative results.

The role of the urban worker has been obscured by the existence of divergent views on its proper utility. Lenin saw workers' leaders properly educated in their role as the vanguard of the workers as a whole, but the combat itself he saw in purely traditional terms. In Leninist terms, the workers' reaction to the inception of a violent transition should be in the first place to go on strike, and in the second place to take over by force control of military strong-points and the economic 'commanding heights' such as factories, warehouses, and banks.[87]

On Lenin's insistence, this role was written into the scheme for the Bolshevik *coup* in Russia in October 1917. It proved

---

[86] Gerald Brenan, *The Spanish Labyrinth, an account of the Social and Political Background of the Spanish Civil War* (C. U. P., Cambridge, 1962), pp. 322 ff.

[87] Lenin's warning on the importance of assessing *real* strength is, however, relevant; cf. Andrew C. Janos, 'The Communist Theory of the State and Revolution', in Cyril E. Black and Thomas P. Thornton, eds., *Communism and Revolution, The Strategic Uses of Political Violence* (Princeton University Press, Princeton, 1964), pp. 34–5.

militarily neither to assist in impairing the immediate capacity
for violence of the state organism, nor to operate to supply
sufficient men sufficiently well armed to resist a possible attack
by professional forces. They were fortunate not to have to cope
with either.[88]

Malaparte was correct in recognizing that the ineffectiveness of the Leninist approach in making use of the urban workers
lay in the fact that his tactics demanded first depriving them of
their functional specialization.[89] Trotsky, he considered,
correctly made use of this functional specialization first to
deprive the Kerensky Government of its symbiotic organism of
command of communication, achieving the effective destruction of that government before diverting the workers' effort to
the Leninist targets. But Malaparte failed to recognize the
parallel between Lenin's priorities and his own action in aiding
Mussolini's victory in 1922 by publishing false rumours of his
success. Lenin was concerned to obviate the danger of leaving
too even a balance between the new government and the old,
in which the advantage of residual loyalties would operate to
his disadvantage. As a politician, he knew well that it was not
enough to be in command, he had to be seen to be in command.

The purest instances of the destruction of government by
making use of the functional specialization of the urban worker
have come in those spontaneous withdrawals of activity which
gave no chance for the government to make alternative arrangements, as in Costa Rica in 1948 (1948 δ) or in El Salvador in
1944 (1944 β).[90] Otherwise it can be said categorically that in
the majority of cases the role of 'worker' has not contributed
materially to the effectiveness of the individual as revolutionary
material.

For the same purpose students, on the other hand, have
shown exceptionally effective qualities allied to their distinctive role. The student group contains a relatively high per-
centage of politically 'aware' people. They are easily aroused
to extremes, of which other groups are seldom capable, because of their youth, *esprit de corps*, and traditions of group inde-

[88] Goodspeed, loc. cit.

[89] Malaparte, *Coup d'Etat, the Technique of Revolution*, trs. Sylvia Saunders (E. P.
Dutton & Co., New York, 1932), p. 73.

[90] Franklin D. Parker, *The Central American Republics* (O. U. P., London, for Royal
Institute of International Affairs, 1964), pp. 267, 152.

pendence from the general restraints of society. Their tendency towards excitable responses to political events is enhanced not only by the pressures of student life and their uncertainty as to their own future place in the country, but in most countries also by the proximity of large universities to the national capital. Similar group consciousness in high-school students, it should be noted, is not uncommon, but is limited by the social proximity of the age group to the responsibilities of everyday life.

5. *Peasantry* The rural worker, or peasant, is distinguished in most societies by being the largest reservoir of manpower. In apposition to the urban worker, the rural worker has an individuality born of remoteness and a dispersal which limits his group's effectiveness in military action, except in large-scale movements. While peasant-based movements can preclude the effective operation of government, they are at a corresponding disadvantage in achieving an actual transition. In modern times it is, however, conceivable that an inspired peasant conspiracy could be, as it were, preformed in the provinces and transplanted to the capital by a sudden invasion. Since the nature of the peasant's response to a revolutionary call, from the nature of his sociological conditioning, tends towards extreme radicalism if he responds at all, the possibility should not be entirely discounted.[91]

It should be noted that out of their role as workers or peasants, those engaged in manual labour may be expected—number for number—to be superior in force over unarmed non-manual workers. There is, however, as we have seen, an important difference between the two roles in the degree to which they afford access to arms. The urban worker, because he lives in a town, is subject to effective police action limiting his access, and unless this is transcended by effective action on the part of his group organization—unless, that is to say, a group to which he belongs buys or steals arms—he is restrained from improvization. The peasant, however, is well armed in primitive societies even as against the regular forces he may expect to meet. Knives, bill-hooks, pitchforks, and their diverse relations are a necessary part of his life. Only with the functional specialization of agricultural machinery in advanced societies does this

[91] Mehmet Beqiraj, *Peasantry in Revolution* (Cornell University Center for International Studies, Ithaca, 1966).

advantage disappear, while the proportion of agrarian to urban workers falls.

6. *Anomic groups*   There remain those purely anomic groups known as riots and demonstrations. Members of these are bound by no functional tie except that of participation in a temporary grouping for a political purpose.

The purely anomic group is transitory and has the corresponding advantage of being insulated from the conventional associational techniques of counter-insurgency investigation. In its urban form it enjoys almost complete anonymity. Even if it has been arranged and incited by agitators, the latter are virtually undetectable, except to a trained observer with photographic aid. Fortunately the social scientist has the advantage of access to sound historical investigations of anomic groups which, because of their success, were recorded for posterity. The work of Rudé has shown that in the advanced countries of Europe in the late eighteenth and early nineteenth centuries what was popularly known as a 'mob' was, in fact, a broadly based assembly of all classes and conditions of people. It was not, in short, just an idle gathering of the anti-social, but it was not a spontaneous rally of the working classes either.[92] Nor can it be said today that the 'mob', trained and directed by Communist agents, which smashes and defiles an American Embassy or library, consists only of workers—or for that matter of Communists.

Certain generalizations about crowd behaviour can accordingly be accepted as valid in the main. The crowd at a demonstration does not consist of people who individually are stupid, and no agitator would wish it to be. Sophistication is essential for a sophisticated application of force. But the normal crowd wields an equivalent force and may be much more pliable.

The collection and maintenance of any crowd depends on suitable climatic conditions. The optimum conditions involve dry weather with a shade temperature between 90° and 95°F and humidity ranging above 50 per cent—conditions well fulfilled in the American Deep South in summer, as in most of the big northern cities. Greater temperatures discourage activity,

[92] George Rudé, *The Crowd in History, a Study of Popular Disturbances in France and England, 1730–1848* (John Wiley, New York, 1964), pp. 195 ff.

and excess humidity brings with it the chance of rain. Potentially threatening riots were ended by rain in Britain in 1848, in Mexico in 1911, and in Algeria in 1960, to take only three widely spaced instances.[93] For this reason, it seems, fire hoses are still used by many police forces in counter-insurrectionary work. If the temperature is hot and dry they often provide nothing much more than ill-timed refreshment and incitement to weary demonstrators.[94]

The crowd also needs a common focus of interest. It loses cohesion, therefore, with action, especially action involving a degree of specialization. A crowd in motion is more easily dispersed or stampeded than one which is massed and threatening.[95] It has, therefore, a limited usefulness. That usefulness is most pronounced while it is but one element, used for a specific purpose, in an overall pattern of revolutionary action. Such a pattern, however, demands an organization and a planning group.

7. *The revolutionary party* The most notorious form of such organizations is the revolutionary party. This is an organization functioning through the anomic structures of revolution in the same fashion as a conventional party operates through the non-anomic structures of the political system.

The popular concept is that a revolutionary party is a political party dedicated to the destruction of the state through the capture of its institutions within the context of its own behaviour pattern. This indeed may be so. But the revolutionary party need not necessarily have a continuous existence, any more than a revolution does. If at the time of a *coup* the transition of power is achieved by the agents of a party, of whatever type, and transferred into the hands of that party in its institutional character, a revolutionary party has been created.

By its nature the revolutionary party is split. It exists simultaneously on two planes, the legal and the illegal. If it is to last through time there must be the minimum contact between the

---

[93] Robertson, *Revolutions of 1848*, p. 405; Calvert, *The Mexican Revolution, 1910–1914*, pp. 71–2.

[94] Anthony Lewis and *The New York Times, Portrait of a Decade; the Second American Revolution* (Bantam Books, New York, 1965), p. 157, their use in Los Angeles in the Watts riots was taken as even stronger incitement.

[95] Hibbert, op. cit.

two planes so as to avoid contamination. This is seldom attempted, since the brief existence of the party before the *coup* prevents the need being felt. But where the party is set up with a long-term goal in mind the need is paramount. The need to devise such a command structure led to the adoption by the Communist Party of the cell system, which in the first instance was devised for the needs and purposes of criminals, just as it has subsequently been copied by the American 'radical Right'.[96]

The cell system, however, is not in itself important. What matters is the adoption of a command structure which does not preclude recruiting 'across the line', and in fact will facilitate it as far as possible; such devices as youth organizations, 'front' organizations, social clubs, and so forth are used for the same purposes by normal political parties. Against these any 'illegal' organization, however skilled at infiltration, must necessarily be at a disadvantage. If, in turn, the illegal organization makes use of its front organization to plan a strategy for disposing of weapons etc. so as to infiltrate the centre of state power, it can survive an element of surprise otherwise difficult to attain. Yet the habit of conspiracy has the same enervating effect upon the party as it has on the secret junta. It predisposes it towards accepting recruits with a mind inclined towards conspiratorial explanations, and in extreme form this can render it almost incapable of exercising power logically and effectively should it ever, somehow, succeed in attaining it. Furthermore, its own strength, in its own membership, obeys the regular rules. If it is delimited too strictly by the need for security it is excessively vulnerable to ruthless and wholesale action, as the massacre in 1965–6 of the greater part of the huge Indonesian Communist Party (P.K.I) has shown.[97]

The significance of an overt party organization to a revolutionary group lies in its incorporating a mechanism for the organization, collection, and distribution of finance.[98]

Revolution is expensive by the standards of regular political activity, though not as expensive as many forms of governmental

[96] Duverger, pp. 2, 5, 27–36.

[97] Vittachi, pp. 138–51.

[98] Harold Blakemore, 'Chilean Revolutionary Agents in Europe, 1891', *Pacific Historical Review*, XXXIII, no. 4 (Nov. 1964), 425.

activity, even on a local level. Money is required for many purposes: to purchase arms, sustain forces for the duration of the action, provide special equipment for the *coup* or ancillary diversions, suborn key personnel either in governments or in gatehouses, print proclamations, and serve as legal fees for representation by legal advisers both at home and in foreign capitals. Examples of these will easily occur to the reader.

Possible sources of revolutionary finance, as for regular political activity unless restricted by law or agreement, will include:

 (a) the contribution of voluntary activity, gifts in kind or small subscriptions from members of front organizations;
 (b) large donations from a few prominent individuals or from foreign governments interested in the diplomatic consequences of a revolutionary transition;
 (c) the sale of bonds having a prospective value in the event of revolutionary success;
 (d) promises to purvey valuable governmental concessions in the same eventuality;
 (e) forced loans and requisitions, or living off the country, as applicable to military organizations in regular combat or under conditions of national emergency.

They may also include:

 (f) illegal (criminal) means, such as forgery, embezzlement, or fraud, such as would form a justifiable basis for criminal prosecution under the pre-revolutionary code of law.

The method employed does not seem to be of great significance to the ultimate success of the movement. One of the few authenticated cases of the use of embezzlement to finance a revolutionary movement is the Madero revolution in Mexico in 1911 (1911 δ).[99] Yet this was conspicuously successful, and the revolutionary government in fact received much more criticism on a purely apocryphal charge of having offered concessions to the Standard Oil Company. The United States Central Intelligence Agency is said to have financed the Castillo Armas *coup* in Guatemala in 1954, but no amount of finance served to save the Cuban exiles from disaster at the Bay

---

[99] This question is discussed at length in Calvert, *The Mexican Revolution, 1910–1914*, pp. 73 ff.

of Pigs.[100] The actual quantity of money available to a revolutionary movement, certainly, must be of some significance. But it is scarcely surprising to find that the structure of revolutionary finance is even more jealously concealed than the *trabajos* and *compromisos* leading to the actual *coup*. One can, however, hope to ascertain reasonably complete details of expenditure if not of income, if one pays particular attention to the effect of a successful transition on the national treasury, reflected in the national balance and taxation changes.

We are now in a position to take account of the variables in personnel expressed in our test sample. Principally we were concerned to delimit the *personnel* as military, civilian, or partaking of the character of both; to discover whether participation rose or fell as the consequence of the *coup*; and to ascertain the strength and disposition of the *forces* in each case. As a cross-check on the figures for strength we also made use of the Richardson concept of *magnitude* of casualties incurred.

(ii) *Personnel composition*

The figures for personnel composition in each quinquennium have been represented in actual numbers on Table 13 (p. 204). The trends here are of particular interest. Until the late 1940s it was civilians who dominated the field of revolutionary activity, and the great surge in revolutionary activity in the periods 1906–10 et seq. was dominated by them, though in the interwar years the balance was much more even. It is only since the late 1940s that military intervention has come to have overwhelming significance.

It must be remembered that, as stated above, the civilian figures throughout do include civilian governing officials even if of military provenance, but these so rarely act on their own that their inclusion does not by any means account for the discrepancy between expectation and practice.

(iii) *Participation*

In the case of the other variable describing the nature of succession in revolutionary transitions, the increase or decrease of participation in the governmental process, the fluctuations were even more clearly and directly related to the incidence,

[100] Wise and Ross, pp. 167-8, 178.

and periodicity, of the events themselves, and hence to the prevailing social climate (Table 18, p. 206).

The categories of 'increase' and 'no change' turned out to be almost exactly equal, with some 40 per cent each. That of 'decrease' was correspondingly rare, and was strikingly associated with the inter-war years 1920 to 1940. Furthermore, while increase was highest for 1916–20 and lowest for 1936–40, and decrease was the reverse, the quinquennium 1911–15 registered the highest proportion of no change, the lowest following in 1916–20. The quinquennium 1916–20 therefore saw the greatest effective increase in participation as the result of violence, and a net loss was recorded only twice, in 1936–40 and 1951–5. On these figures, there is no reason to suppose that revolutionary activity shows any trend as yet towards acting normally to decrease participation.

But it should be observed that since 1945 there has been some sign of a trend towards the 'no change' situation, and that there is every reason to suppose that this will prove to be associated with the increase in military activity noted above in subsection 4.

(iv) *Strength and disposition of forces*

From the data on *strength* and disposition of *forces* it was clear that most revolutions involve forces of formation strength, and that the normal posture of the military towards them, where they are successful, is one of non-intervention or support by a section of them, represented by 149 of 279, and 168 of 351 known instances, respectively ($N = 363$).

(v) *Magnitude*

The data were insufficient to say more than that 131 cases or at least one third of the universe, were of *magnitude* 0. That is to say, they resulted in the deaths of 3 people or less; frequently in no deaths. As observed above, however, more complete returns would probably tend to swell the proportion of higher magnitude. So far only 58 cases of higher magnitude have been established with certainty, another 6 cases being regarded as unascertainable.

VI. GOALS

In the revolutionary scheme of things, the goals of a revolution are usually well publicized. The goals of a revolution are the official objective or set of objectives for taking up arms, for breaking through the framework of traditional legality, or for adopting the anomic course rather than the non-anomic. They may be quite unrelated to objective facts (being either genuine or propaganda in type), and in practice seldom approach either of the paradigm types.

The importance of the goal therefore is to the personnel; it is enunciated by a leader whose motivation is at one remove from that which actuates his followers. Had Karl Marx himself been exploited as a member of a 'proletariat' he would have had no time to sit in the British Museum and write *Das Kapital*. Had Venustiano Carranza starved as a peasant or slaved on a *henequen* plantation he might have become a bandit, but he could not have sat in Díaz's Senate and he would not have had the chance to become the heir to a revolutionary cause.[101]

The significance the goal has lies principally in the way in which it legitimizes the use of violence. But it also has the auxiliary function of canalizing solidarity of purpose and, hence, promoting discipline in the ranks of followers. Provided it is accepted, it matters little, from the point of view of the criterion of effectiveness, what it is. It may be religious, patriotic, sentimental, moral, at will and in turns, but within each field, each antonym of motivation will serve the revolutionary turn. The egalitarian goal is no more attractive to the revolutionary follower than is the elitist; and may even be identical with it.

To convince others, the leader must first convince himself. But if the leader 'believes' in his goal, it does not follow that the goal he proclaims can be used as a guide to the probable social achievement of the revolution he proposes to make. The successful leader modifies his beliefs to attract followers; the followers do not modify theirs to suit his needs for support. The nature of the cause will therefore be a fair guide as to the possibility of a revolt being successful; but in the strict sense, when related to the consequences of that revolt, neither that nor any other goal is ever 'real', though some are more so than others.

Goals are often set out in a written or spoken manifesto. The more elaborate a manifesto, the more support it has been planned to obtain. However, the greater the support it has been

101 Blanco Moheno, I, 23.

planned to obtain, the greater the chances that it has succeeded in nullifying a part of its appeal, through its cross-connection of issues potentially alienating to different support groups. It is not possible to classify goals without allowing for this from the outset. Following fashion in this respect leads to 'bulking' of issues, often reducing the apparent impact of a major cause by dignifying relatively trivial ones with equal prominence. The phenomenon is familiar to those rare people who actually read the correspondence columns of newspapers.

More insight into specifically revolutionary goals can only be obtained from a direct study of actual objectives which have had revolutionary values attached to them. The most outstanding example of a slogan summarizing a revolutionary cause is, of course, the French 'Liberté, Égalité, Fraternité!' In this, 'liberty' stands for the demand for the removal of religious, intellectual, financial, and in some cases physical, restraints; 'equality' for the desire for the raising of the standard of living to that of the rich for the poor, by the forcible rearrangement of the accepted order of the distribution of land and possessions; and 'fraternity' for the recognition of the individual by government as a citizen at the least privileged to make a complaint, whether in fact any notice is taken of it or not.

But slogans are treacherous guides, paradoxical in form and deceptive in substance. For example, 'Independência ou Morte!' the slogan of Brazilian independence does not propound the second alternative as a desirable goal![102] Their significance, however, is undoubted, and their flexibility to the mind of the interpreter the greater part of their value. It is to them, and not to the more lengthy and detailed statements, that we should look in the first instance. It is unlikely that one can do more than classify slogan, or goal, more precisely than as 'strong', 'weak' or 'absent' (negligible in content and impact). But even this is enough to improve one's estimate of a movement's chances when it is applied to an assessment of individual support groups.

---

[102] The context makes this even clearer: 'Comunicando então à comitiva que as Côrtes queriam 'massacrar' o Brasil, arrancou o tope de fita azul claro e encarnado (as côres constitucionais portuguêsas antes do azul e branco) qui ostentava no chapéu armado, lançou-o por terra e, desembainhando e espada, bradou — 'E tempo'... Independência ou Morte!... Estamos separados de Portugal...' (Oliveira Lima, *O Movimento da Independência, O Império Brasileiro (1821–1889)*, 2nd edn. (São Paulo, Edições Melhoramentos, 1928), pp. 277–8).

The belief in the possibilities of the success of a given cause, however, is closely bound up with the degree of acceptance of the society's prevailing theory of revolution, and a different reaction may be expected to each main type.

The inevitability theories would seem to imply that if revolution itself is impossible without fixed 'objective' conditions being satisfied, the proposition of a cause in itself can have no effect. But, as is well known, discontent is a normal state of human life; and conspicuously the only times in which a people as a whole achieves euphoria are times of special dedication, that is to say, times of war or revolution. Inevitablists, therefore, solve their dilemma by assuming that the objective conditions actually are favourable, even in the most stable of societies and in face of the most irrefutable evidence of failure.[103] They are not well placed actually to achieve a revolutionary transition, as the strength of their beliefs restrain them from developing beyond the confines of the ideological values which they have pre-accepted as being the only possible basis for revolution.

Theories of circular motion, on the other hand, positively demand the automatic creation of fresh goals by each movement of a polity through a cycle, though the cause is seen as being a fixed quantity at each stage of the cycle. Thus democracies break down for their own reasons, not for those that afflict tyrannies, and so forth. Where cyclical beliefs prevail, extra strength is given to any cause by representing it as a return to a better past. The past is always with us, everywhere, and is freely available to the romantic to beckon us towards an unimaginable future. In such circumstances, the conservative revolutionary finds special opportunities.[104]

Other evitability theories reproduce divided responses, depending on the stake the believer has in the continuation of the existing order. Believers in evitability theories who lack the rigour of the cyclical pattern may feel at a disadvantage in approaching the subject from a scientific standpoint at all. This

[103] For example, Karl Marx, 'The Eighteenth Brumaire of Louis Bonaparte', ed. cit.; Ghiţa Ionescu, *The Break-up of the Soviet Empire in Eastern Europe* (London, Penguin Books, 1965), pp. 95–8.

[104] The Emperor Augustus is the classical example (C. Suetonius Tranquillus, *The Twelve Caesars* (Penguin Books, London, 1958), Augustus, c. 28, etc.).

study as it happens falls into this category. We allow that, even if a cause must always exist to be found, it is always open to the established order to make a rational response to it. We must further consider why among a range of goals appealing to powerful support groups there is sufficient irrationality to support one particular movement rather than a rival.

Reference has already been made to the phenomenon noted by Crane Brinton in the so-called 'great' revolutions, which has been referred to as the 'theory of leftward displacement'.[105] This holds that revolutions begin with a *coup* by moderates, who fail to satisfy the goals of their followers, and may, indeed, retreat towards conservatism in face of their unsatisfied importunities. They are therefore, it is suggested, overthrown in turn by the extremists, who rule with so many excesses that in time they arouse moderate hostility, which is made desperate by the urgency of survival, and are in turn overthrown in the process identified by Brinton as 'Thermidor'. This theory is, as we have seen, widely accepted today.

In developing the current model it has already been demonstrated that in the great majority of revolutionary sequences such a displacement does not happen. It can happen only when the elements are again in conjunction. Of these the goal is but one.

If a moderate programme is pursued by the initial leadership, it is because the need to maximize support is interpreted by the leadership as being most safely achieved in these terms. Some bias may be expected towards a moderate course, because of the advantage it seems to offer in controlling the bulk of support. If more extreme courses offer a greater chance of support, however, it is unlikely that this bias will be sufficient to prevent them being adopted.

Two possible sets of circumstances can follow the adoption of moderate courses. There may be dissension or there may be general approval. In the former, the dissension may take place on the left or on the right. In either case, the dissension may or may not find expression through a leadership that has the ability to correlate it with an effective exposition of a cause and the means to maximize support for a *coup*.

If we leave out of account for the present the question of

[105] Brinton, pp. 155 ff.
10—S.O.R.

means, this is where, from the point of view of the manifesto writer, the problem arises. The maximization function of the second *coup* must be at least as effective as that of the first, but the grounds for appeal have already altered. The most substantial body of opinion has been pre-empted by the existing regime, and is correspondingly unwilling to change allegiances again. The distinctively conservative nature of revolutionary radicalism, furthermore, is paralleled by distinctively radical features in revolutionary conservatism, so that the revolutionary radical must trump the moderate with the cause which reaches still further into the past.

Consideration of the attitudes of the leading political groups in France in 1789–93 shows, for example, that in their attitudes towards the key institution of the monarchy they reversed the historical course of the development of that institution. Louis XVI received his first opposition from a Valois institution, was arrested and tried as a Capet, and suffered the ultimate fate of many Merovingians.

A final set of problems confronts us when we come to interpret two specialized types of goal which may even be regarded as designating variants of revolution. To avoid confusion, some explanation is needed as to why these two have been singled out for special attention.

There are, in fact, more than two major variations normally identified.

(i) *Official revolution*

The first is that which is represented by the *coup d'état* in its strict sense, such as the Obote *coup* in Uganda (1966 δ), what has here been called an official revolution. The official revolution is the situation ensuing on possession of the powers of the state gained through sub-revolutionary means, when those powers are used to effect changes in the structure of the state by violence. It is therefore an extreme form of centralist action. The constitutional norms in many states allow for a very considerable use of violence by the government, but specific opponents may well be unwilling to admit this fact. If the norms are in fact not exceeded, no revolution can by definition have occurred; and if they are extended, in revolutionary terms this is the equivalent of a constitutional change. Either instance is excluded from the definition given above. If, however, the actual mechanism of political change is examined in the remaining cases, it will be found that the absence of violence is nominal, in that it took the form of sub-revolutionary activity over a long period.

(ii) *Counter-revolution*

Next may be taken the counter-revolution, the effort of a former governmental group to resume their former position by violent means. It is related to the official type in that the promoters have the expectations of power as a group accustomed to wield it, and indeed enjoy the advantages of their already having acquired the skills of government. Here, however, no separate variety seems to carry analytical value. Counter-revolution is, after all, merely the use of revolutionary means to carry out a revolutionary transition for a particular ideological reason, in this case, to divert, change, or pre-empt a prevailing trend of 'progressive' thought expressed in terms of violence. Even if a so-called counter-revolution does not follow any overt revolutionary act, the ostensible cause being the need to pre-empt an official revolution (real or imaginary), it follows the same forms in terms of disposition and application of power.

(iii) *Separatism*

The other category which we have accepted is that characterized by the goal of altering the boundaries of the state in which it occurs. This may take the form either of their extension (revolutionary imperialism) or of their contraction (separatism).

Separatist revolutions, successful or not, are easily defined, but in terms of power they follow the same rules as movements covering the entire territorial extent of the polity. Their strong ideological bent makes them of great interest to the investigator. By this very fact they distract his attention. Their distinction does not rest on their ideological characteristics, but on their strategic ones. In attempting to establish a new polity from a section of a larger one, they find themselves directed in the first instance not towards the centre of government in the larger polity but towards that government's agents in their own.

This distinction has been recognized already by strategists as carrying the implication that some modification of technique is necessary. Certainly, subordinate officials are unable to fight—or, indeed, to capitulate—in the style of a fully sovereign government.[106] But they can call on reserves of actual force, which the limited aims of the separatists restrain them from equalling, without that absolute control of the state machine which in normal cases by definition they cannot easily attain. Successful separatist movements, therefore, are rare.

(iv) *Revolutionary imperialism*

The same problem, in different form, arises in the case of revolutionary imperialism. The fact that a state which has just undergone a revolutionary change declares war on or invades a neighbouring territory does not of itself cause a revolutionary situation in that neighbouring territory. It must attempt to extend to its neighbours the same kind of social change as internally it has undergone itself. Whether or not this is properly an attribute of the revolution, or of the people who carry it out or attain power as a result of it, is another question.

Theorists of international relations are not in agreement, it seems, on whether or not there is a discontinuity of kind between the state and the international community.[107] If there is no discontinuity, then the type of revolution which exhibits imperialism would be a distinct sub-category, seen from the field of international relations. Indeed, it might be regarded as a distinct phenomenon in that it forms an extension of the internal mechanism of political change into the extra-societal environment of which that system forms a part. Such an extension would have to be distinguished, however, from the accepted tendency (the reasons for which will be considered later) for revolutionary movements to involve the intervention of outside powers. If it is not distinguishable, or if there is no discontinuity, this of itself raises no particular problem, and the extension of revolution into the international community will be seen to fit neatly into the schematic pattern of the model used here.

---

[106] Goodspeed, p. 65.
[107] Sigmund Neumann, 'The International Civil War', *World Politics*, I (1949), 341 ff.; Morton A. Kaplan, *System and Process in International Politics* (John Wiley, New York, 1967), p. 19.

The two sub-types of goals isolated for separate consideration in our sample did, as expected, prove to form a very small sub-sample: a total of 36 separatist and 40 official revolutions during the period under review (Table 19, p. 207).

Separatist revolutions were most successful in the quinquennium 1916–20. In view of the number of new states that have gained independence since 1945, they have been conspicuously unsuccessful since then.[108]

The official revolution is basically an act of centralization, unlikely to be initiated by anyone who is not likely to benefit directly from it. Yet most governments seem to have enough power to do anything they can reasonably want to do, within the norms of the society; and this power is often embodied in a clearly defined code of rules. There is no direct association between revolution as defined here and the presence or absence of dictatorship. Official revolution marks an extreme not only of ordered political life but of revolutionary politics as well. In this century, the peak number of official revolutions occurred in the quinquennium 1931–5, reflecting the authoritarian climate of the early thirties. In these years we must look for other factors to explain the need to reconcile fact with theory as revealed by these incidents.

VII FACILITIES

The facilities of revolution include all that is necessary for the successful deployment of force, except what relates directly to the directorate and personnel, their personalities, and private resources. They include not only the tools of violence, but also the opportunity to use them. It may safely be assumed that, given time, the opportunity can always be found. The nature of the tools themselves, therefore, is of prime importance.

(i) *Firearms*

The most effective weapons for revolutionary purposes are firearms. Hence the widespread prevalence of restrictions on their sale and use. Firearms have, however, many different

---

[108] Between 1945 and 1960 inclusive the number was 5, of 47 new states; see also Amitai Etzioni, *Political Unification, A Comparative Study of Leaders and Forces* (Holt, Rinehart & Winston, New York, 1965).

qualities. The emphasis in revolutionary conditions tends to be, often erroneously, placed on the short-range, rapid-firing weapon. This is suitable either for street fighting or for guerrilla combat in or on the outskirts of villages, but the old-fashioned rifle, still relatively cheap, has pride of place in open country.[109] Revolutionaries seldom have the financial resources to afford weapons bigger than the light machine-gun. By an irony, most modern projectile weapons over this size are too powerful and too indiscriminate in their effects to be used for counter-revolutionary warfare except in mountain, desert, or swamp. The lack therefore is not as damaging to the revolutionary as it seems.

Shortage of funds may, however, lead the revolutionary to shift emphasis away from projectile weapons altogether. The use of home-made bombs was pioneered by anarchists in the nineteenth century at the time when they were still too un-reliable to be used in conventional warfare.[110] Since the First World War military use has refined them into reliable weapons, but the attitudes of mind of the nineteenth century have been carried over to the new age, and they are in any case, rela-tively speaking, expensive. Furthermore, the same period has seen a substantial development by governments for internal security purposes of non-lethal weapons and the refinement of social control techniques to the point at which no one relying on home-made bombs today stands much of a chance of success.

In military terms these and other developments mean that if large-scale artillery and air power be excluded from considera-tion, the balance of advantage has come increasingly to rest with the defence.[111] In the initial stages, this implies a value to possession of the initiative and a premium on surprise being achieved by the revolutionary side. Equally, it implies that if this advantage is not gained, the revolutionary side is unlikely to achieve its goal of a successful transition of power. It does

---

[109] The rifle has the advantage of combining a bayonet at will. Since, as U.S. Army tests showed, a comparatively small number of troops remember to fire their weapons in battle, this can be a considerable advantage.

[110] Explosions in ammunition factories in the First World War showed that even under professional conditions, bomb manufacture was perilous. Their use was no less so.

[111] Maude, 'Strategy', *Encyclopaedia Britannica*, 13th edn.

mean also that the revolutionaries can continue to maintain their position more readily in a state of stalemate, in the hope that the government may capitulate or external factors come to their aid.[112] Where this might be possible, however, it does happen often that it is not achieved, since it involves a rapid change of plan in the course of action. This is a manoeuvre which, as every armchair strategist knows, carried considerable dangers in its own right.

(ii) *Primitive weapons*

No modern government is forced to rely, for its official means of violence, on primitive (non-explosive) weapons. Even the least economically developed of nations have today invested in a status symbol range of military hardware, often of very little use for the sort of tasks which it could reasonably be expected to fulfil.[113] But in agrarian communities non-explosive weapons are common. As noted above, further supplies of them may easily be improvized out of instruments of primarily agricultural function. The numerical superiority which they give, properly used, may be expected to be capable of defeating a moderate display of force. The capacity for effective use is much increased when combined with high mobility, particularly when used in conjunction with the convenient and self-maintaining horse as the primary source of transport.[114]

The revolutionist who is unable to command resources of modern weapons will attempt to devise alternative sources of supply. One way is to take them from the government, either by theft deliberately concealed (by substitution), or else by local application of sub-revolutionary force under conditions of temporary superiority.[115] It may well be equally effective to deny the government the use of the weapons that in normal circumstances it would expect to have at its disposal; and a

[112] In the Spanish Civil War this posture was reversed (Thomas, p. 566 and footnote).

[113] The fate of these has been dramatically shown by the Arab–Israeli war of 1967.

[114] Not now effective, however, outside limited areas of Central Asia and Latin America.

[115] Instances in which the first objective of revolutionary action is the capture of arms are very numerous.

whole range of possible methods of sabotage have been used for this purpose.[116]

Other ways include capture or theft from private individuals, negotiations with official or unofficial supply agencies in a neighbouring territory, or acquisition of weapons on a legal pretext. The last is normally only open to members of the armed forces who may use the resources of the state to arm and supply their private forces, before defecting and leading them into battle against the state.[117]

(iii) *Mobility*

Mobility has already been mentioned as a characteristic that lends effectiveness to weapons. The ability to dispose of forces rapidly and precisely, to distribute to them food and supplies of ammunition, and to maintain communication between all parts of the operation, if necessary making use of communications to bring up additional reinforcements to hard-pressed areas—all these have to be taken into account. It is possible, and for the revolutionist very desirable, simultaneously to deny transport to the government, since this is, after all, to assist in the obtaining of local superiority.[118]

(iv) *Communications*

Many revolutions fail through neglect of communications. However dangerous the varying of plans may be, it is never possible to plan for all contingencies of the behaviour of opponents under irregular conditions. At all times the effective leader is nevertheless fortunate if he can achieve a fraction of the control normally enjoyed by the military leader; and he is in a rare position indeed if, like Trotsky in 1917, he can be so well in control as to keep accurate time and to check that each stage of the operation has in fact been achieved before proceeding to the next.[119]

---

[116] As in the Egyptian Revolution of 1952 (Finer, pp. 158–9).

[117] As in the unsuccessful revolt of Pascual Orozco in Mexico, 1912.

[118] As in the Batista *coup* in Cuba in 1952 (*Keesing's* 12136A); also Stokes, pp. 314–15. The government is most often sealed off from access, e.g. Russia in 1953 (Wolfgang Leonhard, *The Kremlin since Stalin* (O. U. P., London, 1962), pp. 50–9), or removed, Robert J. Alexander, *The Venezuelan Democratic Revolution* (Rutgers University Press, New Brunswick, 1964), p. 40.

[119] Goodspeed, p. 92.

Communications must be denied to the government, whatever else may be overlooked. Plans, to be effective, must allow for access to all centres of communications and for equipment with which to immobilize all telephone services; all radio, television, and telegraph stations; all rail, road, and air links; and ports (if applicable) within, and on the perimeter of, the area of operations. Care taken not to immobilize his own means of retreat is, to some writers, the last hallmark of a leader's well-thought-out plan.[120] To others, neglect of this precaution argues the sort of confidence that leads to victory.[121]

(v) *Access*

Many an otherwise well-thought-out plan has foundered on the neglect of the problems of access. This question is not so obvious as those of communications or transport, but is just as important. As Goodspeed has shown, it was a major blemish on the effectiveness of the Serbian *coup* of 1903.[122] In order to secure the person of the executive, or the members of the government, or to secure control of the governmental precinct, or of the capital, one must first be able to reach them. Mobility is not enough. Loss of surprise in a preliminary repulse at the stage of access, as in the Serbian *coup*, is, however, less easy to avoid than total failure to gain access through faulty planning, as in Guatemala in the abortive 1960 *coup*.[123]

Access also implies maintenance of a watch and securing of an exit for strategic retreat or an entrance for the advance of reinforcements. It implies the timing of each stage of the operation so as to reduce its duration to the minimum as a guard against surprise. Equally, it implies the desirability of provision for a firm base for attack, designed to minimize risk of governmental pre-emption in the event of a failure of security. The need for security implies that time spent before a revolutionary act preparing propaganda leaflets or the like is not only wasted but positively dangerous, except in the case of provincial revolutions or civil war, where the first priority is no longer surprise

[120] Stokes, p. 320.
[121] Retreat can be deliberately rejected as an alternative with positive results. The campaigns of Cortés in Mexico and Pizarro in Peru are instructive in this and other respects.
[122] See above, p. 44.
[123] See above, Ch. 3.

but the securing of publicity and hence of extended support. The firm base in other cases, one would have thought, should only be used for essential planning moves and the actual launching of an attack. This rule is, however, more honoured in the breach than in the observance.

Tabulation alone did not yield a great deal of useful information from the survey for the variables relative to facilities, often, as indicated above, because those data were incomplete.

In very few cases were sophisticated *weapons* an important part of the action, all 46 being supplementary to the use of small arms. There was no marked increase in the use of such weapons after 1930, when their distribution would have become general, though the introduction of aircraft and tanks and the relative decline of ships and the disappearance of cavalry were important changes registered on the data.[124]

VIII. FOREIGN AID AND INITIATIVES

It is generally well known that revolutionary groups endeavour to obtain as much support as possible from territories outside the control of the government they wish to overthrow, for obvious reasons. Though prohibited in international law from fomenting revolutions in neighbouring territories, they well may find sufficient sympathy to succeed in doing so, and so avoid the reprisals of the domestic law; for they are not open to extradition on purely political offences or for any offence committed outside the jurisdiction of the complainant state.[125]

The purchase of arms, however, is a legitimate activity if carried out under the correct procedures, even if those arms are in fact intended for an ultimate destination in revolutionary hands; moreover, the raising of money in various forms is difficult to control. It is not always appreciated that such activities, however successful, are a poor substitute for active political organization within the national territory, and that resources diverted to such activities are correspondingly inclined to be wasted.

This being so, it is very important to note how much money

[124] Sophisticated weapons were counted only when used as an integral part of the action.
[125] Schwarzenberger, pp. 201, 211–12.

has, in fact, been spent on the overseas representation of revolutionary bodies without bringing conspicuous returns. The case is most marked with Latin-American revolutions maintaining representation in Washington, about which there is a reasonable amount to be learnt.

Between the years 1890 and 1920 legal representation in Washington of Latin-American revolutions was almost, if not completely, monopolized by the single law firm of Hopkins and Hopkins. *Inter alia* this firm acted for the Congressional side in the Chilean Civil War of 1891, for the forces of Juan José Estrada in Nicaragua in 1909, for the forces of Madero, Carranza, and de la Huerta in Mexico in 1910–11, 1914–17, and 1920 respectively. At the same time it also acted for the Dictator Estrada Cabrera of Guatemala (1898–1920), so that its function was ethically neutral, just as the younger Hopkins claimed before a Congressional committee in 1913.[126]

The investigations of this committee show that the function of legal representation for these revolutionary groups was threefold.

The primary function was, naturally, that of ensuring that arms purchase and fund-raising activities conducted in the United States were in conformity with the law and did not lay their organizers open to charges of conspiracy. Secondly, the firm specialized in acting as lobbyists before Congress and the agencies of the Federal Executive in creating a climate of opinion favourable to these activities, and representing the actions of the revolutionaries in the best possible light to press reporters and other influential people. In this they worked closely with a formal delegation of the revolutionary movement, who maintained a 'shadow Embassy' empowered to receive and transmit code messages to and from the revolutionary headquarters in their own country or, if necessary, take decisions and make contracts on behalf of the revolutionary command.

It is the third role which is of particular interest, however; for it was openly admitted, again by Sherburne G. Hopkins, that he was to advise the movement on how best to carry out its

---

[126] United States, Congress, Senate Committee on Foreign Relations, *Revolutions in Mexico* (etc.) (United States Government Printing Office, Washington, 1913), pp. 743 ff.

intended revolutionary transition. It is this function alone that would seem to justify the very high fee—$50,000—for the Maderista revolution; it was drawn from the treasury and handed to him personally in Mexico City as one of the first acts of the revolutionary side under the post-revolutionary interim government. Clearly, the existence of such advisers implies the existence of a supra-national body of expertise in the political uses of violence that predates the inception of the Cold War and the setting up of revolutionary training schools in the Soviet Union, China, and Cuba, not to mention Ghana.[127] The relationship between revolutions then is based on something more than mere fashion, and as the historian pushes exploration of these facts backward into the nineteenth century, it will be very interesting to see if the development of such institutions does in fact correlate closely with the marked increase in revolutionary activity with a successful outcome in the first decade of the twentieth.

As for the *reaction* of governments to the threat presented by revolutionary events, this appeared to be fairly constant throughout the period of our sample. In 116 known cases concessions were made by the governments to their opponents; in only 57 known cases was hostility uncompromising. The broad range of the 168 unassigned cases included many in which the action was so brief that it was not possible to establish that any reaction was registered other than surprise, occasionally varied by relief. External *aid* and *initiatives* did not, at this stage, present any features calling for special comment.

IX. ANALYSIS AND CORRELATION

Detailed analysis of relationships between pairs and multiple variables did not alter any basic conclusions drawn from the tabulation of data, but it did suggest different shades of emphasis, and suggest possible answers to a number of questions not previously covered. The information disclosed could be grouped under six headings: periodicity, duration, personnel, direction, succession and authority, and aid and initiatives.

---

[127] Tibor Szamuely, 'The Prophet of the Utterly Absurd', *The Spectator* (11 Mar. 1966), p. 281.

Except where otherwise stated, the sample consisted of the entire universe of events between 1901 and 1960 ($N = 363$).

(i) Periodicity

From Table 20 (p. 207) it will be seen that short periodicity exhibits a small correlation with short duration, so that the main index of governmental stability exhibits the relationship with the speed of governmental collapse which might reasonably be predicted. This facility must in part be due to a degree of organizational competence on the part of the revolutionaries as well as of incompetence on the part of the government they challenge.

That this is the case is confirmed by the fact that for all types of revolution small directorates are most common, but that for movements challenging governments of high stability (periodicity ten to thirty years) group leadership clearly has advantages over that of an individual. The relationship is set out in Table 21 (p. 208). It will be noted that in governments of exceptionally long periodicity (over one generation) this rule does not hold good, indicating that a really secure government may in the passage of time have become more insecure than it suspects, and be vulnerable to relatively small challenges.

However short or long the interval since a preceding revolution it is also evident that the strength of the forces challenging is often at a disproportionately high level for the tasks which they seek to do. It is reasonable to suppose that this is due to the disproportionate penalties attending the risk of failure (Tables 22, 23, pp. 208 and 209). This suggests that the strategy employed by revolutionaries has more in common with traditional military doctrine than with the strategy of minimum coalitions observed by Riker.[128] The strategy of minimum coalitions is, of course, derived from the theory of games and has been considered by some (though not all) to be applicable to the condition of competitive non-violent politics.[129] Traditional military doctrine, on the other hand, called for amassing the largest possible force with which to meet the enemy, having

---

[128] William H. Riker, *The Theory of Political Coalitions* (Yale University Press, New Haven and London, 1962).

[129] Anatol Rapoport, *Fights, Games and Debates* (Ann Arbor, University of Michigan Press, 1960).

resort to stratagem and surprise largely as a substitute for deficiencies in men and material. Its principal disadvantage lies in the total commitment of resources to the chances of a single battle, which is essentially the situation with which the revolutionist is normally faced.

If he is not constrained to accept it, and yet does so, he is seriously reducing his chances of meeting unforeseen eventualities. The strategy (raised to a dogma by Napoleon) which is open as an alternative is that of holding back a substantial, even the greater, part of his forces in order to achieve the main attack after the opening gambit has disclosed the position and strength of the enemy's forces.[130] This is seldom possible under revolutionary conditions, but it was this element in the planning of Antonov-Ovseenko, the former Tsarist cavalry officer, which made the October Revolution in Russia (1917 ε) a text-book example. It would not have been possible but for the extreme weakness of the Provisional Government, who were well aware that a *coup* was in preparation and had taken only the traditional steps to meet it.

It is not possible to say how far these constraints are real and how far they may be the product of excessive caution or of misunderstanding of the mechanics of a given situation in conditions of incomplete information. From the evidence of the correlation between periodicity and level of revolutionary action it is, however, possible to suggest that with improved communications the room for manoeuvre has been substantially reduced over the greater part of the Earth's surface. This is particularly noticeable in the case of events at province level with a periodicity of less than three years (Table 22). Between 1901 and 1930 there were 51 such events, but from 1931 to 1960 there were only 13.

Periodicity did not yield any significant correlation with personnel, authority, succession, forces, or governmental reaction.

(ii) *Duration*

When the duration of revolutionary movements was considered in terms of the categories of personnel taking part in

---

[130] Maude, 'Strategy', loc. cit.

them, the distinction between short and long period movements was further amplified (Table 24, p. 209). While it was very rare for military movements to exceed a duration of one month, one third of civilian movements did so. Thus while there was on that account good reason to agree with Sorokin's contention that 'most of the internal crises in the life process of a social body . . . come and pass their acute stage within the period of a few weeks',[131] there was at least a suggestion that the differences were due to essentially political causes.

The relationship between duration and direction (Table 25, p. 210) exhibited a very pronounced positive correlation, tending to support the tentative conclusions as to their value as indicators of efficiency. In particular, the advantage in maintaining the element of secrecy must not be overlooked. The conclusion was reinforced by the clear relationship between duration and level, despite the shifts already noted in the passage of time towards the centralization of revolutionary activity. Table 26 (p. 210) exhibits the relationship. It will be noted that the smallness of the actual sample of government-level actions against those at capital level introduced a possible element of distortion.

The relationship between duration and post-revolutionary participation changes, which was not postulated in advance, has some interesting features. Very short periods of duration correlate with negative trends in participation (no change or decrease). The longer the period the more the chances of the outcome being an increase (Table 27, p. 211). This is attributable to purely organizational criteria, for a movement that endures must necessarily involve the mobilization of a greater number of people than one that does not. This is not, however, to suggest that longer revolutions mobilize greater strength of actual participants. In fact, the reverse is the case (Table 28, p. 211), an an inverse correlation exists between duration and strength. The relationship between duration and magnitude seems (given the limitations of the data) to be a direct one (Table 29, p. 212). The mobilization of the longer revolution is one of sympathizers rather than participants; it is the mobilization of the people who provide the political base for military operations by giving tacit and overt financial and other aid,

[131] Sorokin, *Social and Cultural Dynamics*, III, 479.

and by hampering the efforts of the governmental machine to identify and destroy the force challenging it.

The data presented in Table 30 (p. 212) confirms to some extent the hypothesis that the absence of marked governmental reaction in so many cases is due to the short period of time in which the governors have time to become aware of the challenge before being overcome by it.

(iii) *Personnel*

It has already emerged that there are in fact distinct differences between the military and civilian approaches to revolution, as indeed has been traditionally believed. The fact that such a large proportion of revolutionary events are of civilian origin suggests, however, that there may have been some inadvertent misattribution of other characteristics normally attached to one group or the other. The evidence presented here appears to confirm that certain aspects in particular might well receive further considerations.

It does not come as any surprise to find that the joint military/civilian revolution type is correlated with action on the higher levels (Table 31, p. 213). The military are not in a position to fight a protracted action without the support of civilians forming an economic and social substructure to supply their wants. They are unlikely to be afforded this without having to accept in return a measure of equality for the civilian element in the struggle, including participation in the directorate. The figures show quite clearly that the military do not in fact fight such actions.

It is therefore of more than incidental interest to observe that it is the civilian revolution, not the military, that is associated with the direction of a single leader rather than a group (Table 32, p. 213). Furthermore, the convention as a succession device, popular with civilians before 1930, has not been used by them since, while the four military/civilian instances dropped to one. The two other occasions on which it has been used have been military; they parallel the rare military use before 1930. Civilians used designate succession proportionately just as often as did the military, each in 41 per cent of their actions, as is demonstrated by Table 33 (p. 214). The constant use of interim succession may well conceal an important change of emphasis which these tests do not disclose.

That this is at least a possibility is hinted by the fact that it is the military who account for a very marked increase in the claim of traditional authority—from 10 cases before 1930 to 31 cases since. It must be said, however, that since the concept of traditionality is in itself a product of the passage of time, some increase in this correlation was to be expected, and may be purely attributable to a change of emphasis in the authors of source material.

Emphasis on this relationship should further be diminished by consideration of the evidence of Table 34 (p. 214) that the military supported the government in no less than 78 cases in which civilian personnel succeeded in bringing about a revolutionary transition. Tradition was therefore much more important as a factor promoting stability than as one promoting instability. This stability was not, however, of sufficient strength to support the governments in question against the challenges with which they were faced, and in only a small proportion of cases could this reasonably be attributed to the effect of surprise.

Cases in which revolutionary action was followed by decrease in participation resulted equally from military and civilian intervention. Increase in participation, on the other hand, was indeed correlated positively with civilian action (Table 35, p. 215).

Governments tended more often to make concessions to movements of civilian composition (Table 36, p. 215). It seemed probable that this was associated not only with their type of claim to legitimacy (for this was not a clear relationship) but also with their slight tendency towards higher magnitude. The evidence for this (Table 37, p. 216) is scanty, but it is reasonable to suppose that the higher magnitude of a province-based movement would be a necessary corollary of its effect in impressing a central government remote from the scene of action.

Civilian movements were significantly strongly associated with extremist goals. While by the definition of official revolution adopted here their monopoly of this type was given beforehand, their ascendancy over separatist revolutions was equally certain (Table 38, p. 216).

(iv) *Direction*

Evidence drawn from this variable tended to confirm data

11—S.O.R.

given previously. It was particularly noticeable that its correlation with level strongly supported the efficiency hypothesis (Table 39, p. 217).

(v) *Succession and authority*

The variables of succession and authority, on the other hand, suggested some substantial modifications in comments presented so far.

To begin with, the relationship between succession and level suggested that the raw values for participation, and still more their correlation with military and civilian personnel, might require an important qualitative modification (Table 40, p. 217). It will be recalled that civilian action correlated strongly with high level and with subsequent increase in participation. It was therefore of significance to find that a marked association existed between action on province level and the category of designate succession. From this evidence one could not go so far as to suggest that the increase in participation associated with civilian action is largely illusory, but certainly it would be fair to say that it would be unlikely to become fully operational until the conclusion of the first term of the successor's office (Table 41, p. 218). The relationship between designation and the claim of legal rational authority supported this (Table 42, p. 218), although the category of authority was not necessarily an accurate representation of an important consideration. The reason for supposing that it might be, at least in this particular instance, lay in the observation that legal/rational authority was correlated negatively with a decrease in post-revolutionary participation (Table 43, p. 219).

Introduction of a qualitative measure of participation in future studies should go far to resolve this question.

(vi) *Aid and initiatives*

Aid either to government or opposition does not appear to be very common. It may alter the duration of a revolutionary movement substantially from the norm, but has no discernible influence on the level on which that movement operates, as is shown by Tables 44 and 45 (pp. 219 and 220).

Both internal and external social initiatives are positively correlated with short duration and to a slight extent with high level (Tables 46, 47, pp. 220–1). The association between military personnel and internal initiatives (Table 48, p. 221) seemed especially worthy of note. Taken together, these associations seemed to tend to support the hypothesis advanced in Chapter 2 that social initiatives derive from movements which generate force in excess of that required to carry out the task of transition.

Advanced weapons were associated above the norm with revolutions of long duration (Table 49, p. 222). Since such weapons are normally associated with the military, and in recent years in particular in the public mind with military enjoying the benefits of foreign aid, it is a salutary reminder to note that the rarity of foreign aid to the military short-term revolution makes it clear that this contingent aid is the type of real importance, not that actually afforded in the course of revolutionary action.

The use of advanced weapons, moreover, was associated with increase in post-revolutionary participation, while implicit force was associated with a decrease (Table 50, p. 222).

X. CONCLUSION

The major purpose of this study was to see in what way and to what extent it was possible to use statistical methods to form a picture of revolutionary action within the broad political definition used here. The study itself was developed on the basis of a model. This model was shown by it to be a reasonable functional representation of the revolutionary process and to have utility in facilitating the major purpose.

This picture of revolutionary action will be examined in the next chapter, which seeks to offer some suggestions on its significance to the further development of the study of revolutionary behaviour, its motivation, and its relation to technical factors. Here it is only proposed to summarize the major conclusions that seem to emerge from the picture as it stands.

It is clear, to begin with, that in association with the progress of weaponry, and even more importantly with the development of modern communications, the twentieth century has seen the development of revolutionary expertise. This has been marked by shorter duration and the narrower limitations of the field of revolutionary action. The role of communications is emphasized, because it is clear that the development of modern communications has greatly accelerated the process of absorption of foreign ideas noted by Edwards as a contributory factor in the generation of the 'Great Revolutions'.[132] As recent experience has shown, it is not so much that there is a world-wide conspiracy to seize power, but that those who wish to seize power now have much less difficulty in hearing of the experience of others.

This in turn suggests that it is in centres of tradition that we must look for the links between tradition-orientated revolutions, and that it is at Sandhurst, Eaton Hall, and West Point that the patterns of behaviour are inculcated with such startling results that when they are activated by local circumstances they result in similar types of action. The revolution orientated towards legal-rational goals is likely to benefit too, however; and when the present wave of military *coups* falls back to a more normal level in a few years, we can expect a return to the dominance of civilian action for as long as the greater part of the world's surface continues to lie outside the effective operation of governmental control, as in South-East Asia and over large tracts of Latin America.

Such a process would not necessarily be one that increased the freedom of individuals in the sense in which people associated the liberation of peoples in the nineteenth century with dramatic incidents of violence. No account has been taken here of the many occasions on which authority has been yielded peacefully, and it may well be that the number of these occasions, could they be counted, would outweight those on which governments have moved into authoritarian patterns.

[132] Edwards, p. 23.

5
THE INDIVIDUAL AND REVOLUTION

IT is a fundamental proposition of this study that political revolution is not necessarily associated with social change, or vice versa. It follows that recent sociological treatments, which assume such a connection, need re-examination.

These treatments may broadly be divided into three classes. The dominant view, the Marxist one, sees revolution as purely social, and as the product of the clash of interests represented in organized classes.[1] The political revolution is seen only as a minor part of a process in historical inevitability which leads to the replacement of one class by another. In this process individuals have no part, and the Marxist offers no theory of individual behaviour beyond the degree to which the individual is incorporated in the structure of the class of which he is a part. It is a fundamental part of the Marxist proposition that members of the ruling class will be conscious of their membership of it, while membership of the supplanting class is not fully realized. Marxist theory therefore ascribes key importance to the role of a few devoted people whose job it is to educate the members of the supplanting class into consciousness of their duties. No explanation is offered as to which class these people will belong or how they will become aware of their mission to educate others.

The second theory is basically one of dysfunction in the social system.[2] It differs therefore from the Marxist analysis in presuming that the social system should be in a normally healthy state but that for some reason it has failed to maintain its normal state of health. This dysfunction leads in the individual to a sense of what Pettee calls 'cramp'. This social cramp consists in a desire to enlarge the individual range of options; for which

---

[1] Marx and Engels, ed. cit.; Vladimir Ilyich Lenin, 'What is to be done? Burning questions of our movement', in *Selected Works* (Lawrence & Wishart, London, 1947), I, 147. How far the old-line Communists have been at times from understanding Lenin's principles is well shown by R. Palme Dutt, *Fascism and Social Revolution; A Study of the Economics and Politics of the Extreme Stages of Capitalism in Decay*, revsd. edn. (International Publishers, New York, 1935); see also Janos, 'The Communist Theory of the State and Revolution'.

[2] Pettee, op. cit.

purpose it is not sufficient just to change the constitution of the state but to make fundamental and far-reaching alterations in the basic political 'culture'.

The similarity of these two models to one another is not altogether unintentional. Paradoxically the existence of each tends to support the analysis of the other, since each appears to the other to evolve from the state of affairs which they presuppose. The impartial observer may prefer to consider that they are opposed aspects of the same view of society; the difference being that the former is based on an essentially pessimistic interpretation and the latter on one which is essentially optimistic. The trend of each is towards a more balanced view of acceptance. For example, Sigmund Neumann, in his discussion of 'the international civil war', outlined the development of forces tending towards a merging of the two points of view,[3] recognized in recent American writing by the tendency to place increasing amounts of blame for a revolutionary situation on the existence of a *status quo* elite.[4] A broad similarity between the theories, however, is their acceptance of the principle that it is broad social forces that motivate human behaviour, and not human behaviour that produces in aggregate broad social forces.

In sharp contra-distinction to both stands the view, best enunciated by Lyford P. Edwards, of the Darwinian model of revolutionary change. This model is established from the experience of the individual, which Edwards renders as the search for and the achievement of 'the four wishes of Thomas'. These are respectively: new experience, security, recognition, and response.[5] The pattern of motivation here is much more satisfying, but the theory still lacks the element of completion. The basic motivation is not carried to the point at which a satisfactory explanation is given as to why the pressures for these goals should result in a pattern specifically of *revolutionary* change. Indeed, the whole of Edwards's work is geared to the consideration of revolutions as rare, emergency phenomena

---

[3] Neumann, 'The International Civil War'.

[4] Ralf Dahrendorf, 'Über einige Probleme der sociologistischen Theorie der Revolution', *Archives Européenes de Sociologie*, II, no. 1 (1961), 153; Stone, op. cit.; cf. Dale Yoder, 'Current definitions of Revolution', *The American Journal of Sociology*, XXXII, no. 3 (Nov. 1926), 433.

[5] Edwards, pp. 2–3.

cutting sharply across normal trends of history. In more recently developed terms Edwards's concept of revolution could be reformulated as a theory of 'quantum jump' in human development.

In his recent pamphlet published by the Hoover Institute for War, Peace and Revolution, Chalmers Johnson has attempted to establish guide-lines on past American experience for a typology and study of revolution. This is of much value in provoking discussion and comment.[6] This discussion has little to do, on the other hand, with the question of motivation. What are mysteriously referred to as psycho-dynamic theories of revolutionary motivation are vaguely mooted, but have failed so far to get off the ground—still less to be accepted as part of the working tools of motivational research. Clearly despite the recent work of sociologists such as Smelser and Meadows there is still much room for development in this field.[7]

It is, however, entirely correct at this time to stress the urgency of developing a satisfactory psycho-dynamic theory in the light of the dominant simplistic views of commentators that revolution must either be antisocial or else a boon to mankind. The analysis of motive, which this dilemma implies, is based in itself on an inaccurate perception of the circumstances of revolutionary behaviour.

It assumes a fully accurate foreknowledge of the consequences of political actions. It assumes, secondly, the existence of positive and (by derivation) specific goals. The maintenance of a regular hierarchy of goals in all the circumstances of a highly confused political situation is taken as read. Lastly, a remarkable confidence is placed in the ability of a revolutionary to obtain access to accurate and complete sources of information.

We would attribute none of these to the politician operating in a peaceful political situation. The revolutionary is a politician, but one who operates in a negative and not a positive state of society, in which inhibitions against violent action by individuals are for some reason suspended. Consequently

---

[6] Chalmers Johnson, op. cit.

[7] Neil J. Smelser, *Theory of Collective Behavior* (Routledge, London, 1962); Paul Meadows, 'Sequence in Revolution', *American Sociological Review*, VI, no. 5 (Oct. 1941), 702.

revolutionaries fail in their endeavours for reasons that are essentially political, or, in other words, derive from their own limitations in understanding the situation in which they find themselves. Equally, their motivation is personal to themselves.

In reassessing the element of motivation, and in proposing alterations of earlier theories, we shall necessarily take account of developments of general theories of the nature of human beings. In particular we have to accept that recent years have seen changes in assumptions about the biological make-up of the human animal. These are peculiar to our time and may well be superseded in their turn. Though they support an assessment of motivation which is in some respects more intellectually complete than their predecessors, they cannot be regarded as being definitive. The assessment in the following section should be read, therefore, with this caution in mind.

REVOLUTIONARY ACTIVITY

Revolution is a common phenomenon in society and is generally recognized as such. Even in the most ordered of societies, people seem to accept with surprising ease the fact that revolutions are common in other societies. Their attitudes are, of course, quickly modified if the governmental transitions in question are marred by an especially high degree of savagery or bloodshed.

This refers only to private reactions. Official reactions are often forced for reasons of diplomacy to establish positions that are widely different. Popular opinion may well not follow them, as in the celebrated case in which British brewery workers threw General Haynau into the Thames. The General had been a leader in suppressing the forces of a foreign revolutionary movement. Yet the workers' loyalty to their own government—only a generation after similar repressive measures at Peterloo—was not questioned; and their action met with positive approval from members of the government, notably Lord Palmerston.[8]

Revolution as concerned with the fundamental problem of securing changes in political leadership, is an important part of the political process. As such it is essentially a group activity. A successful transition purports to be a collective decision of

[8] Herbert C. F. Bell, *Lord Palmerston* (Longmans, London, 1936), II, 40.

society, but at the least it requires acceptance of a change in the source of authority for the ultimate defence of the state from other states and groups. The fact that it involves individual replacement of individual leaders, who are subject to personal attack, makes clear that the kind of action involved is pre-civilized. Though the action takes place in a social context, the motivation of individuals is individual.

Three recently stressed aspects of human behaviour merit special attention. An important element in it is the instinctive reaction of aggression[9]; a reaction which biologically has been so effective that, despite its hazards, species that have evolved it have found it more profitable to inhibit it in their relations with one another than to dispense with it altogether. One way in which it has been regulated and in which it has proved useful for survival is in the establishment of authority over areas of territory,[10] a pattern of behaviour which human beings have adopted and which, despite communal living arrangements, they have actually felt the need to extend. The reasons why they have felt the need to do so are more complex.

Basically, it has been suggested, the human being is a typical primate—a migratory animal living on a largely vegetable diet —that has taken up a carnivorous diet in order to survive, and, hence, with it the patterns of action and restraint necessary in animals potentially lethal to their own species.[11] This process has been so recent in biological terms that it is not complete. Human beings, therefore, retain the pattern of hierarchical dominance characteristic of the primate alongside the patterns of co-operative activity characteristic of the carnivore. They have in addition to both developed a capacity for speech. This, though a necessary attribute for their particular pattern of adaptation to a new way of life, has been a mixed blessing in that it has enabled them to reason (erroneously) that their motivation is primarily or exclusively social or even ethical.

These conclusions, arrived at by chains of reasoning based on evidence falling outside the normal sphere of reference of

9 Konrad Z. Lorenz, *On Aggression.*
10 Robert Ardrey, *The Territorial Imperative* (Collins, London, 1967).
11 Desmond Morris, *The Naked Ape* (Transworld Publishers, London, 1968).

the political scientist, have nevertheless a great deal of relevance for him. Observers of political behaviour in each generation have had to take account of the prevailing views of their time on the nature of man. Some, such as Machiavelli, have made comments on human political behaviour which show implicit acceptance of these propositions solely on the evidence available to them.[12] A 'scientific' study of politics can hardly reject such evidence without a detailed knowledge of it, a knowledge that the political scientist is not in a position to supply. What he can do is to test the propositions against his own experience. In this instance, this means testing them in their application to the existing phenomena of revolution.

Undoubtedly revolution is an applied act of aggression. It is designed to secure a specific, limited end: the replacement of the centre of authority in the community. As an act of intra-specific violence we would expect it to be inhibited once it had achieved this end. This, as we have seen, is just what does happen in the majority of cases. Violence against other parties is restrained to the level normal in the appropriate society, and the deposed leader or leaders, on displaying appropriate signs of submission, are allowed to escape, or even in some cases to remain in a subordinate role.

The principle of territoriality is conspicuous in two ways. Firstly, revolutionaries often act because their position in society, their personal estate, or even their lives have been threatened, directly or indirectly, by the ruling group. They see their action basically as one of self-defence. They justify it by referring to traditional rights or principles of limitation on the uses of authority. Secondly, they amplify this justification by suggesting that if these rights and principles are transgressed, the welfare of the community as a whole will be endangered, thus summoning up the 'patriotic' response of their fellow-members of that community. We find both themes stressed not only in the classical form of the American Declaration of Independence[13] and of the earlier Grand Remonstrance,[14] but also in briefer form from the leaders of recent military *coups* such as

[12] Machiavelli, *Discourses*, I, xxxvii, xlvi; II, xxii.

[13] Henry Steele Commager, ed., *Documents of American History*, 6th edn. (Appleton-Century-Crofts, New York, 1958), pp. 100–3.

[14] J. R. Tanner, *English Constitutional Conflicts of the Seventeenth Century 1603–1689* (C. U. P., Cambridge, 1957), pp. 109–10.

that which overthrew the Government of President Grunitzky of Togo in 1967 (1967 β).[15]

If this were all, the analysis of revolutionary motivation would be a relatively simple matter. But of course it is not. On the one hand, individuals are restrained from revolutionary action by their own social conditioning. On the other, in any modern society they meet with complex problems in implementing their actions which are part social and part technical.

Revolutionaries behave as if authority for their actions mattered intensely to them as individuals. This is what we would expect from human beings who feel very much part of a group and yet alienated from the centre of authority in their society. The primitive loyalty to the hierarchical pattern of the community is in conflict with their loyalty to those of their fellows with whom they normally work and associate. Generally such a conflict has been reduced for human societies by the adoption of a myth of a higher authority that limits the power of the hierarchical superior to the point at which such co-operative endeavour is not stultified. Such myths are necessarily 'official', however, and the individual revolutionary can counter them only in two ways. He has either to claim superior knowledge of the 'official' myth or to proclaim an alternative myth which can replace it.

This is a problem that faces any individual trying by any means to replace the ruling group. There is a striking parallel between the consequences of the acts of successor governments to violent revolutionary transitions and those of the rare civilian politicians who have succeeded in obtaining power through constitutional means and who have faced the same problems in consolidating their position. Woodrow Wilson deposed more European monarchs than Robespierre, and Luther condemned more peasants to the gallows than Cromwell. Any change in society as fundamental as the alteration of the 'official' myth is dangerous, even if attempted by a 'moral' politician. Nor must we forget that the most adept of the moral politicians at managing the political system have achieved their political dominance at the expense of their moral dominance, by the astute manipulation of semantic terminology. They develop

[15] *The Guardian* (Sat., 14 Jan. 1967).

a conceptual reality whose difference from the reality as perceived by others lies purely in the terminology which they are prepared to give it. Recent instances have included the governments of President Sukarno in Indonesia[16] and the transitional phase of the Cuban Revolution under Fidel Castro.[17]

Leadership in a revolutionary situation has everything to do with the manipulation of human passions by symbols and evocative language. The importance of semantic analysis to revolution is therefore unquestionable.[18] Nevertheless we cannot yet undertake it in the absence of an effective tradition of semantic analysis in political studies.

All we can say here is that its significance to revolutionary studies is the fact that it obviates the search for a feeling of 'cramp'. The efficient manipulation of semantic symbols goes far to eliminate the sense of cramp which is felt under regimes less adept in recreation of an artificial reality. The importance of semantic analysis lies in the realization itself of the gap between theory and reality. It is precisely that this necessity for the revolutionary to create an artificial reality is most effective in the weaning of potential supporters from a tradition of assuming as normal the overwhelming dominance of the political machine.

The gap between theory and reality is not constant. It widens and narrows according to the shifts and turns of interests and the degree of efficiency with which they are integrated into the decision-making process.[19] If the theory and reality are close, society may be violent, but it will be healthy and non-revolutionary. The stability of democratic systems, for example, lies in the assumption of a wide dispersal of a claim to rule. However, it is the assumption and not the fact that gives democracy its strength; and if too wide a disparity exists between the fact and the assumption, then the possibility of

---

[16] Donald E. Weatherbee, *Ideology in Indonesia; Sukarno's Indonesian Revolution*, Yale University Southeast Asia Studies, Monograph Series No. 8 (New Haven, 1966).

[17] Goldenberg, pp. 185 ff.

[18] See Charles E. Osgood, George J. Suci, and Percy H. Tannenbaum, *The Measurement of Meaning* (University of Illinois Press, Urbana, 1957).

[19] Cf. James C. Davies, 'Toward a Theory of Revolution', *American Sociological Review*, XLIII, no. 1 (Feb. 1962), 5–19.

violent self-expression becomes very probable. Conversely the power of a dictatorship lies in the assumption of its authority. Dictatorships are therefore stable in societies in which legitimacy has a traditional base, and unstable in societies in which it is believed that more than one individual may possess a claim to power.[20]

In essence, the claim to rule is an attribute of ability of the so-called specialist techniques of decision-making. In so far as these exist, they are separated from the functional specialization of society. There is no such activity as political decision-making that is separable from the manifold operations of the society as a whole. In every small group and every organization, whether it be a large business or a voluntary society, the activity which we term politics can be identified.[21] Those holding authority within these groups are performing the function performed by government in a society as a whole. The separation of function in society results from the assertion of a specific ability to carry out these particular techniques, but the assertion of this ability in itself leads to its own contradiction.[22] This opposition takes the form of an assertion of functionalist independence. The functionalist opposition bases its claim to independence upon its specific techniques and its specific abilities in its own particular field.

Examples of milieux in which functionalist opposition redevelops include the military, the literati, and trade unions. These are not necessarily separated from the existence of a non-functionalist opposition, often based upon an *emigré* centre. The assumption of functional self-control leads to the self-realization that the continuance of society involves something more than the ability to operate one's own organization. Functional separation of authority therefore breaks down for three main reasons.

To begin with it involves too much strain on the specialist group. It means that that group is unable to continue to perform its functional specialization in society without annoying perturbations occasioned by its need to assume a higher, or

---

[20] Cf. John L. Enos, *An Analytical Model of political allegiance and its application to the Cuban Revolution* (The Rand Corporation, Santa Monica, Calif., Aug. 1965).

[21] Merriam, pp. 182 ff.

[22] i.e. to argument and objection.

wider, role within the society. By attempting to exercise this wider authority it destroys its own specialist claim to rule.

Secondly, its specialist claim to rule is challenged by the assertion of rival claims. As long as government is clearly vested in a specialist organ, for which the expertise of government is the main qualification, other forms of expertise are not necessarily pathways to power.[23] Once, however, this has been broken by the successful assumption of a functionalist authority in one sphere, this assumption of authority will be challenged from others.

In the third place, the assault phase of the assumption of power demands a new commitment. The act of commitment implies in itself questioning the traditional bases of authority, and this in turn implies the questioning of the new basis as well. Such questioning may well arise even among the members of the functionalist organism. They are, after all, brought up in the belief that this organ is separate, remote, and authoritative in its own sphere, and when it comes in contact with the realities of power politics, it is all too probable that it will sustain invasion from without.[24] All these, it will be noted, are occupational hazards of military intervention in politics. It is clear, however, that the same phenomena will apply in any sphere, and hence the military have much in common with other functionalist groups attempting to exercise authority within the state.

This analysis is just as applicable to the acts of political assassination, military intervention, or of the supplanting of a government as it is to the complex of events known as the Russian Revolution. In it is to be found the basis of the motivation of revolutionary behaviour. In each case the resort to violence marks a reversion to the occasion of the development of the primitive specialization of government. This is made possible because society does not *eliminate* political violence, but instead suppresses it or regulates it on behalf of the state. Indeed, the state commonly educates its citizens in the virtues of using violence against the alien and hence anti-social mem-

---

[23] Herbert Hiram Hyman, *Political socialisation; a study in the psychology of political behaviour* (The Free Press, Glencoe, Ill., 1959).

[24] Cf. Harold D. Lasswell and Daniel Lerner, eds., *World Revolutionary Elites: Studies in Coercive Ideological Movements* (The M.I.T. Press, Cambridge, Mass., 1966).

bers.[25] It follows that the revolutionary is a person who identifies himself as a normal person doing a normal job of work in a normal (though intermittent) stage of social development.

With all his functional awareness, however, the revolutionary may still be a very simple-minded political animal. This explains the paradox that although revolution is to a large extent a military phenomenon, military specialists are not necessarily good at it. Certainly they are more likely than civilians without military training to appreciate that the technical problems involved in achieving power by violent means are in themselves complex in a modern society. The increased technical proficiency which has multiplied the number of successful military *coups* in the recent period has not brought with it an equivalent increase in political awareness, and military *coups* therefore continue to be frequent, and the governments formed by them correspondingly short-lived.

To sum up, therefore, the conflict between the co-operative impulse and the pattern of hierarchical dominance is in modern times compounded by the complexity of society. The simple impulse of self-defence has to be applied in conditions of complexity in which the assessment of the consequences of revolutionary action are more than ever difficult to comprehend.

THE REVOLUTIONARY AND THE OUTSIDE WORLD

The most important feature of the twentieth century has been that development in systems of communication which has brought different societies into relative proximity with one another. Further, they have developed ways of injuring one another, up to and including total annihilation. Modern states maintain their individuality by the creation of an essentially secular myth of their own uniqueness. The re-creation of such myths involves hazards not only for the society concerned, but also for all others. Special attention must therefore be focused on the development of the phenomena of revolutionary war and imperialism.

The sharp discrepancy has already been noted between the prevailing levels of internal political violence during the

25 Cf. Seymour Martin Lipset, *Political Man* (Mercury Books, London, 1964), pp. 120–2.

times covered by the First and Second World Wars. The latter period was distinguished by many fewer successful transitions induced by force than the former. Writing in 1937 Sorokin saw the first quarter of our century as being exceptional in its magnitude of violence, and the figures he put forward seemed to indicate that, although the second quarter was unlikely to be as peaceful as the last quarter of the nineteenth century, for example, it was nevertheless to be expected that in its level of violence it would fall well below that achieved by its predecessor.[26]

This in fact appears to have been the case, and accordingly the Second World War must be regarded as being a discrepancy from the prevailing order of violence[27] (although one of colossal magnitude!). In fact, the quarter-century was characterized by a very low level of political violence for the kinds of social and economic problems people might reasonably be expected to have had to tackle, and the aspects of political violence which appear in the causation of the Second World War appear, characteristically enough, in countries with a recent tradition of a relatively rapidly developing political system.

However, the discrepancy must also be attributed to a number of other causes. To begin with, the Second World War involved a much larger mobilization of forces involving the greater part of the world's surface. It followed that the large majority of the countries of the world operated during this period under emergency legislation, vesting exceptional powers in the government and tending towards the maintenance in the short-term of political stability. However, this does not entirely satisfactorily account for the very sharp falling off in violence during the mid-thirties, though it does tend to harmonize with the out-break of war in Spain[28] and Paraguay[29]

[26] Sorokin, *Social and Cultural Dynamics*, III.

[27] Charles Tilly and James Rule, *Measuring Political Upheaval*, Woodrow Wilson School of Public and International Affairs, Princeton University, Research Monograph No. 19 (Center of International Studies, Princeton, 1965).

[28] Gerald Brenan, *The Spanish Labyrinth, An Account of the Social and Political Background of the Civil War* (C. U. P., Cambridge, 1962), pp. 302–15; Thomas, op. cit.

[29] Efraim Cardozo, *Paraguay Independiente* (Salvat Editores, Barcelona, 1949); Harris Gaylord Warren, *Paraguay, An Informal History* (University of Oklahoma Press, Norman, 1949).

and the very rapid recrudescence of political violence at the end of the war.

Thirdly, the Second World War originated from the consolidation, rather than the dissolution, of empires. The development of the Japanese 'co-prosperity sphere' in South-East Asia, and the extension to continental hegemony of the power of greater Germany, both carried with them a consequent reduction of the number of states available for revolutionary developments. In contrast, both the immediate cause and the approximate causes of the First World War are to be found in separationist movements tending to result in the overall increase in the number of states; and although the greater part of these culminated in the two remarkable revolutionary years of 1917 and 1918, it is of some interest to note that these peaks form part of a continuous rise from 1911 onwards. Then, although the First World War itself and the immediate conclusion of peace coincide with a peak in revolutionary activity, that peak falls away very rapidly in 1920, and the early 1920s are a period of relative peace and quiet. These very years, however, were years of intense social dislocation and economic catastrophe in central Europe, and the fact that the revolutionary movements of the inter-war period are grouped in the thirties rather than in the 1920s seems to cast some doubt upon de Tocqueville's association of revolution with periods in which circumstances, having been worse, are actually tending to get better.[30]

It is particularly interesting to note also that movements for independence tend on the whole to be fairly peaceful affairs, and even in the early years of the century, at the time of the separation of Norway from Sweden in 1905, the tensions liberated could be successfully contained within the constitutional order.[31] It is not, therefore, as surprising as it seems that so many states have been given their independence in the last decade under relatively peaceful auspices, while at the same time the social tensions in these newly liberated states

[30] Alexis de Tocqueville, *L'Ancien Régime et la Révolution* (Paris, 1856); cf. Melvin Richter, 'Tocqueville's contribution to the theory of revolution', *Nomos VIII: Revolution*, ed. Carl J. Friedrich (Atherton Press, New York, 1966).

[31] Ingvar Andersson, *A History of Sweden* (Weidenfeld & Nicolson, London, 1956), pp. 400–13; Raymond E. Lindgren, *Norway–Sweden: Union, Disunion, and Scandinavian Integration* (Princeton University Press, Princeton, 1959).

proved sufficient to create violent *internal* revolutionary situations, resulting in violence of considerable magnitude and extensive loss of life. On the Richardson scale most of the crises recorded in modern history fall well short of the number of deaths which occur at reasonably frequent intervals from natural causes. The magnitude of the First and Second World Wars alone exceed the magnitude of the great revolutionary battles originating from purely internal causes, such as the T'aip'ing Rebellion in China, the American Civil War, or the Mexican Revolution.[32] But more people are killed in some decades in China in floods than were killed in the whole of the the T'aip'ing Rebellion.[33]

Imperialism, it seems, produces more complicated effects. We have seen that the reduction of the number of states in which revolution can occur does not have any direct relationship to the absolute total of revolutionary transitions. As in the case of war, the opportunities for the legitimate use of violence do to some extent divert the elements of society available for political violence into the goal of expansion; while concentration on the goals of expansion reduces the dangers of revolution in the imperial power. The exercise of imperial authority, certainly, requires the inculcation of political attitudes designed to be those of obedience, respect, and loyalty to the authority of the imperial power.

Insufficient attention, however, has been given to the fact in devoting its attention to imperial expansion, the host country is unconsciously making itself into the model which it expects the conquered territory to follow. It exports its more violent elements, thus facilitating the retention of an organized constitutional order during the period of expansion, and its difficulties are not likely to become great again until the point at which sufficient national self-consciousness builds up in the dependent territory for it to seek to reassert its own power. The imperial power is therefore in a position, as it seems, to point to a real, rather than a theoretical, example of good social

[32] Richardson, pp. 40, 48, gives magnitudes 6.3, 5.8, and 5.4 respectively; the Spanish Civil War had external causes for its exceptional magnitude of 6.3.

[33] Tibor Mende, *China and her Shadow* (Thames & Hudson, London, 1966), pp. 197–8. Mende's figure for the T'aip'ing Rebellion includes deaths from disease, etc.; cf. Richardson, loc. cit. above.

behaviour.[34] If this is inculcated in common with an active social culture and a well-articulated system of beliefs tending to confer authority upon the believer, the situation that results, in default of outside influences, is likely to be a very stable one.

It will be seen that behavioural pattern engendered by war and imperialism in itself gives good reason for separating the sub-type of separatist revolution. It is an equally good reason for placing in a separate category the class which has been here described as official revolutions. The official revolution, it will be recalled, is what traditionally and correctly has been called *coup d'état*; that is to say, the use of the legitimate powers of government in order to make a forcible alteration in the societal structure. It is the vagueness of the definition of this activity which makes it so distinctive. When a government has been deposed by an outside movement, the result is clear for all to see. The amount of violence available to a government in exercising social control, and the ways in which it can be deployed in order to strengthen its own position, vary so widely from state to state that no generalization here is very convenient.[35]

Hence, it is only possible to incorporate a satisfactory cut-off point in the model if the concept of legitimacy is entirely banished from it. This has been achieved here by requiring for the execution of such a *coup*, the actual physical presence of force, whether it is exercised or not. In other words, a *coup* which involves the deployment of troops in order to meet a possible objection, even if that objection does not come, falls within the scope of the model; while the exclusion of members of a legislature by vote alone, the strengthening of an existing government by electoral devices such as a plebiscite, and similar devices are not revolutionary, even if force is present to ensure

[34] The touchstone for this interpretation would be the reasons for the retention of Cuba by Spain, owing largely to internal class divisions. For Portugal and its relations with Angola and Moçambique see H. V. Livermore, *A New History of Portugal* (C. U. P., Cambridge, 1966).

[35] Some of the more extreme cases can be found in George I. Blanksten, *Ecuador, Constitutions and Caudillos* (Russell & Russell, New York, 1964); James C. Carey, *Peru and the United States, 1900–1962* (University of Notre Dame Press, Notre Dame, Ind., 1964); Harry Kantor, *Ideology and Program of the Peruvian Aprista Movement* (University of California Press, Los Angeles, 1953); Guillermo Morón, *A History of Venezuela*, trs. John Street (Allen & Unwin, London, 1964).

that they are successful. Nor do the most extensive social changes, with their inevitable repercussions on the maintenance and extension of governmental power, necessarily fall within this category.

Taken together, these observations raise some very interesting points about revolutionary motivation. The most obvious of these is that the general improvement of communications has given governments techniques to project images of themselves to the outside world which they find facilitate their official dealings with the neighbouring and, by extension, remote states. Such images may be used by revolutionaries in other countries to illustrate the secular myth which they are attempting to establish. Their remoteness makes them in some respects more plausible, but revolutionary leaders who have travelled in order to study other countries derive from them no less useful lessons.[36] The observer of a foreign country carries his own preconceptions with him.

Countries project on the world stage the images which their leaders have found effective in achieving hierarchical superiority in their own communities. These images accordingly involve a substantial element of aggression in the sense of preparedness to defend the cause or causes for which they stand. This is important to leaders in other countries who share those causes, but it is even more important to their followers in reassuring them that others think the way they do and are prepared to back them.

Though actual official support from other countries to revolutionary movements is in fact fairly rare, as we have seen, few people are aware of this. In any case, prospective support may be more important than real in convincing a revolutionary of the overwhelming power of his cause. The fact that technically he does not need overwhelming power is less important than the probability that psychologically he does. The assumption that uncommitted power is neutral in the balance of advantage is one that few strategists are prepared to make when their lives are at stake.

Conversely, governments, who spend much of their time on the alert for external threats, are easily persuaded that manifestations of internal dissent are externally inspired. The

[36] Cf. Edwards, pp. 27 ff.

probability that this is so has much increased during the century with the increase in awareness of foreign countries. But the superficial nature of this awareness suggests that the external element is still much overrated. What must not be overrated is the extent to which governments tend to use the 'external' response, that is, the response appropriate to attack from another community, in meeting movements of largely internal origin. It is precisely in this way that governments commit those excesses of force which call up in turn hostility from the more traditional elements in society on whose support they must depend.

After all, in the past governmental stability has been maintained with relative ease in some countries in which there was a prevailing atmosphere of approval for revolutionary movements abroad. In nineteenth-century England, stability has been attributed to many causes, ranging from the export of violent elements to the demilitarization of the homeland. Sociologists add that the existence of the 'career open to talent' enabled the replacement of the ruling group to take place by peaceful means rather than by force. Publicists will point to the existence of strong symbols of unity in the make-up of the British system of government: the monarchy, the Church, the widespread Empire, and the far-flung language.[37]

All these as reasons in themselves are, of course, open to a considerable degree of criticism. Regiments were after all trained in England before being sent overseas. The openness of career to talent did not mean that the education to be found at Eton and at Christ Church, Oxford, was not immensely more efficient in preparing one for higher office than any other. The monarchy was very unpopular indeed in the 1860s and 1870s. In any case comparative studies in monarchy as between, for example, Denmark and Greece do not suggest that the existence of a crowned rather than uncrowned parliamentary system necessarily promotes stability and freedom from violence.[38] A similar comparison may be made in very different circumstances as between the effectiveness of the monarchies

[37] It has, however, been recently suggested that on the other hand the very universality of English lessens the sense of community imparted by it, as against, e.g., French.

[38] See William Miller, *Greece* (Ernest Benn, London, 1928); and J. H. S. Birch, *Denmark in History* (John Murray, London, 1938).

in Burma and Thailand, two countries with a very similar tradition of resistance to imperial expansion in the context of a common history and political background.

Until recently, it might well have been accepted also that the existence of a high standard of living in England was of some particular significance in maintaining stability. This is considerably more difficult today, not so much because of the excesses of a Hitler or Mussolini, but because the case of France in 1958 has proved that the difference between revolution in a highly articulated modern state and revolution in a primitive and under-developed one consists mainly in the extent of the arena which it occupies and the spectacular features which accompany its use.[39] Nevertheless, certain attributes of a high standard of living must necessarily have important political consequences. The prevalence of a high degree of literacy is one that deserves more attention than it has so far received; especially, perhaps, it should be studied in a Western political culture in which there is an increasing tendency for the literati to abandon the use of language in favour of a series of grunts. The particular importance of literacy is the maintenance of a homogeneous political culture. Britain in the nineteenth century is particularly characterized by just this sense of unity and the degree to which information was capable of being rapidly systematized and disseminated.[40] That is to say, Britain as opposed to Ireland; for the case of Ireland was another matter.

It is at least arguable that the existence of Irish disaffection was a major factor in promoting the consolidation of the British political system. The existence of an organized body of dissent held the parliamentary system together for a whole generation after 1886, though at the price of considerable turbulence among the structure of political parties themselves. As in the parallel case of Austria, whose scattered fringes of empire were consolidated by their common desire not to be identified with Hungarian nationalism, the British found unity in their prevailing agreement that the Irish were separate and unique.

[39] Merry and Serge Bromberger, *Les 13 Complots du 13 Mai* (Librairie Arthème Fayard, 1959); James H. Meisel, *Military Revolt in France, the fall of the Republic* (University of Michigan Press, Ann Arbor, 1962).

[40] It is important not only that the facilities exist but that they should also be used. Where the literati maintain a distinct culture and guard knowledge from the 'masses' the same effect is attained.

As this separateness and uniqueness consisted in large measure in their resistance to constituted authority, it followed that the maintenance of this separateness and uniqueness was at least in part dependent on the maintenance of a state of constituted authority in Britain itself. Political socialization set out to provide this. Multiplied a hundredfold it found its mechanism for articulation and dissemination in the expanding universities and the newly developed public schools. These institutions stressed higher loyalties than loyalty to government (as those readers familiar with Kipling's *Stalky and Co.* will recall); higher also than the organized belief system of the Church of England, to whom unity was a prime article of faith. The secular faith was in the existence of a kind of Empire-wide secret society of ex-schoolboys, whose duty it was to maintain the structure of this informal network before all other factors tending to promote unity. The effect of this particular political solution upon the evolution of Empire into Commonwealth in the present century is so obvious as scarcely to need emphasis.

We may conclude, therefore, that although the revolutionary can seldom get physical help from the world outside his community, his awareness of that world and his government's response to it are both important in understanding his motivation. The revolutionary of today has the opportunity to know more about other countries and their societies than his predecessors. But the improvement in communications which has made this possible has accompanied an increase in levels of literacy which has brought corresponding strength to governments. Techniques have improved on both sides; the duration of revolutionary movements has gone down, they have become more centralized and more efficient.

THE COMMUNICATION OF REVOLUTIONARY IDEAS

So far we have been considering motivation as spontaneous and internal. What then of the deliberate propagation of ideas designed to promote revolutionary responses? On the subject of 'scientifically' designed propaganda a great deal has been written, but, perhaps fortunately, very little effort has so far been made to apply it to specifically revolutionary situations.

The high degree of sophistication attained by propaganda under the Nazi regime in Germany was attained by a government that reached power by constitutional means and then shattered the constitutional order with the use of an official revolution; hence the scientific studies that had been made and the records that have been left of the work of Dr. Goebbels and his associates are of little value to the student of revolution.[41] Much more important would be studies evaluating scientifically the impact of the works of Marx, Engels, and Lenin as put out by the Foreign Languages Publishing House in Moscow and of the cheap reprints of Marx's texts circulated in Africa, Asia, and Latin America by the Chinese Government. Unfortunately, however, owing to our proximity to this material a great deal that is known about it is necessarily covered by the blanket of military security. What is clear, however, is that this kind of propaganda is still—in the Marxist case as a result of deliberate choice—erroneously aimed at people in the mass and not at the individuals whom it is designed to convert.

The problem about directing propaganda, or any other form of political exhortation, at a mass rather than at a body made up of complex individuals, lies in the modifications of language made in the specialist worlds of all societies. The will to communicate is basic to the effect which communication has upon the auditors. An over-simple interpretation of the pattern of social behaviour imposed on the receptor will stultify the effort to communicate as effectively as the absence of media with which communication can be carried on, but it is a great deal harder for the communicator to understand.[42]

It is clear that the obsessive mentality of many revolutionary leaders leads them consistently to fall into this trap. That is to say, the propaganda that they put out is directed in the main towards people of like mind as themselves. By definition, in most societies the numbers of such people are limited, and in each society they are bound to be further restricted in their interactions by their functional specialization. The degree to which revolution in its constructive stages is a matter of com-

[41] Z. A. B. Zeman, *Nazi Propaganda* (O. U. P., London, 1964); Serge Chakotin, *The Rape of the Masses, the Psychology of Totalitarian Political Propaganda* (Routledge, London, 1940).

[42] Cf. George Sorel, *Reflections on Violence* (The Free Press, Glencoe, Ill., 1950), ed. and intro. Edward A. Shils.

munication, therefore, is of high importance in determining the ineffectiveness of widespread movements; and ineffectiveness is as great on the communication sphere as it is in terms of the energy model itself.

The problems of communication are that they have an effect on both sides of the equation in the revolutionary situation; they relate not only to the reactions of the revolutionaries themselves but also to the apparently suicidal moves of governments threatened by revolutionary disturbances. The generation of revolutionary energy implies the creation of a rival centre of ideological interpretation. The actual efficiency of the revolutionary machine, therefore, is not necessarily as important as it seems.

The revolutionaries will be devoting their maximum attention to trying to win support outside governmental circles, or, within governmental circles, to win the support of those furthest removed from the centre of power. They aim to create the impression of power, invincibility, and effectiveness, representing themselves as being a force which inevitably must assume supremacy, and indicating as vaguely as they may the kind of programme which they propose to follow should opportunity be afforded to them. Now, all this may well not succeed in being disseminated to the people that they intend to reach. But it is the function of government to be well informed about such movements within its sphere of activity, and the government, therefore, in exercising its power of supervision and surveillance actually enables this propaganda to be sucked into its own organization.

It follows, therefore, that a substantial number of governments collapse from internal disillusion and decay, not because this decay would necessarily be present in the absence of a revolutionary centre, but because the government is using its maximum efforts to induct the views of the revolutionaries into its own system for its own purposes, and in the process is enabling that propaganda to rot its own structure. In many cases this acts to convince government of its own failure before it convinces onlookers of the success of the revolution. With the disappearance of the will to resist, its members abdicate their responsibility and retire from active political resistance. Sometimes they do this, as noted above, before the threatening

revolutionary movement has developed the technical superiority to succeed.

Such a reaction is consistent with the fact that these individuals are those who are best placed to pick up the traditional
signs of submission by which the ruling group acknowledge
defeat. They are in the main the same people who, by consistently projecting an image of loyal endeavour, often deceive
governments into overestimating their degree of popular support. For the majority of human beings, whatever their occupation or position, know well only a relatively small number of
people.[43] It is this, rather than the effectiveness of revolutionaries at maintaining secrecy about their preparations, that
accounts for the surprising speed with which so many recent
governments have been overturned.

REVOLUTIONARIES IN COMPLEX SOCIETIES

We can now begin to discern why, in a century in which
revolutionary technique has developed, there is more confusion
than ever about what revolution actually is; for greater understanding only leads to greater wonder that in certain cases
human beings have perpetrated spectacular atrocities on one
another in its name, or on the pretext of averting it.

What has happened, it seems, is that it is not revolution
that has become more complex, so much as the societies in
which it takes place. Actors may be more aware of their circumstances but they are less able to predict the consequences
of their actions. Four aspects of this are of particular importance.

The most obvious is that technical improvement of weapons
which enables human beings to kill one another at relatively
greater distances. The increase in distance is sufficient to prevent the aggressive instinct of the user of weapons from being
controlled by the normal restraints of face-to-face fighting.
Though, as it has been noted, this gives an advantage to the
defence where forces are evenly matched, it also enables one
deviant individual to kill a very large number of people single-
handed. In times of revolutionary upheaval men revert to
primitive attributes of authority. So they find in such individuals

[43] Morris, pp. 162–3.

the outstanding characteristics on which they can refocus their loyalties. And they follow his example.

No less important is the social development of the bureau-cratic machine, the 'staff' of the governmental group, the military formation, and, for that matter, of the modern revo-lution. This important development in command structure enables a small group to retain overall control of much larger numbers of men. But it insulates them from those whom they control, so that an order to kill is carried out in a quasi-judicial capacity by individuals who are persuaded of the necessity of maintaining order and obeying superior commands.

The modern myth of the state, and hence of the counter-state, is an essentially secular one. Hence propitiation of it has to be cast in essentially secular terms. If there are demons to be cast out, they are demons in human form, enemies of the state, or of the cause. If blood has to be spilt, it must be human blood, and not goats' or bullocks'. Secularization has, certainly, had some very admirable consequences. Women are no longer drowned for witchcraft (or at least not in more advanced societies), children are no longer hanged for stealing property or flogged for swearing. But the idealization of the state is not one of those consequences. It remains a mere generalization of a collection of very fallible and uncertain human beings. And a generalization of its more deviant elements is not necessarily any more admirable.

On the other hand, the increase in social controls in the modern state is two-edged. It can screen out harmful impulses for political change. It can also screen out beneficial ones. The more power that is concentrated in the hands of modern rulers, the more important it becomes that they be frequently changed. Frequent changes of political personnel are not necessarily a sign of a healthy society, but in healthy societies such changes are frequent. This statement should, however, be qualified with the proviso that the society be autonomous. Where the society is inhibited or restrained from taking decisions in those areas which affect its survival, the frequency of change is noticeably less.

Other complexities of the so-called 'Great Revolutions' (and some of the less great) originate to a greater extent outside the specifically 'revolutionary' framework. Their link to the

process of revolution, however, is made through the same compound of primitive motivation and sophisticated rationalization. It is no easy task for ordinary human beings to co-ordinate
these aspects, particularly when their needs in an unstable
social environment impel them towards self-preservation in the
most narrow sense.

The greatest burden falls on the revolutionary leader. If he
is to be successful, he has first to prepare, and subsequently
consolidate, a revolutionary event. This in itself is a full-time
activity demanding minute-to-minute alertness and great
technical expertise. Yet it has to be performed by an individual
whose psychic state is by no means rational and while he is in
a social situation in which his particular form of deviancy exposes him to serious physical danger.

At one and the same time he has a number of very concrete
tasks to perform. He must regulate the technical level of the
forces at his command in order to secure maximum effect. He
must maintain effective command both of his staff and of the
personnel whom they control. He has to proclaim a rival myth
to the official one, while at the same time evading the social
controls designed to restrain him (controls which do not cease
on the deposition of a government but which continue to
function autonomously by virtue of being social rather than
political in origin). And he has to retain a sensitive awareness
of external influences both positive and negative.

It is not surprising that on occasions his calculations of power
should be inexact, especially when he does not know or care
about the grounds on which they must necessarily be based.

As the transfer of power is achieved and rival systems of
authority coexist in the popular mind, his followers—and in
particular those who arrive late on the scene—orient themselves by reference to their own internal norms. The degree of
uncertainty as to where and how those norms are to be applied
determines whether they act with comparative rationality by
doing as they are told, follow a conservative impulse of withdrawal from involvement, or succumb to primitive impulses
in an attempt to re-create order. Since the members and
followers of the erstwhile government behave in a similar
fashion, the unpredictability of the consequences is correspondingly multiplied.

To conclude, therefore, revolutions are a regular political activity. Typically they occur according to regular cycles, frequently, and on a low level. They are subject to certain general rules about the amount and quality of force employed on each side. Though they arise principally from individual motivation, they appeal to instincts that are not only general but basic to the emergence of human society. They reflect the survival in modern man of a primitive form of social organization. Therefore the process of the fall and rise of governments tends to recapitulate the features of the emergence of society itself. It is for this reason that they have acquired the exaggerated respect characteristic of our own time.

One can only hope that in all ways a better understanding of the human condition may make the world a more humane place in which to live, without unduly restraining those idealistic impulses intended by many of those who today speak loosely about the subject of revolution. It is in this hope that this study of revolution was undertaken. There is still a long way to go.

APPENDIX A

CHECK LIST OF TRANSITIONS, 1901–60

1901 α	Nepal	30 June	Fall of Deb Shamsher
β	United States	14 September	Assn. of McKinley
1902 α	Paraguay	9 January	Fall of Aceval
β	Arabia	15 January	Ibn Saud takes Riyadh
γ	Dominican Rep.	2 May	Fall of Jiménez
δ	Haiti	12 May	Fall of Simon Sam
ε	Haiti	22 December	Nord Alexis President
1903 α	Dominican Rep.	23 March	Fall of Vázquez
β	Serbia	10 June	*Coup* agst. K. Alexander
γ	Panama	3 November	Independence
δ	Dominican Rep.	25 November	Fall of Wos y Gil
1904 α	Russia	28 July	Assn. of Plehve
β	Paraguay	12 December	Liberal *coup*
1905 α	Russia	30 October	October manifesto
β	Dominican Rep.	24 December	Fall of Morales
1906 α	Ecuador	15 January	Fall of García
β	Arabia	April	Fall of Ibn Rashid
γ	Cuba	25 September	Fall of Estrada Palma
δ	Persia	7 October	Revolution for Majlis
1907 α	Rumania	24 March	Agrarian revolt
β	Portugal	2 May	Franco *coup*
γ	Russia	3 June	Stolypin *coup*
δ	Korea	19 July	Depn. of Emperor
ε	Persia	31 August	Assn. of Amin es Sultan
ζ	Persia	15 December	Shah's first *coup*
1908 α	Portugal	1 February	Assn. of K. Carlos
β	Persia	23 June	Shah's second *coup*

1908 (*continued*)

γ	Paraguay	5 July	Fall of Ferreira
δ	Turkey	24 July	Young Turk revolt
ε	Morocco	23 August	Fall of 'Abd el 'Aziz IV
ζ	Bulgaria	5 October	Independence
η	Crete	7 October	Union with Greece
θ	Haiti	13 December	Fall of Nord Alexis
1909 α	Turkey	13 April	Revolt of 1st Army Corps
β	Turkey	26 April	Fall of Abdul Hamid
γ	Colombia	8 July	Fall of Reyes
δ	Persia	12 July	Depn. of Mohammed Ali
ε	Nicaragua	16 December	Fall of Zelaya
ζ	Venezuela	19 December	*Coup* of Gómez
1910 α	Nicaragua	20 August	Fall of Madriz
β	Portugal	5 October	Fall of Manoel
1911 α	Paraguay	17 January	Fall of Gondra
β	Honduras	8 February	Revolt of Bonilla
γ	Nicaragua	15 May	Fall of Estrada
δ	Mexico	16 May	Fall of Díaz
ε	Paraguay	5 July	Fall of Jara
ζ	Haiti	14 August	Fall of Simon
η	Russia	14 September	Assn. of Stolypin
θ	Outer Mongolia	18 November	Independence
ι	Dominican Rep.	19 November	Assn. of Cáceres
κ	Persia	24 December	'Russian' *coup*
1912 α	China	12 February	Revolution for republic
β	Paraguay	28 February	Fall of Rojas
γ	Paraguay	22 March	Fall of Peña
δ	Haiti	8 August	Assn. of Leconte
ε	Spain	12 November	Assn. of Canalejas
ζ	Albania	26 November	Independence
η	Dominican Rep.	26 November	Depn. of Eladio Victoria
1913 α	Turkey	23 January	Young Turk *coup*
β	El Salvador	9 February	Assn. of Araújo
γ	Mexico	18 February	Huerta *coup*

1913 *(continued)*

δ	Greece	18 March	Assn. of K. George
ε	Dominican Rep.	13 April	Fall of Nouel
1914 α	Haiti	27 January	Fall of Oreste
β	Peru	5 February	Fall of Billinghurst
γ	Serbia	24 June	Regency for Peter I
δ	Mexico	15 July	Fall of Huerta
ε	Dominican Rep.	6 August	Fall of Bordas Váldes
ζ	Mexico	13 August	Flight of Carvajal
η	Albania	3 September	Fall of William of Wied
θ	Haiti	27 October	Fall of Zamor
1915 α	Mexico	16 January	Fall of Gutiérrez
β	Portugal	28 January	Dict. of Pimenta de Castro
γ	Haiti	22 February	Fall of Theodore
δ	Portugal	14 May	Democratic *coup*
ε	Portugal	15 May	Assn. of Chagas
ζ	Mexico	11 June	Fall of González Garza
η	Haiti	27 July	Fall and assn. of Sam
θ	China	9 December	Yüan assumes Empire
ι	China	25 December	Yunnan rebellion
1916 α	Mexico	1 January	Fall of Lagos Cházaro
β	Dominican Rep.	6 May	Fall of Jiménez
γ	Arabia	7 June	Revolt of the Hejaz
δ	Ethiopia	27 September	Fall of Lij Yasu
ε	Austria	21 October	Assn. of Count Stürgkh
1917 α	Costa Rica	27 January	Fall of González Flores
β	Russia	15 March	February revolution
γ	China	1 July	Rstn. of Ch'ing
δ	China	12 July	*Coup* of Tuan
ε	Russia	6 November	October revolution
ζ	Russia	20 November	Secession of Ukraine
η	Esthonia	28 November	Independence
θ	Portugal	5 December	Fall of Machado
ι	Finland	6 December	Independence

1918 α	Latvia	12 January	Independence
β	Russia	24 January	Secession of Bessarabia
γ	Russia	22 April	Secession of Transcaucasia
δ	Russia	26 May	Secession of Georgia
ε	Russia	26 May	Secession of Azerbaijan
ζ	Russia	28 May	Secession of Armenia
η	Lithuania	4 June	Independence
θ	Bulgaria	3 October	Fall of Tsar Ferdinand
ι	Czechoslovakia	21 October	Independence
κ	Fiume	24 October	Secession from Hungary
λ	Yugoslavia	29 October	Formation in Croatia
μ	Poland	3 November	Independence
ν	Germany	9 November	Republic
ξ	Austria	13 November	Republic
ο	Russia	15 November	Socialist *coup* in Ukraine
π	Hungary	16 November	Republic
ρ	Montenegro	26 November	Depn. of K. Nicholas
σ	Portugal	14 December	Assn. of Paes
1919 α	Afghanistan	19 February	Assn. of Habibullah
β	Hungary	22 March	Béla Kun
γ	Peru	4 July	Fall of Pardo
δ	Costa Rica	12 August	Fall of Tinoco
ε	Honduras	11 September	Fall of Bertrand
ζ	Fiume	12 September	Italian *coup*
η	Turkey	1 November	Nationalist revolt
1920 α	Guatemala	8 April	Fall of Estrada Cabrera
β	Mexico	21 May	Fall of Carranza
γ	Bolivia	11 July	Fall of Gutiérrez Guerra
δ	China	July	Fall of Tuan Chi-jui
ε	Poland	9 October	Vilna *coup*
1921 α	Outer Mongolia	19 February	Independence
β	Persia	21 February	*Coup* of Reza Khan
γ	Spain	8 March	Assn. of Dato
δ	Portugal	20 May	Dism. of Machado

1921 *(continued)*

ε	Outer Mongolia	6 July	Communist *coup*
ζ	Portugal	19 October	Assn. of Granjo
η	Paraguay	29 October	Fall of Gondra
θ	Japan	4 November	Assn. of Hara
ι	Guatemala	5 December	Fall of Herrera
κ	Ireland	6 December	Independence
1922 α	Fiume	3 March	Fall of Zanella
β	China	June	Fall of Hsu Shih-chang
γ	Ireland	22 August	Assn. of Collins
δ	Greece	27 September	Depn. of K. Constantine
ε	Italy	27 October	Mussolini March on Rome
ζ	Poland	16 December	Assn. of Narutowicz
1923 α	Lithuania	11 January	Memel revolt
β	Bulgaria	9 June	Fall of Stamboliiski
γ	China	11 June	Fall of Li Yuan-hung
δ	Spain	13 September	Primo de Rivera's *coup*
ε	Greece	18 December	Depn. of K. George
1924 α	Honduras	10 March	Fall and d. of Gutiérrez
β	Albania	10 June	Fall of Zogu and Shefket
γ	Chile	5 September	Fall of Alessandri
δ	Arabia	3 October	Fall of Hussein
ε	China	25 October	Fall of Ts'ao Kun
ζ	Albania	12 December	Fall of Fan Noli
1925 α	Chile	23 January	Recall of Alessandri
β	Greece	25 June	Pangalos *coup*
γ	Ecuador	9 July	Fall of Córdoba
δ	Bolivia	1 September	Fall of Villanueva
ε	Chile	1 October	Second fall of Alessandri
ζ	Nicaragua	25 October	Chamorro revolt
η	Persia	31 October	Elevn. of Reza Shah
1926 α	Greece	3 January	Fall of Kondouriotis
β	Arabia	8 January	Proc. of Ibn Saud
γ	Nicaragua	14 January	Chamorro President
δ	China	20 April	Fall of Tuan Chih-jui

		1926 (*continued*)		
	ε	Poland	14 May	Pilsudski revolt
	ζ	Portugal	28 May	Second fall of Machado
	η	Portugal	9 July	Fall of Gomes da Costa
	θ	Greece	22 August	Kondylis *coup*
	ι	Nicaragua	23 September	Sandino revolt armistice
	ϰ	Lithuania	17 December	Fall of Grinius
1927	α	Chile	6 May	Fall of Figueroa Larráin
1928	α	China	8 June	KMT to power
	β	Yugoslavia	20 June	Assn. of Radich
	γ	Albania	1 September	Zog king
1929	α	Yugoslavia	5 January	K. Alexander dict.
	β	Afghanistan	14 January	Fall of Amanullah
	γ	Afghanistan	17 January	*Coup* of Bacha-i-Saquao
	δ	Afghanistan	8 October	*Coup* of Mohd Nadir Shah
1930	α	Dominican Rep.	23 February	Fall of Vázquez
	β	Rumania	8 June	Depn. of Michael
	γ	Bolivia	28 June	Fall of Siles
	δ	Peru	25 August	Fall of Leguía
	ε	Argentina	6 September	Fall of Irigoyen
	ζ	Brazil	30 October	Fall of Prestes
	η	Japan	14 November	Assn. of Hamaguchi
	θ	Guatemala	16 December	Fall of Palma
1931	α	Panama	2 January	Fall of Arosemena
	β	Chile	26 July	Fall of Ibáñez
	γ	Ecuador	23 August	Fall of Ayora
	δ	Ecuador	15 October	Fall of Luis Alba
	ε	El Salvador	2 December	Hernández Martínez dict.
1932	α	France	6 May	Assn. of Doumer
	β	Japan	15 May	Assn. of Inukai
	γ	Chile	5 June	Fall of Montero
	δ	Chile	17 June	Dávila *coup*
	ε	Siam	24 June	Revolution of 2475
	ζ	Germany	20 July	v. Papen *coup* in Prussia

	1932 (*continued*)		
η	Chile	13 September	Fall of Dávila
θ	Chile	2 October	Fall of Blanché
1933 α	Germany	23 March	Hitler's Enabling Act
β	Uraguay	31 March	Terra *coup*
γ	Siam	3 April	Royal *coup*, fall of Pradit
δ	Peru	30 April	Assn. of Sánchez Cerro
ε	Siam	20 June	*Coup* of Phya Phahon Sena
ζ	Cuba	12 August	Fall of Machado
η	Cuba	5 September	Fall of Céspedes
θ	Afghanistan	8 November	Assn. of Mohd Nadir Shah
1934 α	Cuba	20 January	Fall of Grau
β	Austria	4 March	Dollfuss counterrevn.
γ	Esthonia	12 March	Paets *coup*
δ	Latvia	15 May	Ulmanis *coup*
ε	Bulgaria	19 May	Army *coup*
ζ	Austria	25 July	Assn. of Dollfuss
η	Yugoslavia	9 October	Assn. of K Alexander
θ	Russia	1 December	Assn. of Serge Kirov
ι	Bolivia	27 October	Fall of Salamanca
1935 α	Ecuador	20 August	Fall of Velasco Ibarra
β	Ecuador	26 September	Fall of Antonio Pons
γ	Greece	10 October	Restn. of K. George
1936 α	Paraguay	17 February	Fall of Ayala
β	Bolivia	17 May	Fall of Tejada Sórzano
γ	Nicaragua	12 June	Somoza revolt
δ	Spain	18 July	Fall of Casares Quiroga
ε	Spain	19 July	Fall of Martínez Barrio
ζ	Greece	4 August	Metaxas *coup*
η	Spain	4 September	Fall of Giral
θ	Iraq	29 October	*Coup* of Sidqi
ι	Peru	8 December	Benavides *coup*
κ	Cuba	23 December	Fall of Gómez
1937 α	Spain	16 May	Fall of Largo Caballero

1937 (*continued*)

β	Bolivia	14 July	Fall of Toro
γ	Iraq	11 August	Assn. of Sidqi
δ	Paraguay	15 August	Fall of Franco
ε	Ecuador	22 October	Fall of Paez
1938 α	Rumania	10 February	Royal *coup*
β	Austria	11 March	Fall of Schusschnigg
1939 α	Spain	28 February	Fall of Azaña
β	Spain	5 March	Casado *coup*
γ	Spain	28 March	Fall of Miaja
δ	Bolivia	24 April	Dict. of Busch
ε	Rumania	21 September	Assn. of Calinescu
1940 α	Paraguay	14 February	Presidential *coup*
β	France	10 July	Vichy govt. estd.
γ	Rumania	6 September	K. Carol deposed
1941 α	Yugoslavia	27 March	Regency overthrown
β	Syria	17 September	Independence
γ	Panama	9 October	Fall of Arnulfo Arias
δ	Lebanon	26 November	Independence
1942 α	Algeria	1 December	Darlan *coup*
β	Algeria	24 December	Assn. of Darlan
1943 α	Argentina	4 June	Fall of Castillo
β	Argentina	7 June	Fall of Rawson
γ	Italy	26 July	Fall of Mussolini
δ	Bolivia	19 December	Fall of Peñaranda
1944 α	Argentina	25 February	Fall of Ramírez
β	El Salvador	8 May	Fall of Hernández Martínez
γ	Ecuador	28 May	Fall of Arroyo del Río
δ	Guatemala	1 July	Fall of Ubico
ε	Bulgaria	9 September	Fatherland Front *coup*
ζ	El Salvador	21 October	Fall of Menéndez
η	Guatemala	22 October	Fall of Ponce
θ	Albania	28 November	Hoxha to power
1945 α	Egypt	24 February	Assn. of Ahmed Maher
β	Cambodia	15 August	Son *coup*
γ	Vietnam	26 August	Fall of Bao Dai

1945	*(continued)*			
δ	Argentina	12 October	Camp de Mayo rising
ε	Venezuela	19 October	Fall of Medina Angarita
ζ	Laos	27 October	Fall of Sisavang Vong
η	Yugoslavia	29 October	People's Republic
1946 α	Haiti	11 January	Fall of Lescot
β	Thailand	9 June	Assn. of K. Ananda
γ	Bolivia	21 July	Death of Villaroel
δ	Brazil	30 October	Fall of Vargas
ε	Indonesia	November	Linggadjati agrt.
1947 α	Nicaragua	25 May	Fall of Argüello
β	Hungary	31 May	Fall of Nagy
γ	Burma	19 July	Assn. of Excom. members
δ	Ecuador	23 August	Fall of Velasco Ibarra
ε	Ecuador	2 September	Fall of Mancheno
ζ	Thailand	9 November	Fall of Luang Dhamrong
η	Rumania	30 December	People's Republic
1948 α	Iraq	27 January	Fall of Sayed Saleh Jabr
β	Yemen	17 February	Assn. of Imam Yahya
γ	Czechoslovakia	25 February	Communist *coup*
δ	Costa Rica	20 April	Fall of Picado
ε	Israel	14 May	Independence
ζ	Paraguay	3 June	Fall of Moriñigo
η	Peru	29 October	Fall of Bustamante
θ	Venezuela	23 November	Fall of Gallegos
ι	El Salvador	14 December	Fall of Castañeda Castro
1949 α	El Salvador	6 January	Fall of de Cordoba
β	Paraguay	30 January	Fall of González
γ	Paraguay	26 February	Febrerista revolt
δ	Syria	30 March	Zaim's *coup*
ε	Syria	14 August	Fall of Zaim
ζ	China	1 October	People's Republic
η	Panama	20 November	Fall of Chanis
θ	Panama	24 November	Fall of Chairi
ι	Panama	24 November	Imposn. of Arias
κ	Syria	19 December	Shishakli *coup*

1950	α	Haiti	10 May	Fall of Estimé
	β	Nepal	7 November	Depn. of Tribhuvana
	γ	Venezuela	13 November	Assn. of Delgado Chalbaud
1951	α	Nepal	12 January	Restn. of Tribhuvana
	β	Persia	7 March	Assn. of Gen. Ali Razmara
	γ	Panama	10 May	Fall of Arias
	δ	Bolivia	16 May	Fall of Urralagoita
	ε	Jordan	20 July	Assn. of K. Abdullah
	ζ	Thailand	29 November	Military *coup*
	η	Syria	29 November	Shishakli *coup*
1952	α	Cuba	10 March	Fall of Prío Socarrás
	β	Bolivia	13 April	Fall of Ballivan junta
	γ	Egypt	26 July	Fall of K. Farouk
	δ	Venezuela	30 November	Pérez Jiménez dictator
1953	α	Russia	7 March	Beria *coup*
	β	Colombia	13 June	Fall of Laureano Gómez
	γ	Russia	10 July	Fall of Beria
	δ	Persia	19 August	Fall of Mossadegh
1954	α	Egypt	25 February	Depn. of Naguib
	β	Syria	25 February	Fall of Shishakli
	γ	Egypt	27 February	Restn. of Naguib
	δ	Egypt	17 April	Fall of Naguib
	ε	Paraguay	5 May	Fall of Chavez
	ζ	Guatemala	27 June	Fall of Arbenz
	η	Guatemala	29 June	Ousting of Díaz
	θ	Brazil	24 August	Depn. of Vargas
1955	α	Panama	2 January	Assn. of Remón
	β	Argentina	19 September	Fall of Perón
	γ	Vietnam South	26 October	Depn. of Bao Dai
	δ	Brazil	11 November	Fall of Coimbra da Luz
	ε	Argentina	13 November	Fall of Lonardi
	ζ	Brazil	22 November	Depn. of Café Filho
1956	α	Tunisia	20 March	Independence
	β	Nicaragua	29 September	Assn. of Somoza
	γ	Honduras	21 October	Fall of Lozano Díaz

1956	*(continued)*			
δ	Hungary	24 October	Hungarian uprising
ε	Haiti	12 December	Fall of Magloire
1957 α	Haiti	4 February	Fall of Pierre-Louis
β	Haiti	2 April	Fall of Sylvain
γ	Colombia	10 May	Fall of Rojas Pinilla
δ	Haiti	21 May	Dissn. of Exec. Council
ε	Haiti	14 June	Fall of Fignolé
ζ	Guatemala	26 July	Assn. of Castillo Armas
η	Thailand	17 September	Fall of Pibul Songgram
θ	Guatemala	24 October	Fall of González López
1958 α	Venezuela	23 January	Fall of Pérez Jiménez
β	Algeria	13 May	Massu *coup*
γ	France	31 May	Fall of IV Republic
δ	Iraq	14 July	Iraqui Revolution
ε	Pakistan	7 October	Abrogn. of constn.
ζ	Thailand	20 October	*Coup* of Sarit Thanarat
η	Sudan	17 November	Fall of Khalil Govt.
1959 α	Cuba	1 January	Fall of Batista
β	Cuba	17 July	Fall of Urrutia
γ	Laos	31 December	Phoumi Nosavan *coup*
1960 α	Korea South	27 April	Fall of Syngman Rhee
β	Turkey	27 May	Fall of Menderes govt.
γ	Congo (Leo.)	11 July	Secession of Katanga
δ	Laos	9 August	Kong Lae *coup*
ε	Cyprus	16 August	Independence
ζ	Jordan	29 August	Assn. of Hazza Majali
η	Congo (Leo.)	14 September	Mobutu *coup*
θ	El Salvador	26 October	Fall of Lemus
ι	Congo (Leo.)	13 November	Gizenga govt. estd.
κ	Laos	9 December	Fall of Souvanna Phouma

APPENDIX B

CHECK LIST OF TRANSITIONS SINCE 1961

1961	α	El Salvador	25 January	Fall of mil. junta
	β	Korea South	18 May	Pak *coup*
	γ	Dominican Rep.	30 May	Assn. of Trujillo
	δ	Syria	28 September	Secession from UAR
	ε	Ecuador	8 November	Fall of Velasco Ibarra
1962	α	Dominican Rep.	18 January	Fall of Balaguer
	β	Burma	2 March	Fall of U Nu
	γ	Algeria	18 March	Evian agreement
	δ	Syria	28 March	Fall of Dawalibi
	ε	Argentina	29 March	Fall of Frondizi
	ζ	Peru	18 July	Fall of Prado
	η	Yemen	27 September	Military *coup*
1963	α	Togo	13 January	Assn. of Olympio
	β	Iraq	8 February	Fall of Kassem
	γ	Peru	3 March	Fall of Pérez Godoy
	δ	Syria	8 March	Fall of Azem govt.
	ε	Guatemala	30 March	Fall of Ydígoras
	ζ	Ecuador	11 July	Fall of Arosemena
	η	Congo (Braz.)	15 August	Fall of Youlou
	θ	Dominican Rep.	25 September	Fall of Bosch
	ι	Honduras	3 October	Fall of Villeda Morales
	κ	Dahomey	28 October	Fall of Maga
	λ	Vietnam South	1 November	Fall of Diem
	μ	Iraq	18 November	Fall of Bakr
	ν	United States	22 November	Assn. of Kennedy
1964	α	Zanzibar	12 January	Fall of Sultan Seyid
	β	Vietnam South	30 January	Fall of Duong
	γ	Gabon	18 February	Fall of Mba
	δ	Brazil	2 April	Fall of Goulart
	ε	Laos	19 April	Mil. *coup* forces comp.
	ζ	Vietnam South	26 August	Fall of Khanh
	η	Arabia	2 November	Depn. of K. Saud

1964 *(continued*			
θ	Bolivia	4 November	Fall of Paz Estenssoro
ι	Sudan	15 November	Fall of Abboud
1965 α	Burundi	15 January	Assn. of Ngendandumwe
β	Persia	26 January	Assn. of Ali Mansur
γ	Vietnam South	27 January	Fall of Tran Van Huong
δ	Dominican Rep.	25 April	Fall of Reid Cabral
ε	Dominican Rep.	26 April	Est. of Wessin y Wessin
ζ	Algeria	19 June	Fall of Ben Bella
η	Rhodesia	11 November	Independence
θ	Congo (Leo.)	25 November	Depn. of Kasavubu
ι	Dahomey	27 November	Fall of Apithy
ϰ	Dahomey	22 December	Fall of Congacou
1966 α	Cent. Afr. Rep.	1 January	Fall of Dacko
β	Upper Volta	3 January	Fall of Yameogo
γ	Nigeria	15 January	Fall of Tafawa Balewa
δ	Uganda	22 February	Obote *coup*
ε	Syria	23 February	Fall of Bitar
ζ	Ghana	24 February	Fall of Nkrumah
η	Indonesia	11 March	Army control estb.
θ	Ecuador	29 March	Fall of junta
ι	Argentina	28 June	Depn. of Illía
ϰ	Burundi	8 July	Depn. of Mwambutsu IV
λ	Nigeria	29 July	Death of Ironsi
μ	China	31 July	Fall of Liu Shao-chi
ν	South Africa	6 September	Assn. of Verwoerd
ξ	Burundi	29 November	Fall of Ntare V
1967 α	Lesotho	5 January	Chief Jonathan *coup*
β	Togo	13 January	Fall of Grunitzky
γ	Sierra Leone	21 March	Army *coup*
δ	Ghana	17 April	Assn. of Kotoka
ε	Greece	21 April	Fall of Kanellopoulos
ζ	Biafra	May	Secession from Nigeria
η	Anguilla	16 June	Secession from St. Kitts
θ	Yemen	3 November	Fall of Sallal

1967 *(continued)*

ι	South Yemen	29 November	Independence
κ	Dahomey	17 December	Fall of Soglou
1968 α	Sierra Leone	18 April	Sergeant's *coup*
β	Iraq	17 July	Fall of Aref
γ	Congo (Braz.)	3 August	Army *coup*
δ	Congo (Braz.)	4 September	Fall of Massemba Débat
ε	Peru	3 October	Fall of Belaúnde
ζ	Panama	11 October	Fall of Arias
η	Mali	19 November	Fall of Keita
1969 α	Pakistan	24 March	Fall of Ayub Khan
β	Sudan	25 May	Fall of Mahgoub
γ	South Yemen	22 June	Fall of Shaabi
δ	Brazil	31 August	Repl. of Costa e Silva
ε	Libya	1 September	Depn. of King Idris
ζ	Bolivia	26 September	Fall of Siles Salinas
η	Somalia	15 October	Assn. of Shermarke
θ	Dahomey	10 December	Fall of Zinšou

TABLES

TABLE 1

Causes of Governmental Transition in Guatemala, 1839–1966

Cause	Occasions	Total
Natural death	1865, 1885, 1926	3
Resignation	1885, 1930, 1931*	3
Election	1871, 1873, 1885, 1891, 1931, 1944, 1945, 1951, 1966	9
Defenestration	1898, 1957	2
Golpe	1897, 1930, 1957, 1963	4
Cuartelazo	1920, 1920, 1944, 1944	4
Pronunciamiento	1871, 1954, 1954*	3
		28

* Under diplomatic pressure.

TABLE 2

Dates of Selected Political Events in Guatemala since 1944

Type	Successful*	Unsuccessful†
Defenestration	16 July 1957	
Golpe	24 October 1957	5 November 1950
	31 March 1963	25 November 1962
Cuartelazo	1 July 1944	18 July 1949
	20 October 1944	18 July 1950
		12 July 1952
		February 1953
		20 January 1955
Pronunciamiento	June 1954	6 August 1948
		31 November 1948
		January 1949
		29 March 1953
		13 November 1960
		6 February 1962‡

* Date of transition.
† Date of overt inception.
‡ In progress.

TABLE 3

Balance of Forces in Revolutionary Situations, 1954 to 1963

							Land

Year		Revolutionaries			Government		
	R	n	Rn^2	B	m	Bm^2	$Rn^2 - Bm^2$
1954	0·9	5,000	25m	1·0	7,000	49m	See Table 5 (p. 199)
1955	0·9	100	9,000	1·0	8,000	64m	−63,991,000
1957	1·0	1	1	0·2	1*	0·2	0·8
1960	1·0	30	900	1·0	8,000	64m	−63,999,100
1962	0·8	500	200t	1·0	8,000	64m	−63,800,000
1963	1·0	200†	40t	1·2	6	43·2	39,956·8

							Air
1954	0·8	2	3·2	1·0	20†	400	−396·8
1955		0	nil	1·0	20†	400	−400
1957		0	nil		0	nil	nil
1960		0	nil	1·0	20†	400	−400
1962	1·0	20†	400		0	nil	400
1963		0	nil		0	nil	nil

NOTE: In 1954 there was also present a hypothetical force of 5,000 civilians which when armed would at a value of 0·8 have represented 20m units.

* Or 2.   † Estimated.

TABLE 4
Guatemala: Balance of Forces, 1957 (Symbolic)

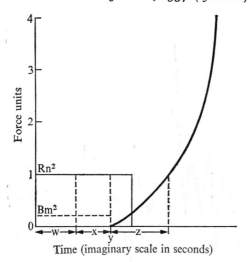

Time (imaginary scale in seconds)

TABLE 5
Guatemala: Balance of Forces, 1954

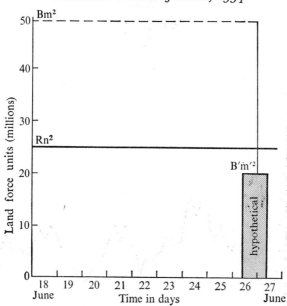

NOTE: This table represents gross values only. Since Rn^2 and Bm^2 were deployed over comparable areas, the hypothetical force in $B'm'^2$ the capital would locally have been superior to either.

TABLE 6
Annual Incidence of Revolution, 1901–60

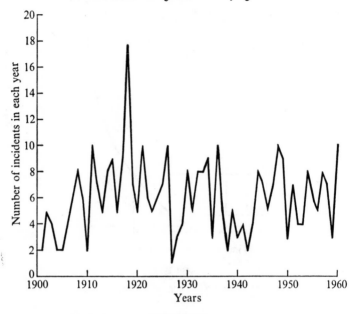

TABLE 7
Mean Incidence of Revolution, 1901–60

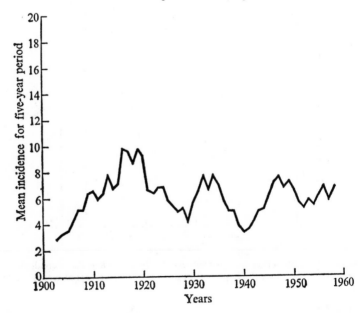

TABLE 8

*Annual Revolutionary Incidence by Number of Autonomous
States, 1901–60*

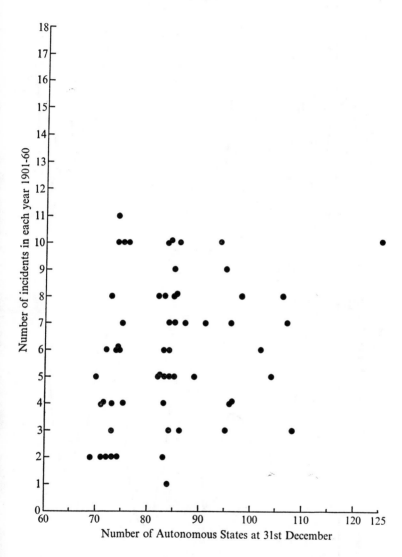

Tables

TABLE 9

Periodicity of Revolution by Years, 1901–60

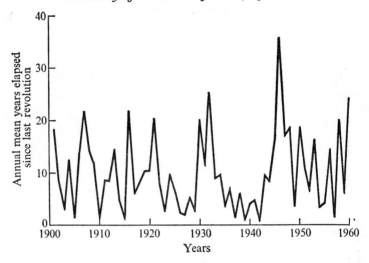

TABLE 10

Mean Periodicity of Revolution, 1901–60

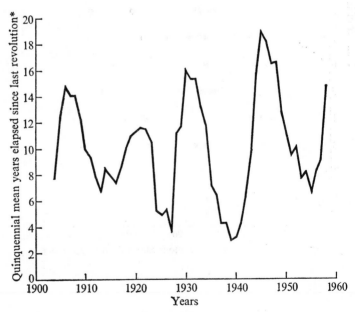

* NOTE: Vertical scale $2\frac{1}{2}$ × horizontal scale.

TABLE II

Incidence of Revolution by Quinquennium, 1901–60

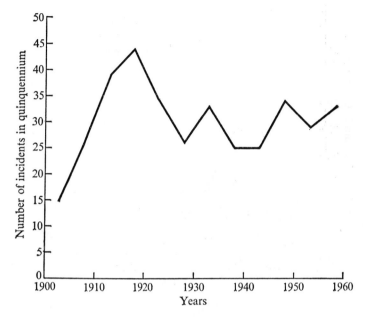

TABLE 12

Duration of Revolutions, 1901–60

N=363

Years	Under 1 day		1–30 days		1–12 months		Over 1 year		Uncertain		Total
		%		%		%		%		%	
1901–5	3	20	8	53	3	20	—	—	1	7	15
1906–10	6	23	10	38	6	23	3	12	1	4	26
1911–15	9	23	11	28	12	31	4	10	3	8	39
1916–20	7	16	15	35	18	41	3	7	2	2	44
1921–5	10	29	16	47	6	18	2	7	—	—	34
1926–30	3	12	12	46	6	23	3	12	2	8	26
1931–5	19	58	14	41	—	—	—	—	—	—	33
1936–40	14	56	7	28	2	8	2	8	—	—	25
1941–5	12	48	8	32	4	16	1	4	—	—	25
1946–50	18	53	10	29	3	9	3	9	—	—	34
1951–5	17	59	8	29	4	15	—	—	—	—	29
1956–60	15	45	14	42	1	3	3	10	—	—	33
ALL	133	37	133	37	65	17	24	7	8	2	363

TABLE 13
Personnel Composition of Revolutions, 1901–60

TABLE 14
Level of Revolutionary Action, 1901–60
$N=363$

Years	Execu-tive		Govern-ment		Capital		Province		Total
		%		%		%		%	
1901–5	3	20	3	20	2	13	7	47	15
1906–10	5	19	2	8	8	31	11	42	26
1911–15	13	33	3	8	4	10	19	49	39
1916–20	4	9	4	9	10	23	26	59	44
1921–5	12	35	8	24	3	9	11	33	34
1926–30	8	31	3	12	9	35	6	23	26
1931–5	12	36	9	27	7	11	5	15	33
1936–40	8	32	8	32	5	20	4	16	25
1941–5	7	28	7	28	6	24	5	20	25
1946–50	10	29	8	24	10	29	6	18	34
1951–5	10	34	6	21	9	31	4	15	29
1956–60	9	27	7	11	10	30	7	11	33
ALL	101	28	69	19	83	23	111	30	363

TABLE 15
Direction of Revolutionary Organization, 1901–60
$N=363$

Years	Individual		Junta		Party		Convention		Uncertain		Total
		%		%		%		%		%	
1901–5	6	40	4	27	4	27	0	—	1	7	15
1906–10	6	23	4	15	12	46	2	8	2	8	26
1911–15	19	49	7	19	6	15	2	5	5	13	39
1916–20	12	27	9	21	7	16	15	35	1	2	44
1921–5	16	47	12	32	4	12	1	3	1	3	34
1926–30	18	70	6	23	2	8	0	—	—	—	26
1931–5	13	39	13	39	5	15	2	6	—	—	33
1936–40	12	48	7	28	5	20	1	4	—	—	25
1941–5	9	36	10	40	3	12	3	12	—	—	25
1946–50	15	44	10	29	6	18	2	6	1	3	34
1951–5	9	31	16	56	3	10	1	3	—	—	29
1956–60	12	36	13	39	5	15	3	9	—	—	33
ALL	147	40	111	30	62	17	32	9	11	4	363

TABLE 16
Authority of Revolutionary Leaders, 1901–60
$N=363$

Years	Charismatic		Legal/Rational		Traditional		Unclassifiable		Total
		%		%		%		%	
1901–5	1	7	8	53	4	27	2	13	15
1906–10	5	19	13	50	3	12	5	19	26
1911–15	11	28	11	28	7	19	10	26	39
1916–20	6	14	29	66	5	11	4	9	44
1921–5	11	32	12	35	7	21	4	12	34
1926–30	11	42	10	38	4	15	1	4	26
1931–5	3	9	18	55	8	24	4	12	33
1936–40	6	24	7	28	10	40	2	8	25
1941–5	1	4	14	56	6	24	4	16	25
1946–50	3	9	15	44	10	29	4	18	34
1951–5	2	7	13	45	11	38	3	10	29
1956–60	1	3	20	61	9	27	3	9	33
ALL	61	17	170	47	84	23	48	13	363

TABLE 17

Succession Resulting from Revolutionary Transitions, 1901–60

N=363

Years	Auto-matic		Desig-nate		Interim		Conven-tion		Total
		%		%		%		%	
1901–5	4	27	7	47	3	20	1	7	15
1906–10	8	31	13	39	2	8	3	12	26
1911–15	12	31	10	26	13	33	4	10	39
1916–20	4	9	13	30	12	27	15	35	44
1921–5	10	29	14	41	8	24	2	6	34
1926–30	2	8	16	62	8	31	0	—	26
1931–5	11	33	11	33	10	30	1	3	33
1936–40	8	32	13	52	4	16	0	—	25
1941–5	6	24	11	44	6	24	2	8	25
1946–50	15	44	12	35	7	21	0	—	34
1951–5	5	17	17	59	7	24	0	—	29
1956–60	5	15	13	39	15	45	0	—	33
ALL	90	24	150	42	95	27	28	8	363

TABLE 18

Increase/decrease in participation following revolutions, 1901–60

N=363

Years	Increase		Decrease		No change detected		Total
		%		%		%	
1901–5	7	47	2	13	6	40	15
1906–10	10	38	5	19	11	42	26
1911–5	14	36	5	13	20	51	39
1916–20	28	64	5	11	11	25	44
1921–5	12	35	10	29	12	35	34
1926–30	8	31	7	27	11	42	26
1931–5	12	36	12	36	9	27	33
1936–40	5	20	12	48	8	32	25
1941–5	14	56	4	16	7	28	25
1946–50	10	29	8	24	16	47	34
1951–5	6	21	9	31	14	48	29
1956–60	13	39	4	12	16	48	33
ALL	139	38	83	23	141	39	363

TABLE 19

Extreme Types of Goals of Revolution, 1901–60

$N=363$

Years	Separatist	Official	All other	Total
1901–5	2	2	11	15
1906–10	2	6	18	26
1911–15	3	2	34	39
1916–20	18	1	25	44
1921–5	2	1	31	34
1926–30	0	4	22	26
1931–5	0	9	24	33
1936–40	0	5	20	25
1941–5	4	2	19	25
1946–50	2	3	29	34
1951–5	0	4	25	29
1956–60	3	1	29	33
ALL	36	40	287	363

TABLE 20

Relationships between Periodicity and Duration of Revolutions, 1901–60

$N=363$

Periodicity (Time since last revn.)	Duration of assault phase					Total
	Under 1 day	1–30 days	1–12 months	Over 1 year	Uncer-tain	
Under 1 year	37	36	27	4	1	105
1–3 years	26	22	16	8	2	74
3–10 years	28	35	11	3	3	80
10–30 years	24	28	7	4	2	65
Over 30 years	18	12	4	5	0	39
TOTALS	133	133	65	24	8	363

$$X^2 = 21.8 \qquad C = 0.24$$

TABLE 21

Relationships between Periodicity and Direction of Revolutions,
1901–60

$N = 363$

Periodicity (Time since last revn.)	Size of directorate					
	Individual	Junta	Party	Convention	Uncertain	Total
Under 1 year	43	30	15	13	4	105
1–3 years	31	23	13	4	3	74
3–10 years	37	25	10	6	2	80
10–30 years	18	26	13	7	1	65
Over 30 years	18	7	11	2	1	39
TOTALS	147	111	62	32	11	363

$$X^2 = 16{\cdot}9 \qquad C = 0{\cdot}21$$

TABLE 22

Relationships between Periodicity and Level of Revolutionary
Action, 1901–60

$N = 363$

Periodicity (Time since last revn.)	Level of revolutionary action				
	Executive	Government	Capital	Province	Total
Under 1 year	32	17	21	35	105
1–3 years	18	12	15	29	74
3–10 years	23	21	22	14	80
10–30 years	15	12	16	22	65
Over 30 years	13	6	9	11	39
TOTALS	101	68	83	111	363

$$X^2 = 13{\cdot}1 \qquad C = 0{\cdot}19$$

TABLE 23

Relationships between Periodicity and Strength of Revolutionary Forces, 1901–60

$N = 363$

Periodicity (Time since last revn.)	Strength of revolutionary forces						
	Individual	Detachment	Unit	Formation	Unknown	Uncertain	Total
Under 1 year	5	13	21	41	5	20	105
1–3 years	3	10	8	37	2	14	74
3–10 years	8	10	15	30	2	15	80
10–30 years	4	5	12	26	5	13	65
Over 30 years	9	5	2	15	2	6	39
TOTALS	29	43	58	149	16	68	363

$$X^2 = 26 \cdot 6 \qquad C = 0 \cdot 26$$

TABLE 24

Relationships between Duration and Personnel of Revolutions, 1901–60

$N = 363$

Duration	Personnel			
	Military	Civilian	Military/ Civilian	Total
Under 1 day	62	59	12	133
1–30 days	51	50	32	133
1–12 months	8	40	17	65
Over 1 year	—	16	8	24
Uncertain	2	5	1	8
TOTALS	123	170	70	363

$$X^2 = 45 \cdot 5 \qquad C = 0 \cdot 33$$

TABLE 25

Relationships between Duration and Direction of Revolutions, 1901–60

$$N = 363$$

Duration	Size of directorate					
	Individual	Junta	Party	Convention	Uncertain	Total
Under 1 day	65	50	12	4	2	133
1–30 days	49	46	19	15	4	133
1–12 months	21	11	19	10	4	65
Over 1 year	7	1	12	3	1	24
Uncertain	5	3	—	—	—	8
TOTALS	147	111	62	32	11	363

$$X^2 = 59 \cdot 5 \qquad C = 0 \cdot 38$$

TABLE 26

Relationships between Duration and Level of Revolutionary Action, 1901–60

$$N = 363$$

Duration	Level of revolutionary action				
	Executive	Government	Capital	Province	Total
Under 1 day	55	39	31	8	133
1–30 days	34	21	45	33	133
1–12 months	8	7	5	45	65
Over 1 year	1	—	1	22	24
Uncertain	3	1	1	3	8
TOTALS	101	68	83	111	363

$$X^2 = 141 \cdot 6 \qquad C = 0 \cdot 53$$

TABLE 27

Relationships between Duration of Revolution and Subsequent Variation in Participation, 1901–60

$N = 363$

Duration	Variation in participation			
	Increase	Decrease	No change detectable	Total
Under 1 day	29	38	66	133
1–30 days	56	34	43	133
1–12 months	36	8	21	65
Over 1 year	16	1	7	24
Uncertain	2	2	4	8
TOTALS	139	83	141	363

$$X^2 = 36.5 \qquad C = 0.30$$

TABLE 28

Relationships between Duration of Revolutions and Strength of Forces Deployed, 1901–60

$N = 363; \ n = 276$

Duration	Strength of revolutionary forces					
	Individual	Detachment	Unit	Formation	Uncertain	Total
Under 1 day	23	31	17	31	31	133
1–30 days	4	10	25	67	27	133
1–12 months	1	1	14	29	20	65
Over 1 year	1	—	1	21	1	24
Uncertain	—	1	1	1	5	8
TOTALS	29	43	58	149	84	363

$$X^2 = 74.4 \qquad C = 0.46$$

TABLE 29
Relationships between Duration and Magnitude of Revolutions, 1901–60

$N = 363; \; n = 187$

Duration	Magnitude (total casualties)					
	Below 3	4–31	32–316	Over 317	Uncer-tain	Total
Under 1 day	80	13	6	1	33	133
1–30 days	39	11	5	7	71	133
1–12 months	7	1	—	5	52	65
Over 1 year	3	—	—	9	12	24
Uncertain	2	—	—	—	6	8
TOTALS	131	25	11	22	174	363

$$X^2 = 69 \cdot 2 \qquad C = 0 \cdot 52$$

TABLE 30
Relationships between Duration of Revolution and Governmental Reaction, 1901–60

$N = 363; \; n = 202$

Duration	Reaction by government					
	Reform	Conces-sion	Co-op-tion	Suppres-sion	Residual	Total
Under 1 day	2	34	5	11	81	133
1–30 days	4	45	10	27	52	138
1–12 months	4	22	2	14	26	68
Over 1 year	3	11	3	5	5	28
Uncertain	—	4	—	—	4	8
TOTALS	13	116	20	57	168	374*

* Total exceeds N owing to overlapping.

$$X^2 = 8 \cdot 2 \qquad C = 0 \cdot 20$$

TABLE 31

Relationships between Personnel and Level of Revolutions,
1901–60

$$N = 363$$

Personnel	Level of revolutionary action				
	Executive	Govt.	Capital	Province	Total
Military	44	29	35	15	123
Civilian	49	27	30	64	170
Military/Civilian	8	12	18	32	70
TOTALS	101	68	83	111	363

$$X^2 = 37 \cdot 6 \qquad C = 0 \cdot 31$$

TABLE 32

Relationships between Personnel and Direction of Revolutions,
1901–60

$$N = 363; \; n = 352$$

Personnel	Size of directorate					
	Indivi-dual	Junta	Party	Conven-tion	Uncer-tain	Total
Military	51	62	7	1	2	123
Civilian	79	26	33	26	6	170
Military/Civilian	17	23	22	5	3	70
TOTALS	147	111	62	32	11	363

$$X^2 = 70 \cdot 3 \qquad C = 0 \cdot 41$$

TABLE 33

Relationships between Personnel of Revolutions and Type of Successor Government, 1901–60

$N = 363$

Personnel	Type of successor government				
	Automatic	Designate	Interim	Convention	Total
Military	26	49	44	4	123
1901–30	6	21	16	2	
1931–60	20	28	28	2	
Civilian	55	69	27	19	170
1901–30	29	34	17	19	
1931–60	26	35	10	—	
Military/Civilian	9	32	24	5	70
1901–30	5	18	13	4	
1931–60	4	14	11	1	
TOTALS	90	150	95	28	363

$$X^2 = 27 \cdot 8 \qquad C = 0 \cdot 27$$

TABLE 34

Relationships between Personnel of Revolutions and Attitude of Forces, 1901–60

$N = 363; \ n = 353$

Personnel	Attitude of forces					
	Aid Govt.	Divided	Aid Oppn.	Nonin-tervn.	Uncer-tain	Total
Military	5	28	91	—	—	123
Civilian	78	30	—	50	12	170
Military/Civilian	8	36	27	—	—	70
TOTALS	90	92	118	50	12	363

$$X^2 = 113 \cdot 7 \qquad C = 0 \cdot 49$$

TABLE 35

Relationships between Personnel of Revolutions and Subsequent Variation in Participation, 1901–60

$$N = 363$$

Personnel	Subsequent variation in participation			
	Increase	Decrease	No change detectable	Total
Military	43	38	42	123
Civilian	60	35	75	170
Military/Civilian	36	10	24	70
TOTALS	139	83	141	363

$$X^2 = 12\cdot3 \qquad C = 0\cdot18$$

TABLE 36

Relationship between Personnel of Revolutions and Governmental Reaction, 1901–60

$$N = 363; \ n = 206$$

Personnel	Governmental reaction					
	Reform	Concession	Co-option	Suppression	Residual	Total
Military	2	37	8	11	67	125
Civilian	7	55	7	23	85	177
Military/Civilian	4	24	5	23	16	72
TOTALS	13	116	20	57	168	373*

* Total exceeds N owing to overlapping.

$$X^2 = 10\cdot5 \qquad C = 0\cdot22$$

TABLE 37
*Relationship between Personnel and Magnitude of Revolutions,
1901–60*

$N = 363$

Personnel	Magnitude (total casualties)					
	Below 3	4–31	32–316	Over 317	Uncertain	Total
Military	62	9	5	2	45	123
Civilian	52	13	5	12	88	170
Military/Civilian	16	3	1	8	42	70
TOTALS	131	25	11	22	175	363

$$X^2 = 15 \cdot 2 \qquad C = 0 \cdot 27$$

TABLE 38
Personnel of Revolutions with Specialized Goals, 1901–60

$n = 76$

Personnel	Goals	
	Separatist	Centralist
Military	1	4
Civilian	26	33
Military/Civilian	9	3
TOTALS	36	40

$$X^2 = 5 \cdot 4 \qquad C = 0 \cdot 26$$

TABLE 39

Relationships between Direction and Level of Revolutionary Action,
1901–60

$$N = 363$$

Size of directorate	Level of revolutionary action				
	Execu-tive	Govern-ment	Capital	Province	Total
Individual	48	33	30	36	147
Junta	42	22	24	23	111
Party	6	10	15	31	62
Convention	3	2	11	16	32
Uncertain	2	1	3	5	11
Totals	101	68	83	111	363

$$X^2 = 39.8 \qquad C = 0.31$$

TABLE 40

Relationships between Level of Revolutionary Action and Type of
Successor Government, 1901–60

$$N = 363$$

Level of revolu-tionary action	Type of successor government				
	Auto-matic	Desig-nate	Interim	Conven-tion	Total
Executive	49	28	21	3	101
Government	10	36	19	3	68
Capital	14	42	25	2	83
Province	17	44	30	20	111
TOTALS	90	150	95	28	363

$$X^2 = 64.3 \qquad C = 0.39$$

TABLE 41

Relationships between Level of Revolutionary Action and Subsequent Variation in Participation, 1901–06

$N = 363$

Level of revolu- tionary action	Subsequent variation in participation			
	Increase	Decrease	No change detectable	Total
Executive	27	15	59	101
Government	14	34	20	68
Capital	35	24	24	83
Province	63	10	38	111
TOTALS	139	83	141	363

$$X^2 = 68·9 \qquad C = 0·40$$

TABLE 42

Relationships between Type of Succession and Authority of Leadership, 1901–60

$N = 363$

Type of succession	Authority of leadership				
	Charis- matic	Legal/ Rational	Tradi- tional	Unclassi- fiable	Total
Automatic	5	31	18	36	90
Designate	39	65	42	4	150
Interim	16	51	23	5	95
Convention	1	23	1	3	28
TOTALS	61	170	84	48	363

$$X^2 = 101·7 \qquad C = 0·47$$

TABLE 43

Relationships between Authority of Leadership and Variation in Participation, 1901–60

$N = 363$

Authority of leadership	Variation in participation			
	Increase	Decrease	No change detectable	Total
Charismatic	9	28	24	61
Legal/Rational	99	23	48	170
Traditional	19	28	37	84
Unclassifiable	12	4	32	48
TOTALS	139	83	141	363

$$X^2 = 78 \cdot 2 \qquad C = 0 \cdot 42$$

TABLE 44

Effects of External Aid on Duration of Revolutions, 1901–60

$N = 363$

Aid	Duration					
	Under 1 day	1–30 days	1–12 months	Over 1 year	Uncertain	Total
To government	3	6	6	8	1	24
To opposition	13	26	24	12	1	76
Neutral	112	103	34	9	6	264
TOTALS	128	135	64	29	8	364*

* Total exceeds N owing to overlapping.

$$X^2 = 7 \cdot 2 \qquad C = 0 \cdot 26$$

TABLE 45
Relationships of External Aid and Level of Revolutionary Action,
1901–60

$n = 100$

Aid	Level of revolutionary action				
	Execu-tive	Govern-ment	Capital	Province	Total
To government	2	3	4	15	24
To opposition	9	10	10	47	76
TOTALS	11	13	14	62	100

$X^2 = 0.4$ $\qquad$ $C = 0.06$

TABLE 46
Relationships of Social Initiatives to Duration of Revolutions,
1901–60

$N = 196; \; n = 193$

Social	Duration					
	Under 1 day	1–30 days	1–12 months	Over 1 year	Uncer-tain	Total
Internal	45	42	14	7	1	109
Internal and external	8	9	5	8	–	30
External	19	17	16	3	2	57
Totals	72	68	35	18	3	196

$X^2 = 19.3$ $\qquad$ $C = 0.30$

TABLE 47

Relationships of Social Initiatives to Level of Revolutionary Action,
1901–60

n = 196

Social initiatives	Level of revolutionary action				
	Executive	Govern-ment	Capital	Province	Total
Internal	21	26	31	31	109
Internal and external	4	9	7	10	30
External	7	8	13	29	57
TOTALS	32	44	51	69	196

$$X^2 = 9{\cdot}9 \qquad C = 0{\cdot}22$$

TABLE 48

Relationships of Social Initiatives to Personnel of Revolutions,
1901–60

n = 196

Social initiatives	Personnel			
	Military	Civilian	Military/Civilian	Total
Internal	44	40	25	109
Internal and external	8	14	8	30
External	11	32	14	57
TOTALS	63	86	47	196

$$X^2 = 8{\cdot}9 \qquad C = 0{\cdot}21$$

TABLE 49

Relationships of Type of Weaponry to Duration of Revolution,
1901–60

$n = 145$

Type of weaponry	Duration					
	Under 1 day	1–30 days	1–12 months	Over 1 year	Uncer-tain	Total
Primitive	5	18	4	4	—	31
Advanced	15	15	12	4	—	46
Implicit	23	27	11	4	3	68
TOTALS	43	60	27	12	3	145

$$X^2 = 8 \cdot 7 \qquad C = 0 \cdot 23$$

TABLE 50

Relationships of Type of Weaponry to Subsequent Variation in
Participation, 1901–60

$n = 145$

Type of weaponry	Subsequent variation in participation			
	Increase	Decrease	No change detectable	Total
Primitive	13	3	15	31
Advanced	23	11	12	46
Implicit	24	23	21	68
TOTALS	60	37	48	145

$$X^2 = 9 \cdot 3 \qquad C = 0 \cdot 25$$

BIBLIOGRAPHY

ADAMS, RICHARD N., 'Power and power domains', *América Latina*, IX, No. 2 (April–June 1966).

ADAMS, RICHARD N., 'Social change in Guatemala and US policy', in Council on Foreign Relations, *Social change in Latin America today, its implications for United States policy* (New York, 1960).

ADORNO, T. W., FRENKEL-BRUNSWIK, ELSE, LEVINSON, DANIEL J., and SANFORD, R. NEVITT, *The authoritarian personality*, 2 vols. (John Wiley & Sons, New York, 1964).

AFRIFA, Colonel A. A., *The Ghana coup 24th February 1966* (Frank Cass, London, 1966).

ALEXANDER, ROBERT J., *The Bolivian national revolution* (Rutgers University Press, New Brunswick, 1958).

ALEXANDER, ROBERT J., *The Venezuelan democratic revolution: a profile of the regime of Rómulo Betancourt* (Rutgers University Press, New Brunswick, 1964).

ALMOND, GABRIEL A., and COLEMAN, JAMES S., eds., *The politics of the developing areas* (Princeton University Press, Princeton, 1960).

ANDERSON, INGVAR, *A history of Sweden* (Weidenfeld & Nicolson, London, 1956).

ANDRZEJEWSKI, STANISLAW, *Military organisation and society* (Routledge, London, 1954).

ARDREY, ROBERT, *The territorial imperative* (Collins, London, 1967).

ARENDT, HANNAH, *On revolution* (Faber & Faber, London, 1963).

ARENDT, HANNAH, *The origins of totalitarianism*, 2nd enlarged ed. (Allen & Unwin, London. 1958).

ARÉVALO, JUAN JOSÉ, *Discursos en la Presidencia* (Guatemala, 1948).

ARISTOTLE's *Politics*, trs. Benjamin Jowett, intro. H. W. C. Davis (Clarendon Press, Oxford, 1931).

BELL, HERBERT C. F., *Lord Palmerston*, 2 vols. (Longmans, London, 1936).

BELLO, JOSÉ MARÍA, *A history of modern Brazil, 1889–1964* (Stanford University Press, Stanford, 1966).

BENNETT, RICHARD, *The Black and Tans* (Four Square, London, 1964).

BEQIRAJ, MEHMET, *Peasantry in revolution* (Cornell University Center for International Studies, Ithaca, 1966).

BIRCH, J. H. S., *Denmark in history* (John Murray, London, 1938).

Jane's fighting ships BLACKMAN, RAYMOND V. B., comp. and ed. (Sampson Low, Marston & Co., London, 1964).

BLAKEMORE, HAROLD, 'Chilean revolutionary agents in Europe, 1891', *Pacific historical review*, XXXIII, no. 4 (Nov. 1964), 425.

BLAKEMORE, HAROLD, 'The Chilean revolution of 1891 and its historiography', *Hispanic American historical review*, XLV, no. 2 (Aug. 1965), 393.

BLANCO MOHENO, Robert, *Crónica de la Revolución Mexicana*, 3 vols. (Libro-Mex Editores, Mexico, 1965).

BLANKENSTEN, GEORGE I., *Ecuador, constitutions and caudillos* (Russell & Russell, New York, 1964).

BRENAN, GERALD, *The Spanish labyrinth, an account of the social and political background of the Spanish Civil War* (C.U.P., Cambridge, 1962).

Jane's all the world's aircraft, BRIDGMAN, LEONARD, comp. and ed. (Sampson Low, Marston & Co., London, 1947) and later issues.

BROGAN, DENIS W., *The price of revolution* (Hamish Hamilton, London, 1951).

BROMBERGER, MERRY and SERGE, *Les 13 Complots du 13 Mai* (Libraire Arthème Fayard, Paris, 1959).

BUCHAN, JOHN, *Oliver Cromwell* (Hodder & Stoughton, London, 1950).

BUCHANAN, JAMES McGILL, and TULLOCK, GORDON, *The calculus of consent: logical foundations of constitutional democracy* (University of Michigan Press, Ann Arbor, 1962).

BURKE, EDMUND, *Reflections on the revolution in France* (etc.) (W. Watson and others, Dublin, 1790).

CALVERT, PETER, 'The Mexican political system: a case-study in political development', *Journal of development studies*, IV, no. 4 (July 1968), 464.

CALVERT, PETER, *The Mexican Revolution, 1910–1914; the diplomacy of Anglo-American conflict* (C.U.P., Cambridge, 1968).

CALVERT, PETER, 'Revolution: the politics of violence'. *Political studies*, XV, no. 1 (Feb. 1967), 1

CALVERT PETER and SIMPSON, JOHN, 'Attributes of revolution'. Unpublished paper presented to International Sociological Association, Working Group on Armed Forces and Society, Conference of 'Militarism and the Professional Military Man', London, 14–16 Sept. 1967.

CARDOZA Y ARAGÓN, LUIS, *La Revolución Guatemalteca* (Ediciones Cuadernos Americanos, Mexico, 1955, no. 43).

CARDOZO, EFRAIM, *Paraguay Independiente* (Salvat Editores, Barcelona, 1949).

CAREY, JAMES C., *Peru and the United States, 1900–1962* (University of Notre Dame Press, Notre Dame, Ind., 1964),

CARTER, GWENDOLEN M., *The politics of inequality, South Africa since 1948*, 2nd edn. (Thames & Hudson, London, 1958).

CAULFIELD, MAX, *The Easter Rebellion* (Four Square, London, 1965).

CHAKOTIN, SERGE, *The Rape of the masses, the psychology of totalitarian political propaganda* (Routledge, London, 1940).

CHEKREZI, CONSTANTINE A., *Albania past and present* (Macmillan, New York, 1919).

CHORLEY, KATHERINE C., *Armies and the art of revolution* (Faber & Faber, London, 1943).

CHULA CHAKRABONGSE of Thailand, H.R.H. Prince, *Lords of life; the paternal monarchy of Bangkok, 1782–1932, with the earlier and more recent history of Thailand* (Alvin Redman, London, 1960).

COAST, JOHN, *Some aspects of Siamese politics* (International Secretariat Institute of Pacific Relations, New York, 1953, mimeographed).

COMMAGER, HENRY STEELE, ed., *Documents of American history*, 6th edn. (Appleton-Century-Crofts, New York, 1958).

COPER, RUDOLF, *Failure of a revolution; Germany in 1918–1919* (C.U.P., Cambridge, 1955).

CUNLIFFE, MARCUS, *George Washington, man and moment* (Collins, London, 1959).

DAHL, ROBERT A., *Modern political analysis* (Prentice-Hall, Englewood Cliffs, N.J., 1964).

DAHRENDORF, RALF, 'Über einige Probleme der sociologistischen Theorie der Revolution', *Archives Européenes de Sociologie*, II, no. 1 (1961), 153.

DANG XUAN KHU ('Truong Chinh'), *Primer for revolt, the Communist takeover in Viet-Nam: A facsimile edition of the August Revolution and the resistance will win*, Intro. and notes by Bernard B. Fall (Praeger, New York, 1963).

DANIELS, ROBERT VINCENT, *The conscience of the revolution, Communist opposition in Soviet Russia* (Harvard University Press, Cambridge, Mass., 1960).

DAVIES, JAMES C., 'Toward a theory of revolution', *American sociological review*, XLIII, no. 1 (Feb. 1962), 5.

DEBRAY, RÉGIS, 'Latin America: the long march', *New Left review*, 33 (Sept.–Oct. 1965), 17–58.

DEBRAY, RÉGIS, *Revolución en la Revolución?* (Casa de las Américas, Havana, 1967).

DEUTSCHER, ISAAC, *Stalin, a political biography*, revsd. edn. (Penguin Books, London, 1966).

DOWNS, ANTHONY, *An economic theory of democracy* (Harper, New York, 1957).

DROMUNDO, BALTASAR, *Emiliano Zapata* (Imprenta Mundial, Mexico, 1934).

DUNN, H. H., *The crimson jester, Zapata of Mexico* (George C. Harrap, London, 1934).

DUTT, R. PALME, *Fascism and social revolution; a study of the economics and politics of the extreme stages of capitalism in decay*, revsd. edn. (International Publishers, New York, 1935). ..

DUVERGER, MAURICE, *Political parties, their organisation and activity in the modern state* (Methuen, London, 1964).

EASTON, DAVID, 'An approach to the analysis of political systems,' *World politics*, IX, no. 3 (Apr. 1957), 383.

EASTON, DAVID, *A systems analysis of political life* (John Wiley & Sons, New York, 1965).

EASTON, DAVID, *The political system; an inquiry into the state of political science* (Knopf, New York, 1953).

EBEL, ROLAND H., 'Political change in Guatemalan Indian communities', *Journal of Inter-American studies*, VI, no. 1 (Jan. 1964), pp. 91 ff.

ECKSTEIN, HARRY HORACE AND APTER, DAVID ERNEST, eds., *Comparative politics, a reader* (Free Press, New York, 1963).

EDWARDS, LYFORD PATERSON, *The Natural History of Revolution* (Russell & Russell, New York, 1965).

ENOS, JOHN L., *An analytic model of political allegiance and its application to the Cuban Revolution* (The Rand Corporation, Santa Monica, Calif., Aug. 1965).

ETZIONI, AMITAI, *Political unification, a comparative study of leaders and forces* (Holt, Rinehart & Winston, New York, 1965).

EYSENCK, HANS JÜRGEN, *The psychology of politics* (Routledge & Kegan Paul, London, 1954).

FAINSOD, MERLE, *How Russia is ruled* (Harvard University Press, Cambridge, Mass.; London, 1963).

FALL, BERNARD B., ed., *Ho Chi Minh on revolution: selected writings 1920–66* (Pall Mall, London, 1967).

FARMER, PAUL, *Vichy, political dilemma* (O.U.P., London, 1955).

FERGUSON, J. HALCRO, *The revolutions of Latin America*, The Great Revolutions (Thames & Hudson, London, 1963).

FINER, SAMUEL E., *The man on horseback* (London, Pall Mall, 1962).

FIRTH, Sir CHARLES, *Oliver Cromwell and the rule of the Puritans in England* (O.U.P., London, 1961).

FORTES, MEYER and EVANS-PRITCHARD, E. E., *African political systems* (O.U.P., London, 1963).

FRIAS VALENZUELA, FRANCISCO, *Manual de historia de Chile*, 6th edn. Santiago (Editorial Nascimento, Santiago, 1963).

FROMM, ERICH, *The fear of freedom* (Routledge, London, 1960).

FULLER, J. F. C., *Armament and history* (Eyre & Spottiswoode, London, 1946).

GABRIELI, FRANCESCO, *The Arab revival*, The Great Revolutions (Thames & Hudson, London, 1961).

GALICH, MANUEL, *Por Qué lucha Guatemala; Arévalo y Arbenz: Dos hombres contra un imperio* (Elmer Editor, Buenos Aires, 1956).

GOLDENBERG, BORIS, *The Cuban Revolution and Latin America* (Allen & Unwin, London, 1965).

GOODSPEED, D. J., *The Conspirators, a study of the coup d'état* (Macmillan, London, 1962).

GOTTSCHALK, LOUIS, 'Leon Trotsky and the natural history of revolutions', *The American journal of sociology*, XLIV, no. 3 (Nov. 1938).

GROSS, FELIKS, *The seizure of political power in a century of revolutions* (Philosophical Library, New York, 1958).

GURR, TED, *New error-compensated measures for comparing nations: some correlates of civil violence*, Center of International Studies, Woodrow Wilson School of Public and International Affairs, Princeton University, Research Monograph No. 25 (Princeton, 1966).

GUTTERIDGE, WILLIAM, *Armed forces in new states* (O.U.P., London, 1962).

HABIBULLAH, AMIR (Bacha i Saquao), *From Brigand to King* (Sampson Low, Marston & Co., London, n.d.).

HADDAD, GEORGE M., *Revolutions and military rule in the Middle East: the northern tier* (Robert Speller, New York, 1965).

HALL, D. G. E., *A history of South East Asia*, 2nd edn. (Macmillan, London, 1964).

HIBBERT, CHRISTOPHER, *King Mob: the story of Lord George Gordon and the London riots of 1780* (Longmans Green, London, 1958).

HOWARD, MICHAEL, ed., *Soldiers and governments. Nine studies in civil-military relations* (Eyre & Spottiswoode, London, 1957).

HOWARTH, DAVID, *The Desert King, a life of Ibn Saud* (Collins, London, 1964).

HUNTINGTON, SAMUEL P., *The soldier and the state; the theory and politics of civil-military relations* (Harvard University Press, Cambridge, Mass., 1957).

HYMAN, HERBERT HIRAM, *Political socialisation, a study in the psychology of political behaviour* (The Free Press, Glencoe, Ill., 1959).

INMAN, SAMUEL GUY, *A new day in Guatemala, a study of the present social revolution* (Worldover Press, Wilton, Conn., 1951).

International handbook of universities and other institutions of higher education, 1965 (International Association of Universities, Paris, 1965).

IONESCU, GHIŢA, *The break-up of the Soviet Empire in Eastern Europe* (Penguin Books, London, 1965).

JAMES, DANIEL, *Red design for the Americas: Guatemalan prelude* (The John Day Company, New York, 1954).

JANOS, ANDREW C., 'The Communist theory of the state and revolution', in Cyril E. Black and Thomas P. Thornton, eds., *Communism and revolution, the strategic uses of political violence* (Princeton University Press, Princeton, 1964), p. 34.

JANOS, ANDREW C., *The Seizure of power: a study of force and popular consent*, Research Monograph, no. 16 (Center of International Studies, Princeton, 1964).

JOHNSON, CHALMERS, *Revolution and the social system*, Hoover Institution Studies, 3 (The Hoover Institution on War, Revolution and Peace, Stanford University, Stanford, 1964).

JOHNSON, JOHN J., *The military and society in Latin America* (Stanford University Press, Stanford, 1964).

JOHNSON, JOHN J., editor, *The role of the military in underdeveloped countries* (Princeton University Press, Princeton, 1962).

JONES, CHESTER LLOYD, *Guatemala, past and present* (University of Minnesota Press, Minneapolis, 1940).

KAHIN, GEORGE McTURNAN, editor, *Governments and politics of Southeast Asia*, 2nd edn. (Cornell University Press, Ithaca, N.Y., 1964).

KANTOR, HARRY, *Ideology and program of the Peruvian Aprista Movement* (University of California Press, Los Angeles, 1953).

KAPLAN, MORTON A., *System and process in international politics* (John Wiley, New York, 1967).

KELSEY, VERA, and OSBORNE, LILY DE JONGH, *Four keys to Guatemala*, 5th printing, revsd. (Funk & Wagnalls Company, New York, 1946).

KHADDURI, MAJID, *Independent Iraq, 1932–1958*, 2nd edn. (O.U.P., London, 1960).

KORNHAUSER, WILLIAM, 'Revolution and national development', unpublished paper delivered at World Congress of Sociology, Evian, 1966.

LA CHARITÉ, NORMAN A., KENNEDY, RICHARD O., and THIEUL, PHILIP M., *Case study in insurgency and revolutionary warfare: Guatemala 1944–1954* (Special Operations Research Office, The American University, Washington D.C., Nov. 1964).

LANCHESTER, FREDERICK W., *Aircraft in warfare, the dawn of the fourth arm* (Constable, London, 1916).

LANE, MARK, *Rush to judgement: a critique of the Warren Commission's inquiry into the murders of President John F. Kennedy, Officer J. D. Tippit, and Lee Harvey Oswald* (Penguin Books, London, 1966), revsd. edn. with additional material.

LASSWELL, HAROLD D., *The future of political science* (Atherton Press, New York; Prentice-Hall, London, 1963).

LASSWELL, HAROLD D., and LERNER, DANIEL, editors, *World revolutionary elites: studies in coercive ideological movements* (The M.I.T. Press, Cambridge, Mass., 1966).

LEDERER, IVO J., *Yugoslavia at the Paris Peace Conference: a study in frontier making* (Yale University Press, New Haven and London, 1963).

LENIN, VLADIMIR ILYICH, *Selected works*, 2 vols. (Foreign Languages Publishing House, Moscow, 1947; Lawrence & Wishart, London, 1947).

LEONHARD, WOLFGANG, *The Kremlin since Stalin* (O.U.P., London, 1962).

LEWIS, ANTHONY, and *The New York Times*, *Portrait of a decade; the second American Revolution* (Bantam Books, New York, 1965).

LI CHIEN-NUNG, *The political history of China, 1840–1928*, trs. and ed., Ssu-yu Teng and Jeremy Ingalls (Van Nostrand, Princeton, N.J., 1965).

LIEUWEN, EDWIN A., *Arms and politics in Latin America* (Praeger, London, 1963).

LIEUWEN, EDWIN, *Generals versus Presidents, neomilitarism in Latin America* (Pall Mall, London, 1964).

LIMA, OLIVEIRA, *O Movimento da Independência, O Império Brasileiro (1821–1889)*, 2nd edn. (Edições Melhoramentos, São Paulo, 1928).

LIPSET, SEYMOUR MARTIN, *Political man* (Mercury Books, London, 1964).

LIVERMORE, H. V., *A new history of Portugal* (C.U.P., Cambridge, 1966).

LÓPEZ-FRESQUET, RUFO, *My fourteen months with Castro* (World Publishing Co., Cleveland and New York, 1966).

LORENZ, KONRAD, *On aggression* (Methuen, London, 1966).

MACHIAVELLI, NICCOLÒ, *The Prince* and *The discourses* (Random House, New York, 1950).

MACK SMITH, DENIS, *Italy, a modern history* (University of Michigan Press, Ann Arbor, 1959).

MAIR, LUCY, *Primitive government* (Penguin Books, London, 1962).

MALAPARTE, CURZIO, *Coup d'état, the technique of revolution*, trs. Sylvia Saunders (E. P. Dutton & Co., New York, 1932).

MANSFIELD, PETER, *Nasser's Egypt*, Penguin African Library (Penguin Books, London, 1965).

MAO TSE-TUNG and (ERNESTO) CHE GUEVARA, *Guerrilla warfare* (Cassell, London, 1964).

MARTZ, JOHN D., *Colombia, a contemporary political survey* (University of North Carolina Press, Chapel Hill, 1964).

MARTZ, JOHN D., 'Guatemala, the search for political identity', in Martin C. Needler, editor, *Political systems of Latin America* (Van Nostrand, Princeton, N.J., 1964).

MARTZ, JOHN D., *Central America, the crisis and the challenge* (University of North Carolina Press, Chapel Hill, 1959).

MARX, KARL, and ENGELS, FRIEDRICH, *Selected works*, 2 vols. (Foreign Languages Publishing House, Moscow, 1962).

MAUDE, Colonel FREDERIC NATUSCH, 'Strategy', *Encyclopaedia Britannica*, 13th edn.

MEADOWS, PAUL, 'Sequence in revolution', *American sociological review*, VI, no. 5 (Oct. 1941), 702.

MEISEL, ALFRED, 'Revolution and counter-revolution', in *Encyclopedia of the social sciences* (1934).

MEISEL, JAMES H., *Military revolt in France, the fall of the Republic* (University of Michigan Press, Ann Arbor, 1962).

MENDE, TIBOR, *China and her shadow* (Thames & Hudson, London, 1961).

MENDE, TIBOR, *The Chinese Revolution* (Thames & Hudson, London, 1961) (*The Great Revolutions*).

MERRIAM, CHARLES E., *Political power* (Collier Books, New York, 1964).

MILLER, WILLIAM, *Greece* (Ernest Benn, London, 1928).

MODELSKI, GEORGE, 'The international relations of internal war', in *International aspects of civil strife*, ed. James N. Rosenau (Princeton, University Press, Princeton, N.J., 1964).

MONTEFORTE TOLEDO, MARIO, *Guatemala, monografía sociólogica*, 2nd edn. (Instituto de Investigaciones Sociales, UNAM, Maxico, 1965).

MORÓN, GUILLERMO, *A history of Venezuela*, trs. John Street (Allen & Unwin, London, 1964).

MORRIS, DESMOND, *The naked ape* (Transworld Publishers, London, 1968).

MUNRO, DANA GARDNER, *Intervention and dollar diplomacy in the, Caribbean 1900–1921* (Princeton University Press, Princeton, 1964).

NEEDLER, MARTIN C., 'Political development and military intervention in Latin America', *American political science review*, LX, no. 3 (Sept. 1966), p. 616.

NAGUIB, MUHAMMAD, *Egypt's destiny* (Doubleday, Garden City, N.Y., 1955).

NEUMANN, SIGMUND, 'The international civil war', *World politics*, I (1949), p. 341.

NEUMANN, SIGMUND, *Permanent revolution: totalitarianism in the age of international civil war* (Pall Mall, London, 1965).

NEW YORK TIMES, The, *Report of the Warren Commission on the assassination of President Kennedy*, intro. Harrison E. Salisbury (Bantam Books, New York, 1964).

NUNN, FREDERICK M., 'Military rule in Chile. The revolutions of September 5, 1924, and January 23, 1925', *Hispanic American historical review*, XLVII (Feb. 1967), no. 1, 1.

NUTTING, ANTHONY, *The Arabs, a narrative history from Mohammed to the present* (Hollis & Carter, London, 1964).

O'CONNOR, FRANK, *The big fellow; Michael Collins and the Irish Revolution*, revsd. edn. (Clonmore & Reynolds, Dublin, 1965).

ORTEGA Y GASSET, JOSÉ, *La rebelión de las masas*, 36th edn. in Spanish (Revista del Occidente, Madrid, 1962).

OSGOOD, CHARLES E., SUCI, GEORGE J., and TANNENBAUM, PERCY H., *The measurement of meaning* (University of Illinois Press, Urbana, 1957).

OTTO OF AUSTRIA, *Monarchy in the atomic age* (Monarchist Press Association, London, 1960).

PARET, PETER and SHY, JOHN W., *Guerrillas in the 1960s*, revsd. edn. (Praeger, New York, 1962).

PARKER, FRANKLIN D., *The Central American republics* (O.U.P., London, 1964).

PARSONS, TALCOTT and SHILS, EDWARD A., eds., *Toward a general theory of action* (Harper, New York, 1962).

PENDLE, GEORGE, *Argentina* (O.U.P., London, 1961).

PETTEE, GEORGE SAWYER, *The Process of Revolution* (Harper, New York, 1938).

PIVEL DEVOTO, J. E., *Uruguay Independiente* (Salvat Editores, Barcelona, 1949).

POWELL, JOHN DUNCAN, 'Military assistance and militarism in Latin America', *Western political quarterly*, XVIII, no. 2, pt. 1 (June 1965), pp. 382 ff.

PURCELL, VICTOR, *The Revolution in South-east Asia*, The Great Revolutions (Thames & Hudson, London, 1962).

PUSTAY, JOHN S., *Counterinsurgency warfare* (Free Press, New York; Collier-Macmillan, London, 1965).

QUIRK, ROBERT E., *An affair of honor* (McGraw Hill, New York, 1964).

QUIRK, ROBERT E., *The Mexican Revolution, 1914–1915: the convention of Aguascalientes* (Indiana University Press, Bloomington, 1960).

RAPOPORT, ANATOL, *Fights, games and debates* (University of Michigan Press, Ann Arbor, 1960).

RAPOPORT, DAVID C., 'Coup d'état: the view of the men firing pistols', *Nomos VIII: Revolution*, ed. Carl J. Friedrich (Atherton Press, New York, 1966).

RICHARDSON, LEWIS F., *Statistics of deadly quarrels* (Stevens and Sons, London, 1960).

RICHTER, MELVIN, 'Tocqueville's contribution to the theory of

232 *Bibliography*

revolution', *Nomos VIII : Revolution*, ed. Carl J. Friedrich (Atherton Press, New York, 1966).

RIGGS, FRED W., *Thailand: the modernization of a bureaucratic polity* (East-West Center Press, Honolulu, 1966).

RIKER, WILLIAM H., *The theory of political coalitions* (Yale University Press, New Haven & London, 1962).

ROBERTSON, PRISCILLA, *Revolutions of 1848, a social history* (Harper, New York, 1960).

ROBINSON, VANDELEUR, *Albania's road to freedom* (Allen & Unwin, London, 1941).

ROSENAU, JAMES N., 'Internal war as an international event', in James N. Rosenau, ed., *International aspects of civil strife* (Princeton University Press, Princeton, 1964).

ROSENTHAL, MARIO, *Guatemala, the story of an emergent Latin–American democracy* (Twayne, New York, 1962).

ROSS, STANLEY ROBERT, *Francisco I. Madero, Apostol de la democracia mexicana* (Biografias Gandesas, Mexico, 1959).

RUDÉ, GEORGE, *The crowd in history; a study of popular disturbances in France and England, 1730–1848*, New Dimensions in History (John Wiley & Sons, New York, 1964).

RUSSETT, BRUCE M., *World handbook of political and social indicators* (Yale University Press, New Haven, 1964).

SCHEER, ROBERT and ZEITLIN, MAURICE, *Cuba, an American tragedy*, revsd. edn. (Penguin Books, London, 1964).

SCHNEIDER, RONALD M., *Communism in Guatemala 1944–1954* (Praeger, New York, 1959).

SCHRAM, STUART R., *The political thought of Mao Tse-tung* (Praeger, New York, 1963).

SCHWARZENBERGER, GEORG, *A manual of international law*, 4th edn. (Stevens & Sons, London, 1960).

SHAPLEN, ROBERT, *The lost revolution: Vietnam 1954–1965* (André Deutsch, London, 1966).

SHARABI, HISHAM B., *Nationalism and revolution in the Arab world* (Van Nostrand, Princeton, N.J., 1966).

SHORT, ANTHONY, 'Communism and the Emergency', in Wang Gung-wu, ed., *Malaysia* (Pall Mall, London, 1964).

SHUB, DAVID, *Lenin: a biography*, revsd. edn. (Penguin Books, London, 1966).

SILVERT, KALMAN H., *A study in government: Guatemala* (Middle American Research Institute, Tulane University, Publication 21, New Orleans, 1954).

SMELSER, NEIL J., *Theory of collective behavior* (Routledge & Kegan Paul, London, 1962).

SOREL, GEORGES, *Reflections on violence*, trs. T. E. Hulme & J. Roth, ed. and intro. Edward A. Shils (The Free Press, Glencoe, Ill., 1950).

SORENSON, THEODORE C., *Kennedy* (Hodder & Stoughton, London, 1965).

SOROKIN, PITRIM ALEKSANDROVITCH, *Social and cultural dynamics*, III: *Fluctuation of social relationships, war, and revolution* (American Book Company, New York, 1937).

SOROKIN, PITRIM ALEKSANDROVITCH, *Sociological theories of today* (Harper, New York and London, 1967).

SOROKIN, PITRIM ALEKSANDROVITCH, *The sociology of revolution* (Lippincott, Philadelphia, 1925).

SOUTHALL, AIDAN, 'A critique of the typology of states and political systems', in *Political systems and the distribution of power*, A.S.A. Monographs, 1 (Tavistock Press, London, 1965).

Statesman's Year-Book, 1965–66, The (Macmillan, London, 1965).

STOKES, WILLIAM S., *Latin American politics* (Thomas Y. Crowell, New York, 1959).

STONE, LAWRENCE, 'Theories of revolution', *World politics*, XVIII, no. 2 (Jan. 1966), 159.

SZAMUELY, TIBOR, 'The prophet of the utterly absurd', *The Spectator* (11 Mar. 1966), p. 281.

TALMON, JACOB L., *The origins of totalitarian democracy* (Mercury Books, London, 1961).

TANNER, J. R., *English constitutional conflicts of the seventeenth century 1603–1689* (C.U.P., Cambridge, 1957).

TAYLOR, PHILIP B., JR., 'The Guatemalan Affair: a critique of United States foreign policy', *The American political science review*, L, no. 3 (Sept. 1956), pp. 787 ff.

TAYLOR, REX, *Michael Collins* (Four Square, London, 1965).

THAYER, CHARLES, W., *Guerrilla* (Michael Joseph, London, 1963).

THOMAS, HUGH, *The Spanish Civil War*, revsd. edn. (Penguin Books, London, 1967).

TILLY, CHARLES and RULE, JAMES, *Measuring political upheaval*, Research Monograph No. 19 (Center of International Studies, Princeton, 1965).

TOCQUEVILLE, ALEXIS DE, *L'Ancien Régime et la Révolution* (Paris, 1856).

TORIELLO, GUILLERMO, *La Batalla de Guatemala* (Editorial Universitaria, Santiago de Chile, 1955).

TROTSKY, LÉON, *History of the Russian Revolution to Brest-Litovsk* (Gollancz, London, 1966).

TRUONG CHINH; pseudonym of DANG XUAN KHU, q.v.

UNITED KINGDOM, Government, *State Papers, 1953–54*, XXXIII, Cmd. 9277, Guatemala No. 1 (1954), *Report on events leading up to and arising out of the change of regime in Guatemala 1954* (H.M.S.O., London, 1954).

UNITED STATES, Congress, Senate Committee on Foreign Relations, *Revolutions in Mexico: Hearing before a Sub-committee of the Committee on Foreign Relations, United States Senate, Sixty-Second Congress, Second Session, pursuant to S. Res., 335, a resolution authorising the Committee on Foreign Relations to investigate whether any interests in the United States have been or are now engaged in inciting rebellion in Cuba and Mexico* (United States Government Printing Office, Washington, D.C., 1913).

VAGTS, ALFRED, *A History of militarism, civilian and military* (Hollis & Carter, London, 1959).

VANGER, MILTON I., *José Batlle y Ordóñez of Uruguay, The Creator of his Times, 1902–1907* (Harvard University Press, Cambridge, Mass., 1963).

VITTACHI, TARZIE, *The fall of Sukarno* (Mayflower-Dell, London, 1967).

VO NGUYEN GIAP, *People's war, people's army*, 2nd edn. (Prager, New York, 1965).

VUCINICH, WAYNE S., *Serbia between East and West, the events of 1903–1908* (Stanford University Press, Stanford, 1954).

WALTER, GÉRARD, *Robespierre*, 2 vols. (Gallimard, Paris, 1961).

WARREN, HARRIS GAYLORD, *Paraguay, an informal history* (University of Oklahoma Press, Norman, 1949).

WEATHERBEE, DONALD E., *Ideology in Indonesia: Sukarno's Indonesian Revolution, Yale University South-east Asia Studies*, Monograph Series No. 8 (New Haven, 1966).

WEBER, MAX, *The theory of social and economic organization*, ed. and intro. Talcott Parsons (The Free Press, New York, 1965).

WEINERT, RICHARD S., 'Violence in pre-modern societies: rural Colombia', *The American political science review*, LX, no. 2 (June 1966), 340.

WELLS, HERBERT GEORGE, *The war in the air* (Odham's Press, London, 1921).

WISE, DAVID and ROSS, THOMAS B., *The invisible government* (Jonathan Cape, London, 1965).

WOLFENSTEIN, E. VICTOR, *The revolutionary personality: Lenin, Trotsky, Gandhi* (Princeton University Press, Princeton, 1967).

WOLIN, SIMON and SLUSSER, R. M., eds., *The Soviet Secret Police* (Praeger, New York, 1957).

WRIGHT, QUINCY, *A study of war*, 2nd edn. (University of Chicago Press, Chicago, 1965).

YDÍGORAS FUENTES, MIGUEL, *My war with Communism*, as told to Mario Rosenthal (Prentice-Hall, Englewood Cliffs, N.J., 1963).

YODER, DALE, 'Current definitions of revolution', *The American journal of sociology*, XXXII, no. 3 (Nov. 1926), 433.

ZEMAN, Z. A. B., *Nazi propaganda* (O.U.P., London, 1964).

In addition to the above sources, data for the comparative study were drawn from *The Annual Register*, Bank of London and South America *Fortnightly Review*, *Enciclopedia Universal Ilustrado* (Espasa-Calpe, Barcelona), *Encylopaedia Britannica* (13th edn. and 1966 edn.), *Hispanic American Report*, *Keesing's Contemporary Archives*, *The Guardian*, and *The Times*.

INDEX